Rurality, Diversity and Schooling

Also Available from Bloomsbury

Global Citizenship Education and the Crises of Multiculturalism, Massimiliano Tarozzi and Carlos Alberto Torres
Developing Culturally and Historically Sensitive Teacher Education, Yolanda Gayol Ramírez, Patricia Rosas Chávez and Peter Smagorinsky
Doing Diversity Differently in a Culturally Complex World, Megan Watkins and Greg Noble

Rurality, Diversity and Schooling

Multiculturalism in Regional Australia

Neroli Colvin

BLOOMSBURY ACADEMIC
LONDON • NEW YORK • OXFORD • NEW DELHI • SYDNEY

BLOOMSBURY ACADEMIC
Bloomsbury Publishing Plc, 50 Bedford Square, London, WC1B 3DP, UK
Bloomsbury Publishing Inc, 1359 Broadway, New York, NY 10018, USA
Bloomsbury Publishing Ireland, 29 Earlsfort Terrace, Dublin 2, D02 AY28, Ireland

BLOOMSBURY, BLOOMSBURY ACADEMIC and the Diana logo are trademarks of
Bloomsbury Publishing Plc

First published in Great Britain 2024
This paperback edition published in 2025

Copyright © Neroli Colvin, edited by Megan Watkins and Greg Noble, 2024

The Estate of Neroli Colvin has asserted Neroli Colvin's right under the Copyright, Designs and Patents Act, 1988, to be identified as Author of this work.

For legal purposes the Acknowledgements on p. xiv constitute an extension of this copyright page.

All rights reserved. No part of this publication may be: i) reproduced or transmitted in any form, electronic or mechanical, including photocopying, recording or by means of any information storage or retrieval system without prior permission in writing from the publishers; or ii) used or reproduced in any way for the training, development or operation of artificial intelligence (AI) technologies, including generative AI technologies. The rights holders expressly reserve this publication from the text and data mining exception as per Article 4(3) of the Digital Single Market Directive (EU) 2019/790.

Bloomsbury Publishing Plc does not have any control over, or responsibility for, any third-party websites referred to or in this book. All internet addresses given in this book were correct at the time of going to press. The author and publisher regret any inconvenience caused if addresses have changed or sites have ceased to exist, but can accept no responsibility for any such changes.

A catalogue record for this book is available from the British Library.

A catalog record for this book is available from the Library of Congress.

ISBN: HB: 978-1-3503-6828-6
PB: 978-1-3503-6832-3
ePDF: 978-1-3503-6829-3
eBook: 978-1-3503-6830-9

Typeset by Deanta Global Publishing Services, Chennai, India

For product safety related questions contact productsafety@bloomsbury.com.

To find out more about our authors and books visit www.bloomsbury.com and sign up for our newsletters.

This book is dedicated to my parents and grandparents for their lifelong gifts of curiosity, love of learning and educational opportunities.

Contents

List of Tables	viii
Foreword, *Megan Watkins and Greg Noble*	ix
Preface – A Word on Words	xi
Acknowledgements	xiv
List of Abbreviations	xv
Introduction: Rurality, Diversity and Schooling	1
1 'Our Diversity Is Great' (Part 1): Diversity as a Multiplicity of 'Cultures'	15
2 'Our Diversity Is Great' (Part 2): Policies, Discourses and Public Opinion	41
3 Ends and Means: Researching Diversity in Regional Schools and Communities	65
4 'Sprinkles of Everything': Names, Namings and Numbers	89
5 'Yes, but . . .': Discourses, Affects and Sentiments	117
6 'Old Ways Die Hard': Practices and Consequences	147
Conclusion: Towards a Multiculturalism for All	179
Notes	187
References	190
Index	212

Tables

3.1 Selected Population Statistics from the 2021 Census 69
3.2 Research Sample 76

Foreword

Megan Watkins and Greg Noble

In the Introduction to this insightful and timely book, Neroli Colvin recounts how, when conducting the research that informs it, she would often be asked what it was about, to which she would reply, 'cultural diversity in regional schools'. The standard response she received was, 'Is there any?' This, of course, is the general impression of not only regional schools but anywhere outside Australia's major cities. Cultural diversity is viewed as an urban phenomenon, while the rural is seen as the preserve of White Australians, often also neglecting the presence of Australia's Indigenous populations, the first inhabitants of the land. This book engages with these misconceptions as Colvin incisively examines the changing demographics and complex racial dynamics of the place she calls Easthaven, a regional town in New South Wales (NSW), Australia. With particular attention to its two state high schools, Seaview and Hillview, she interrogates how these schools, and their broader communities, navigate the increasing cultural complexity they are experiencing, foregrounding the influence of policies of multiculturalism at varying levels of government and bureaucracy on this process. While discussion of cultural diversity in Australia is generally concerned with migrant-derived diversity, the focus of multicultural policy, Colvin stresses how this is a very partial account, particularly in rural and regional areas. A study of the 'plural rural' in a settler-colonial nation like Australia, she argues, needs to first acknowledge its First Peoples and their status within this racial and cultural mix. Colvin's study of Easthaven, therefore, not only considers those who are recently arrived, such as the growing number of refugees from parts of Africa, South-east Asia and the Middle East – there by dint of government resettlement programmes – but their interrelations with the White *and* Indigenous populations of the town.

Colvin provides an empirically rich analysis of this diversifying landscape, combining policy analysis, interviews with various actors and observation both inside and outside the two schools. She has a particular interest, however, in language and multicultural discourse and the work they do in regulating values, attitudes and practices in relation to cultural diversity. Taking the relatively innocuous refrain 'Our diversity is great', she shows there is contention in terms of whether diversity *is* great in both number and value. In terms of number, Australia often boasts it is one of the most multicultural countries in the world, but this diversity is not evenly spread and so when it 'arrives' in rural contexts such as Easthaven, its impact is amplified, adding another level of complexity to the predominantly 'White' and, to varying degrees, 'Black' racial mix of such towns.

Colvin also closely scrutinizes the other sense of 'great', seen in terms of diversity's value to the nation. Diversity as a 'strength' and diversity as an 'asset' are common descriptors within multicultural discourse and especially within multicultural education. Building on the work of various scholars, she demonstrates how this celebratory mode of multiculturalism tends to deflect attention away from a more challenging treatment of racism and forms of structural inequality, unhelpfully silencing any discomfit around cultural difference which she feels is the role of education to address. It is here that Colvin sees the real impact of her work, promoting dialogue around difference especially within educational contexts.

Throughout the book, there is mention of the practical application of its implications, but, sadly, Neroli will never see this. You will note a shift here in reference from Colvin, the author and scholar, to Neroli, our friend and colleague. We first met Neroli when she was the successful applicant for the PhD scholarship attached to *Rethinking Multiculturalism/Reassessing Multicultural Education*, an Australian Research Council project that we led in collaboration with Professor Kevin Dunn at Western Sydney University, the NSW Department of Education and the then NSW Institute of Teachers. We supervised Neroli's doctorate, together with Associate Professor Tania Ferfolja, which was an easy task. As a former print journalist, Neroli was not only a keen investigator and researcher, adept at interviewing and sourcing information, but a beautiful writer. Over the course of her candidature, as she developed into a gifted scholar, so too did the disease that had plagued her all her life. Ever the fighter, Neroli was determined to finish her doctorate, but passed away the year after she graduated. This book, based on her doctorate, is an important pillar of her legacy. While she managed to publish two journal articles and some online material, the book was simply too much to consider in her remaining months. What is produced here is Neroli's work, but with some minor editing and updated references. We also want to acknowledge Neroli's publications and thank the publishers for permission to reproduce sections from each of these:

Colvin, N. (2013). Resettlement as rebirth: How effective are the midwives? *M/C Journal, 16*(5). Retrieved from http://journal.media-culture.org.au/ index.php/mcjournal/article/viewArticle/706

Colvin, N. (2017). "Really really different different": Rurality, regional schools and refugees. *Race Ethnicity and Education, 20*(2), 225–39.

We are ever grateful to Bloomsbury, and Ally Baker in particular, for supporting the book's publication. There are also many others who assisted with this project: Ivy Vuong, Barbara Pini, Farida Fozdar and Rose Butler. Most of all, thanks to Jock Cheetham, Neroli's partner – who continues the good work through the Neroli Colvin Storytelling Foundation – and to her parents, Lorraine and Barry. This wouldn't have been possible without your love, support and ongoing commitment to Neroli's legacy.

Megan Watkins and Greg Noble
Institute for Culture and Society
Western Sydney University
Australia

Preface – A Word on Words

Australia is home to the world's oldest continuous living cultures. It is home to a large population of people whose forebears came from the other side of the globe – from England, Scotland, Ireland and Wales. And it is home to millions of people with ethnic and cultural origins elsewhere on the planet, many of whom have arrived in the past seventy years.

Culturally and linguistically, Australia remains strongly linked to that cluster of small islands in the North Atlantic Ocean, the British Isles. Geographically, it is perched on the edge of Asia. Socially, it was born, and has been built, on ideals such as fairness, egalitarianism and secularism. All of these facets of Australia – historical, demographic, cultural, linguistic, geographic, social, economic, political – are important to the work that is this book and are explored in the pages that follow.

Above all, language – both 'official' (as, for example, in national policies) and everyday – is a central concern. As Goldberg (2006) notes:

> Languages embed sets of beliefs, collective understandings and experiences, institutional expressions. They reflect and shape prevailing sociocultural and institutionalizing narratives, overriding, even overdetermining, though not necessarily totalizing or even finalizing accounts of historical memory, social arrangement, how things are and are to be done. Languages, in short, entwine the descriptive with the normative in social life. (p. 358)

That words both describe and produce is foundational to this book, and it is for this reason I explain here, at the outset, usage conventions adopted in the writing.

Key Terms in This Book

Aboriginal and Torres Strait Islander, Indigenous

In everyday usage in Australia, the adjectival terms 'Aboriginal', 'Aboriginal and Torres Strait Islander' and 'Indigenous' are often used interchangeably. Technically, 'Indigenous' is the broader term, encompassing both 'Aboriginal' and 'Torres Strait Islander' peoples – peoples who had distinctive ethnic, cultural and linguistic backgrounds, but who today are 'united' in the fact that they pre-dated European settlement of the lands now known as Australia. However, the terms are contested and usage is inconsistent, in academic as well as popular domains (Jamieson, 2012; Paradies, 2006).

Preferences among Australians who identify as Aboriginal and/or Torres Strait Islander are similarly mixed, with some favouring kinship or language-group identifications, or regional identifications such as Koori or Murri (Shaw et al., 2006), or sometimes terms with global currency such as 'First Peoples', 'First Nations' or 'Black'. In short, usage is heavily contingent on geographical location, institutional setting and social or political context. A person may describe themself as 'an Indigenous Australian' to a European-background Australian, for example, but as 'a Warlpiri person' to other people who identify as Indigenous. Other people of Aboriginal or Torres Strait Islander descent eschew 'Indigenous' as scientific and colonial (Jamieson, 2012).

In this book, I use 'Indigenous' and 'Aboriginal and Torres Strait Islander' interchangeably for national contexts. For New South Wales (NSW), I use 'Aboriginal', the term typically used in state policy documents (Wilson, 2016), including Department of Education (NSW DoE) policies and programmes (NSW DoE, 2016a). While I make this distinction in my own writing, others whose work or words I cite do not necessarily use the terms in the same way.

I use 'peoples' (plural) to emphasize the heterogeneity of Indigenous ancestries, knowledges, perspectives and cultural practices.

Anglo, Anglo-Australian

The term 'Anglo-Australian' (sometimes shortened to 'Anglo') is widely used to describe people with English ancestry in Australia. However, the term is also used to refer to people of Anglo-Celtic descent – that is, whose forebears came to Australia from Ireland, Scotland and/or Wales as well as England (DSS, 2014). It is the latter, broader sense in which 'Anglo-Australian' is used in this book.

Backgrounds Other Than Indigenous and Anglo

The millions of non-British immigrants to Australia have been referred to by many terms over the decades, including 'New Australians' and 'ethnics', and more specific identifiers such as 'Chinese' or 'African'. In view of the arguments this book makes about diversity and inclusion, I use terminology such as 'Chinese-background', 'African-background' and so on to emphasize that people's cultural and/or ethnic origins are not necessarily salient in their present identities and everyday lives. Again, others whose work or words I cite may not follow the same convention.

Language Background

Since the 1970s (albeit to different degrees), Australian multiculturalism has promoted cultural maintenance, including maintenance of community languages and dialects, within the context of a nation united by the common language of English (DSS, 2007). Over the decades, various descriptors and acronyms have been used to refer to people whose first language is not English. These include 'NES'/'NESB' (non-English-speaking background); 'ESL' (English as a second language) and its more contemporary version, 'EAL/D' (English as an additional language or dialect); 'LBOTE' (language background other than English) and the related 'LOTE' (language/s other than English); and the broader 'CALD' (culturally and linguistically diverse). Within NSW schools, EAL/D and LBOTE are the current terms for student cohorts (NSW DoE, 2014); CALD is typically favoured in more general contexts. Although NESB and ESL are 'older' terms and have largely been displaced in official documents by, respectively, CALD/LBOTE and EAL/D (Dobinson & Buchori, 2016; Inglis, 2009), all terms are still in wide circulation.

As well as featuring in policies and political discourses, all of the terms above – and contestations about them – are prominent in educational contexts: student data (categorization and counting processes); curriculum priorities and perspectives, such as the cross-curriculum priority of 'Aboriginal and Torres Strait Islander histories and cultures' in the national curriculum (ACARA, 2016a); school classifications and funding; within-school allocation of resources, and so on. Schools in particular play a crucial role in our socialization into groups that are larger than our family and immediate community; in how we identify with and are identified within diverse groups; and in shaping how we perceive and interpret the physical and social worlds in which we live, learn and work. To return to Goldberg (2006), language is crucial to the notions and narratives of 'difference' that govern our every thought, experience and action. The key issue is not difference per se, but concerns questions about 'who defines difference, how different categories. . . are represented within the discourses of 'difference', and whether 'difference' differentiates laterally or hierarchically' (Brah, 1991, p. 71). In short, much is at stake with terminology, given language produces as well as reflects, enables as well as constrains, our positionalities and possibilities.

Acknowledgements

I am so grateful to finally be writing these acknowledgements, and there are many people to thank.

I would like to acknowledge the Aboriginal and Torres Strait Islander peoples as the first inhabitants of Australia, and the traditional custodians of the lands where we all live, learn and work.

I would like to thank the principals of the studied schools for agreeing to participate in this project. This book would not have been possible without their interest, trust and cooperation, and without the generosity of all of the research participants. Special thanks must go to the schools' EAL/D teachers, who were particularly helpful in inviting me to events, giving me access to materials and sharing their insights and experiences.

I am immensely grateful to Professor Megan Watkins, Professor Greg Noble and Associate Professor Tania Ferfolja for their continual guidance and copious reading. Megan and Greg and the *Rethinking Multiculturalism/Reassessing Multicultural Education* research team gave me the opportunity to be involved in their project, from which I have learnt an enormous amount. The financial assistance from the Australian Research Council and Western Sydney University has also been greatly appreciated.

Many other academics have provided inspiration, personal encouragement and useful feedback along the way. Some appear in the references, while some do not, but thank you all.

My heartfelt thanks, too, to the friends who have provided reading, proofing, transcription, listening and general sanity services, including Susan, Aylin, Reuben, John, Louise, Mary, Eve and Anna.

To my parents, Barry and Lorraine and other family members, thank you for your constant interest and caring.

Finally, my gratitude to Jock for giving me the space to do this. Without your patience, love and all-round support, I would never have made it.

Abbreviations

ABC	Australian Broadcasting Corporation
ABS	Australian Bureau of Statistics
ACARA	Australian Curriculum, Assessment and Reporting Authority
AEC	Australian Electoral Commission
AEO	Aboriginal Education Officer
AHRC	Australian Human Rights Commission
AIATSIS	Australian Institute of Aboriginal and Torres Strait Islander Studies
ANZAC	Australian and New Zealand Army Corps
ATSIC	Aboriginal and Torres Strait Islander Commission (federal, 1990–2005)
BOSTES	Board of Studies, Teaching and Educational Standards (NSW)
CALD	Culturally and Linguistically Diverse
CDA	Critical Discourse Analysis
CLS	Critical Legal Studies
CRT	Critical Race Theory
DFAT	Department of Foreign Affairs and Trade (federal)
DHA	Department of Home Affairs (federal)
DIBP	Department of Immigration and Border Protection (federal)
DIMIA	Department of Immigration, Multicultural Affairs and Indigenous Affairs (federal, 2001–6)
DPMC	Department of Prime Minister and Cabinet
DSS	Department of Social Services (federal)
EAL/D	English as an Additional Language or Dialect
ESL	English as a Second Language
FECCA	Federation of Ethnic Communities' Councils of Australia
HSC	Higher School Certificate (NSW)
ICSEA	Index of Community Socio-Educational Advantage
IEC	Intensive English Centre
LBOTE	Language Background Other Than English

LOTE	Language/s Other Than English
MCEETYA	Ministerial Council on Education, Employment, Training and Youth Affairs
MSC	Mapping Social Cohesion (Scanlon Foundation surveys)
NAIDOC	National Aborigines and Islanders Day Observance Committee
NAPLAN	National Assessment Program – Literacy and Numeracy
NES/NESB	Non-English-Speaking Background
NMAC	National Multicultural Advisory Council
NSW	New South Wales
NSW DoE	Department of Education (NSW)
NT	Northern Territory
OECD	Organization for Economic Co-operation and Development
P&C	Parents and Citizens
PBL	Positive Behaviour for Learning
PLP	Personalized Learning Plan
RMRME	Rethinking Multiculturalism/Reassessing Multicultural Education
SA	South Australia
SBS	Special Broadcasting Service
SRC	Student Representative Council
STARTTS	Service for the Treatment and Rehabilitation of Torture and Trauma Survivors (NSW)
TAFE	Technical and Further Education
TESOL	Teaching English to Speakers of Other Languages
UNESCO	United Nations Educational, Scientific and Cultural Organization
UNHCR	United Nations High Commissioner for Refugees
WA	Western Australia
WASP	White Anglo-Saxon Protestant

Introduction

Rurality, Diversity and Schooling

It's Multicultural Day at Seaview High,[1] a government high school in a coastal town in New South Wales (NSW), Australia. A recent addition to the school's calendar (this is only the third year it has been held), the event has become a feature of Seaview's expanding multicultural education agenda.

The day (in reality, an afternoon) is designed for Year 8 students and involves their participation in a range of activities: fan painting, tai chi, salsa, Aboriginal ceramics, Burmese dancing, African drumming and French cooking. Spreadsheets listing the time and place for each activity have been pinned up in the corridors, and students were asked to write their names down for two of the classes on offer.

First up it's Burmese dancing. About thirty students – most of them blond; some tanned, some fair-skinned; all in school uniform – stand around a space in the centre of the room, while two black-haired, brown-skinned girls dressed in ethnic Burmese clothing hover at one side.

As more students straggle into the room ('I was told to come here'; 'the other activities are full'), a tape recorder is produced and a teacher signals that the two girls should begin dancing.

They perform their dance. The students watching clap politely. The teacher remarks: 'It looks as if you were doing something in the fields – threshing, maybe?' The dancers don't understand the question – or perhaps the word 'threshing' – or don't have the language or confidence to explain the meaning of their actions. The question hangs in the air.

The teacher asks for volunteers to join the dancers in the centre of the room. No one moves.

'Come on', she says, urging several students to copy the dancers' movements.

The teacher is enthusiastic and encouraging, while the students feel awkward and self-conscious. The dancers themselves seem more comfortable, however, relaxing into their performance and enjoying their role as leaders.

Down the corridor, students have gathered for African drumming. There's no teacher; instead, a Year 11 student of African background appears to be in charge. She, too, is wearing colourful traditional clothing and has bright flowers in her hair. The students are shouting and randomly slapping their *djembe* (drums). The older student struggles to be heard, let alone to lead the Year 8s in group practice.

Things are much quieter in the Aboriginal ceramics class. The students have almost finished painting various designs – mostly dot patterns and stylized native animals – on mugs and plates. The art teacher checks their progress, asks them about their designs and explains how he'll fire the pieces in the kiln.

Lois, a head teacher and member of the school executive, later explains that Seaview High is 'going through a great change'. It used to be very much a 'monoculture', she says, but now it's 'physically looking different with all our African and Middle Eastern students'. She thinks multicultural events are often 'just top-dressing stuff' – promoting a view that 'I know about a specific culture because I've seen the national dress and I can recognize their flag and I know they eat this' – but adds: 'Well, it's a start. . . . At least [we're] doing something. . . . We had nothing before.'

* * *

Celebrating Our Diversity

Multicultural Day at Seaview High will be familiar to most people involved with Australian schools. In recent decades multicultural events, along with international exchange programmes, have become popular additions to school calendars and curricula across the country (Watkins & Noble, 2019). They are a common way in which schools recognize and celebrate Australia's status as one of the most culturally diverse nations in the world (ABS, 2013b) – a characteristic that has become central to Australian identity, both within and beyond the nation's borders (DSS, 2011). Exhorted and exalted by a raft of policies, this diversity is recognized and celebrated each year through national events such as Harmony Day, Refugee Week and NAIDOC Week,[2] as well as specific cultural and regional festivals. All these events and programmes reveal something of how cultural diversity and multiculturalism (as the official policy response to diversity in Australia) are understood, valued and lived by individuals and groups within communities.

Multicultural Day at Seaview High is presented here as a window on how cultural diversity and multiculturalism are conceptualized and enacted in one particular setting – in this case, a public high school in a regional town which, like many other regional towns across Australia, has undergone significant demographic change over the past two decades. Of central interest to this book is how multicultural policies' promotion of diversity and its merits is refracted through rural imaginaries, identities and materialities to shape these localized conceptualizations and enactments.

Cultural Diversity in Rural Schools – Is There Any?

'Cultural diversity' and 'regional town' are terms that are not commonly thought of together. In writing this book, when people inquired what it was about and I gave them the five-word answer – 'cultural diversity in regional schools' – the main response was along the lines of: '*Is* there any?' As Hugo (2000) has noted, there are many myths about non-metropolitan Australia – one of them being that it remains untouched by the flows of people that have transformed the nation's major cities post the Second World War. The diversity in regional towns, more typically, has been a matter of 'White' and 'Black':[3] the Anglo-Australian majority and the Indigenous Australian minority.[4] But as Hugo (2000) writes:

> The 37.3 percent of Australians living outside of cities with more than 100,000 inhabitants are changing in substantial and important ways under the influence of economic, social, political and environmental changes. . . . [W]hile the dynamics of population change in the metropolitan sector are well known, that occurring in non-metropolitan Australia has not been analysed to the same extent. ('Introduction' section)

At its most basic level, this book aims to reduce this gap in the literature by documenting the significant changes that have occurred in one regional town, and how the town and its public high schools – Seaview High, already introduced, and Hillview High, the town's other public high school – have responded to those changes. The lens applied to this analysis is Australia's multicultural policies: in other words, how do multicultural policies 'hit the ground' (Jakubowicz & Ho, 2013b) in non-metropolitan areas – areas where cultural diversity has not been a part of most longtime residents' lived experience, and is usually not part of community identities?

In answering this question, the book takes up policies as texts that affect discursive and other social practices and thus have material *effects* (Fairclough, 2003) – thereby extending its purpose beyond simply documenting (school) community changes and responses to critically examining situated policy outcomes. Understanding the 'social, political, cognitive, moral and material consequences and effects' of texts is 'vital . . . if we are to raise moral and political questions about contemporary societies' (Fairclough, 2003, p. 14). Two such questions are at the core of this book. First, after De Lepervanche (1980), why is cultural diversity today promoted and celebrated by Australia and many Australians, when only a couple of generations ago it was officially obstructed and popularly opposed? And second, after Bell (1979),[5] why, after more than four decades of multicultural policies and anti-discrimination laws,[6] are racialized discourses and discriminatory practices still so evident in Australia? A third question then arises as to the relationship between these two – namely, how might the change in orientation towards diversity relate to the persistence of racialization and racism, or rather racisms (Amin, 2010; Forrest & Dunn, 2013)? Or, to put it slightly differently, to what extent might the contemporary emphasis on promoting and celebrating diversity, and particularly in schools and school communities, *enable* continued social inequalities?

The answers to these questions overlap to an extent, but a common starting point can be found in the observation that only *some* cultural differences are celebrated (Ang, Brand, Noble, & Sternberg, 2006; Cowlishaw, 2004a). In so-called 'settler societies',[7] such as Australia, the process of decolonization is slow, halting and uneven, with remnant discourses of colonialism such as White superiority, segregation and assimilation competing with more 'modern' discourses such as equality, inclusion, recognition and Indigenous sovereignty (Curthoys, 2000). The primacy of the latter, more recent discourses cannot and should not be assumed – especially in non-metropolitan areas where settler histories and colonial narratives have a continuing salience in both national and local imaginaries (Edgeworth, 2014; Jordan, Krivokapic-Skoko, & Collins, 2009). Nor should it be assumed that the latter discourses are antithetical, and remedial, to the former. Rather, attention must be paid to tensions within and between discourses and to the 'situated and relational nature' of people's understandings, attitudes and practices with regard to diversity (Valentine & Sadgrove, 2014, p. 1982). These tasks are critical to illuminating the complex and often contradictory ways in which official multicultural discourses are taken up – echoed, appropriated, challenged, resisted – in different physical, social and institutional spaces.

Drawing on observational, interview and documentary data, this book explores four key themes, set out and illustrated here with reference to the opening account of Multicultural Day at Seaview High. First, the event reveals that 'cultural diversity', while seemingly a reasonably straightforward term, is in fact understood and used in varied and potentially problematic ways. For a 'commonsense' meaning of 'cultural diversity', one might turn to the Oxford Dictionaries (2016) and find the following: 'The existence of a variety of cultural or ethnic groups within a society' – with 'culture' defined as the beliefs, customs and social behaviours of a group, and 'ethnicity' as belonging to a group with common national or cultural origins. Similarly, the Australian Bureau of Statistics (ABS) defines cultural diversity as 'the variety of languages, religions, ancestries and birthplaces reported by Australians' in population studies such as the Census (ABS, 2012b, para. 1). With their emphasis on 'variety', these definitions imply that national, cultural, ethnic, linguistic and religious categories such as 'Australian', 'French', 'Aboriginal', 'Mandarin-speaking' and 'Muslim' delineate equivalent dimensions of diversity and equivalent 'groups' of people. At Seaview High's Multicultural Day, however, a subtly but powerfully different conceptualization of diversity is implicit in the focus on the performance of selected cultural practices of selected 'other' cultural or ethnic groups – that is, cultures or ethnicities other than the Anglo-Australian norm. The Anglo-Australian students are the spectators, the other-than-Anglos the 'spectacle'. In short, the choice of activities and performers communicates that 'diversity' pertains to, and only to, ethnic minorities. Contrary to its dictionary definition, then, the term may not, in practice, encompass everyone.

Related to this is the issue of how Indigeneity and 'Indigenous culture' are positioned and represented in multicultural Australia. At Seaview High, 'Aboriginal' is just one of the array of (non-Anglo) 'cultures' students can learn about during Multicultural Day – in this case, through applying designs that are assumed to be ubiquitous in 'Aboriginal art' to (non-Indigenous) objects such as mass-produced ceramic mugs. Symbolically, the (hi)stories and practices of Australia's original inhabitants are elided with the (hi)stories and practices of the country's newest settlers to produce cultural diversity as an art form in itself: a 'tapestry' (Turnbull quoted in Davey, 2017) or 'mosaic' of myriad discrete, internally homogenous and more-or-less equal 'cultures'. One effect of this elision is to mute still-unresolved but crucial questions about Aboriginal and Torres Strait Islander peoples' right to be recognized as Australia's first peoples, including in Australia's founding document, the Constitution (AHRC, n.d.-a). The poet and political activist Oodgeroo Noonuccal[8] put it bluntly in 1988, the bicentenary of European settlement of Australia, when she said:

> It must be clearly understood that the Aboriginal nation, yet to be recognized, has little or no enthusiasm for the so-called multicultural society of Australia, for it is unbelievable and a great indictment of European Australians that the Aboriginal people still find themselves . . . at the bottom of the socio-economic scale with regard to multiculturalism. (cited in Colic-Peisker & Tilbury, 2008, p. 47)

Such sentiments, and the allusion to racialized power structures and long-standing inequalities ('bottom of the . . . scale'), sit awkwardly with the explicitly positive orientation towards diversity of Australian multicultural policies. The current national policy, set out in a 2011 document entitled *The People of Australia*, begins by stating that 'Australia's multicultural composition is at the heart of our national identity and is intrinsic to our history and character' (DSS, 2011, p. 2). Multiculturalism, the policy continues, 'is in Australia's national interest and speaks to fairness and inclusion. . . . [It] is about all Australians and for all Australians' (p. 2). Similarly, the state-level Multicultural NSW Act 2000 begins:

> This Act:
> a) promotes the equal rights and responsibilities of all the people of New South Wales within a cohesive and multicultural society in which:
>   i   individuals share a commitment to New South Wales and to Australia, and
>   ii *diversity is regarded as a strength and an asset*, and
>   iii English is the common language, and
> b) recognises and values the different linguistic, religious and ancestral backgrounds of the people of New South Wales. (NSW Government, 2015, p. 2; emphasis added)

Here we see diversity framed *as* something – as 'a strength and an asset' – rather than merely noted as a 'fact' or characteristic of contemporary Australian society. It is this framing that is frequently echoed in official rhetoric about diversity. In 2016, the then prime minister Malcom Turnbull, for instance, declared that 'the richness of [Australia's] diversity is one of [Australia's] greatest strengths' (Turnbull, quoted in Perkins, 2016), while the theme of Harmony Day[9] in 2016 was 'Our diversity is our strength'. Further, there is an implicit directive to institutions in multicultural policies including the Multicultural NSW Act 2000 (made explicit in Section 3, which sets out six multicultural principles) to recognize the varied backgrounds of Australians as a 'valuable resource' (principle 3(f)). Linguistic, religious and cultural differences are seen as no impediment to harmony and social cohesion – despite, for instance, the concerns voiced above by Noonuccal. This raises the question: What happens if differences *do* cause discomfort and division? What space and language are available to discuss tensions that are not supposed to exist?

Flowing from this is a third theme: the role of schools and other educational institutions in twenty-first-century Australia. Historically, schools have played a crucial part in maintaining the political, economic, social and cultural status quo in Western societies (Banks, 2011; Connell, 2011). More recently, however, schools have been reimagined as sites of innovation and transformation, and essential in preparing young people to live, work and compete in a globalizing world (Leonardo, 2002; Education Council (Australia), 2019). Thus, in addition to inculcating the traditional skills of literacy and numeracy, Australian teachers are now tasked with developing in their students technological competency, 'critical and creative thinking' and 'intercultural understanding' (ACARA, 2016b) – this last involving students learning to 'value their own cultures, languages and beliefs, and those of others' (ACARA, n.d.). Schools, then, have been, and are, both agents of and obstacles to change (Edgeworth, 2011, p. 14) – and Multicultural Day at Seaview High illuminates this tension in shifting conceptualizations of schools' function. The event was introduced – in the face of some resistance from students and staff – in response to the resettlement of hundreds of refugees from Africa, South-east Asia and the Middle East in the region from the early 2000s on. Notwithstanding these recent demographic changes, blond hair, fair or freckled skin and 'Aussie accents' are still very much the norm.

Within this context, Multicultural Day is presented in Seaview High newsletters and reports as a forum for 'raising awareness' of the families from new and emerging communities in the region, as an opportunity for the school's students from language backgrounds other than English (LBOTE[10]) to 'celebrate their cultural heritage' and as of benefit to 'all students' in drawing their gaze beyond their provincial town to the 'global'. However, the focus on performance rather than engagement, on action rather than analysis, raises critical questions about how 'culture' and 'difference' are understood, represented and valued at Seaview High, and about the event's potential and likely impacts as opposed to the stated intentions. As Ladson-Billings and Tate (1995) note:

> Current practical demonstrations of multicultural education in schools often reduce it to trivial examples and artifacts of cultures such as eating ethnic or cultural foods, singing songs or dancing, reading folktales, and other less than scholarly pursuits of the fundamentally different conceptions of knowledge or quests for social justice. (p. 61)

Certainly Multicultural Day at Seaview High was a 'less than scholarly' event and one that did not try to touch on epistemological or social justice issues. I do not suggest that the day was the extent of the school's efforts to educate about, and for, diversity; it was not. Nor does this book intend a simple critique of such events; much has already been written and said, in academic and media spaces, along these lines (Nieto, 1995; Phillips, 2004; Troyna & Williams, 2012; Watkins & Noble, 2019) – including Kalantzis and Cope's (1981) criticism more than four decades ago of the 'spaghetti and polka' approach to multicultural education prevalent in Australian schools. Rather, the intent is to unpack the sorts of understandings of 'culture' and 'difference' that continue to inform diversity initiatives, and to trace and explain the broader implications and impacts of these understandings. Critical to this endeavour is paying close attention to discourses around diversity, both official and everyday, and to the space and time in which they occur – space and time, like language, being socially constructed (Fairclough, 2003).

If space is socially constructed, it is equally true that the social is spatially constructed – 'and that fact – the spatial organization of society – makes a difference to how it [society] works' (D. Massey, 1992, p. 70). Hence a fourth theme of this book is the ways in which the regional setting of Seaview and Hillview high schools shape how multiculturalism is understood, valued and lived at the schools. Pertinent here are not only the 'microcultures of place' (Amin, 2002, p. 967) – local demographic, social, political and economic histories, local geographies, local institutions, local resources and so on – but how the 'rural' itself is imagined and experienced (especially vis-à-vis the 'urban'), and the centrality of the rural in national narratives (Garland & Chakraborti, 2006). Against prevailing urban-as-multicultural/rural-as-monocultural constructions (Askins, 2009; R. Butler, 2021; Farrugia, Smyth, & Harrison, 2016), these are issues that have received scant research attention. On the whole, urban settlements *are* more culturally diverse than rural ones (Jupp & Clyne, 2010) – and both the assumption and the reality of this have meant that popular and academic interest in multiculturalism has focused overwhelmingly on cities (Colvin, 2017). R. Butler (2020), for example, highlights the paucity of research on cultural diversity and immigrant experiences in regional Australia, while Dufty (2009) notes the urban bias in racism work, both in Australia and elsewhere, and the limited Australian literature on the processes of racialization in non-metropolitan spaces. At the same time, a growing body of work indicates that racialization and racial discrimination are significant problems in many rural communities (Malcolm, 2004; Pini & Bhopal, 2017). As Hugo (2008) observes:

> Issues remain . . . about the injection of new elements of diversity into regional communities which have not previously been multicultural. . . . [T]he bulk of our understanding of immigrant settlement in and adjustment to Australia is based on metropolitan-based research, and there is an urgent need to better understand regional migration and settlement processes and impacts. (pp. 568, 569)

Part of the 'urgent need' identified by Hugo stems from the fact that for the past twenty years, Australian migration programmes have channelled increasing numbers of immigrants, including humanitarian entrants, into non-metropolitan areas (R. Butler, 2020; Krivokapic-Skoko & Collins, 2014). This trend occurs in other developed countries as well, usually reflecting governments' desire to relieve immigration pressures on major cities while at the same time enhancing the economic and social viability of smaller centres (Boese, 2010; Dufty-Jones, 2014; Hugo & Morén-Alegret, 2008). The trend is important for several reasons, including that while immigrant flows to regional areas may still be weak compared with urban flows, their *relative* impact on receiving communities (and, in the context of this study, school communities) may be strong; and, relatedly, that the settlement and integration experiences of migrants in rural areas may be quite different to those of migrants who settle in cities (De Finney, 2010; Edgeworth, 2014). Further, migrants' settlement and integration experiences may vary markedly depending (among other factors) on their particular ethnic, cultural, linguistic and/or religious background (Malcolm, 2004). This is true in urban contexts as well, but may be more pronounced in rural spaces given common conceptualizations of them as mostly monocultural (i.e. White).

In regions where cultural diversity has been more something seen on the nightly news than encountered in daily life, changing demographics are bringing opportunities and challenges that remain only partially acknowledged and explored. This gap is where this book makes its main contributions, in particular with regard to three interconnected areas. First, the challenges associated with increasing regional diversity cannot be assumed to be simply less intense versions of the challenges in urban locales (Colvin, 2013, 2017; Hugo & Morén-Alegret, 2008). Second, neither are the challenges simply reducible to lack of lived experience of diversity. Rather, this book contends, they are embedded in social constructions that naturalize both 'Angloness' (or 'Whiteness') and the 'rural' – both unbounded and dependent, respectively, on ethnic 'others' and urban settlements for their definition (Dwyer & Jones, 2000; Forrest & Dunn, 2013). The imagined affinity between Whiteness and rurality, colours and complexifies identity and belonging in non-metropolitan spaces in unique ways. Finally, the book contributes to the 'uneasy conversation' (Curthoys, 2000) about Australian multiculturalism and how it relates to, or should relate to, the past, present and future of Indigenous Australians. As noted, decolonization, like diversification, is uneven in Australia, and the nation's settler-society history has major implications for multicultural policy and practice – yet this is rarely recognized, let alone discussed. In schools, as in other spheres (policy, administration, academe), Aboriginal perspectives and programmes are typically separated from multicultural perspectives and programmes. But as population flows change, new and old settlement issues are coming face to face in regional areas in ways they seldom do in Australia's big cities, illuminating theoretical and practical tensions routinely glossed over by 'diversity-is-strength' discourses.

Discourse and Other Tools

This book examines how difference and diversity are perceived and experienced by people in particular institutional and geographical spaces – here, high schools in a regional town. A starting point for this task is recognizing that cultural, ethnic and racial categories such as 'Australian', 'Burmese' and 'Black' – along with spatial categories such as 'rural' and 'urban' – are socially constructed. It is not enough, however, to say that categories are socially constructed. Questions must be asked about who 'constructs' and who is 'constructed', and how; and what names and namings, and the narratives in which names are embedded, *do* in people's daily lives. As Jørgensen and Phillips (2002) write, within any world view 'some forms of action become natural, others unthinkable' (p. 60). Different understandings of the world – reflected in and produced through language – are linked to different possibilities for action, and thus to different consequences.

It is for this reason multicultural policies, as social artefacts, need to be closely interrogated – to see what conceptualizations of 'culture', 'diversity' and Australia/Australians they promote; what actions they render 'natural' and what 'unthinkable'; and how they play out in interpersonal interactions, institutional practices and society at large. In particular, multicultural policies' positive framing of diversity and narratives of Australia's 'multicultural success' should be scrutinized for the moral, political and economic work they perform. As J. Bell and Hartmann (2007) write:

> In the language of diversity, every [person], regardless of background or social standing, is believed to have a place and perhaps even be welcomed. This defining element of the diversity discourse separates discussions about diversity, difference, and multiculturalism from more uncomfortable conversations about inequality, power, and privilege. (p. 906)

To 'inequality, power, and privilege', I would add, in Australia's case, Indigenous sovereignty. As the official discourse of contemporary Australia, multiculturalism has provided the platform for a national identity based on the acceptance and harmonious coexistence of different-but-equal ethnic and cultural groups. However, as Koerner (2011) argues:

> [This] national story of tolerance and acceptance does not include Australia's colonial beginnings and ongoing hegemonic relationships with Indigenous people. As such, the white Australian discourses about identity and the nation continue to disavow Indigenous sovereignty and maintain white privilege. (p. 10)

Unpacking the 'promise and peril' (Hartmann, 2015, p. 636) of multiculturalism as theory and practice requires attention to the temporal, spatial, political, social and affective contexts in which people encounter and engage with each other. This in turn requires a multidisciplinary and trans-theoretical approach – one that draws on literatures on meaning-making as a social process grounded in language and discourse (the first of the four themes outlined earlier); orientations and attitudes (theme 2); colonialism, globalization and diversification (theme 3); and human geography (theme 4). Following Ball (1993), the premise is that in analysing complex social issues such as policies and their enactments,

> two theories are probably better than one. Or to put it another way, the complexity and scope of policy analysis – from an interest in the workings of the state to a concern with contexts of practice and the distributional outcomes of policy – preclude the possibility of successful single theory explanations. What we need in policy analysis is a toolbox of diverse concepts and theories. (p. 10)

Within a broad social constructionist framework, the 'toolbox' assembled for and utilized in this book derives much from critical discourse and race-critical scholarship.

Both fields provide useful analytical tools as well as methodological guidance and, of course, theoretical perspectives. Discourse is foregrounded as an important element of social practice (Fairclough, 2001), but other elements, and the relationships between them, are also crucial in this study. Social interactions always occur in particular places and are always mediated by 'other faces, other encounters of facing, other bodies, other spaces, and other times' (Ahmed, 2000, p. 7). They therefore *affect* us in myriad ways, many of which we are not conscious of. As noted, there is an 'official positivity' regarding diversity in Australia, established and sustained by multicultural policies. Theories that grapple with the embodied nature of human experience are thus part of the toolbox as well – that is, theories about how we perceive, interpret, affect and are affected by the social and material worlds we inhabit.

It is worth clarifying here the choice of 'race-critical theories' rather than Critical Race Theory (CRT). CRT has its origins in Critical Legal Studies (CLS), which developed in the United States in the 1970s with the work of Derrick Bell and others (Ladson-Billings, 1998). Twenty-five years after the landmark 1954 *Brown v Board of Education* case, which ordered an end to race segregation of American schools, D. Bell (1979) noted and sought to explain an increasing trend towards resegregation. *Brown's* failure to effect the radical 'break from the past' it had appeared to promise highlighted that racial segregation was 'much more than a series of quaint customs that can be remedied ... without altering the status of whites' (D. Bell, 1979, pp. 525, 522). This led him to propose the principle of interest convergence, which posits that the 'interest of blacks in achieving racial equality will be accommodated only when it converges with the interests of whites' (D. Bell, 1979, p. 523).

Australia has a different history of nation-building and race relations to the United States and, generally speaking, less 'Black-and-White' language around race, ethnicity and culture. In the Australian context, the principle of interest convergence might be reformulated as: 'The interests of minority groups in achieving equality will be accommodated to the extent that they converge with the interests of the Anglo majority.' Australia also, of course, has a different schooling system – although there is evidence of growing segregation along ethnic/cultural and socio-economic lines in Australian schools as well (Ho, 2020). Ladson-Billings and Tate introduced CRT to educational scholarship in the mid-1990s (Ladson-Billings & Tate, 1995), and CRT's tenets and tools have since been taken up and developed by numerous researchers and practitioners, particularly in the United States (Ladson-Billings, 2003, 2005; Vaught & Castagno, 2008).

While CRT foregrounds its transdisciplinary nature and commitment to intersectionality (Ledesma & Calderón, 2015) – that is, considering how race intersects with class, gender and other social constructs to advantage some people(s) and not others – much CRT scholarship is, in reality, narrowly focused. Its claims to intersectionality notwithstanding, CRT has been criticized for its 'hyper-emphasis on race' (Ledesma & Calderón, 2015, p. 207) and its reductionist and reifying use of racial categories, in defiance of the ethnic and cultural hybridity that characterize most people's identities and lived experience. Bourdieu and Wacquant (1999) have been scathing, too, about the *uncritical* application of particularist American categories, perspectives and arguments to quite dissimilar sociopolitical contexts – hence the point above about Australia not being the United States is an important one. In short, CRT's Black-and-White framing of racialization and racism can be criticized as not only theoretically underdeveloped but practically problematic, given its US-centrism and the way it perpetuates the very boundary-making CRT sets out to challenge (Hesse, 2007; Ledesma & Calderón, 2015). A *race-critical* approach, in contrast, allows for a more nuanced, multifaceted and spatially sensitive reading of racialization and racisms while retaining CRT's focus on categories, discourses and institutional structures and practices.

Three particular reasons informed the construction and use of the toolbox sketched above. The first relates to discourses and the need to unsettle commonsense understandings and familiar narratives about diversity, identity and achievement in Australia and Australian schools – to interrogate the 'comforting myths that self-avowedly "democratic" states [and institutions] tell about themselves' (Gillborn, 2007, p. 487). The second relates to space and the characteristics, real and imagined, of non-urban settlements in Australia. Historically, as noted, social relations in rural and regional areas have been enacted primarily within a Black/White (Indigenous/Anglo) binary, despite increasingly mixed ancestries (Paradies, 2006). Colonization proceeded not only through the takeover, privatization and pastoralization of Indigenous lands but through the Europeans' defining and policing of racial identities (Hall, 1990a; Paradies, 2006), and the legacy of these practices remains pronounced in many rural communities. The third reason for drawing on critical discourse and race-critical work was practical. Scholars in these fields have proposed a range of concepts and tools that seemed increasingly relevant to the research informing this book. In addition to the notion of interest convergence, for instance, CRT offers the concept of 'Whiteness as property' – the historical importance of property ownership in establishing and cementing European dominance in settler societies, and the continuing dominance of White people not only in law-making and policy-making (D. Bell, 1979) but in decisions about whose knowledge and practices are valued, and in organizing people into groups in the first place (Zembylas, 2010). Critical discourse perspectives likewise emphasize the importance of the historical, political and social contexts of texts – that what is said is always underpinned by understandings, beliefs, conventions and so on that are *unsaid* (Fairclough, 2003, p. 11). Identifying what is assumed in texts, as well as interrogating what is explicit, thus becomes pivotal to demystifying the connections between language and power (Fairclough, 1989).

Structure of the Book

The book begins by troubling two key assumptions in Australian multicultural policies with regard to diversity. The first, implicit assumption is that after more than half a century of large-scale, broad-based immigration, diversity is now part of everyday life in Australia. The second assumption (this one explicit) is that diversity is unequivocally 'good' for the nation and all its citizens – this value being, in theory, the primary rationale for events such as Seaview High's Multicultural Day. Against the first assumption, Chapter 1 examines the uneven distribution of diversity in Australia, geographically and politically, and the ways in which diversity is represented in official texts (such as policy documents). Drawing on the work of Brubaker, Lakoff and Zerubavel, the chapter emphasizes the constructed nature of categories, but also the ways in which this 'constructedness' is often obscured by the automaticity of routine categorization processes – how categories become commonsense. It distinguishes between *classification* as a macro-level categorization process and *identification* as a more localized process, and considers the relationship between the two. It also considers the affective dimension of categories and identities, and theoretical debates about affect and emotion, in view of the celebratory orientation towards diversity promoted by multicultural policies. Recognizing the link between 'who' one is and 'where' one is – Massey's (1992) point about the connection between social and spatial – the chapter concludes with an exploration of the construction of spaces and places, and in particular notions of rurality and rural communities.

Chapter 2 focuses on the second assumption and proposition, that of diversity as a strength and an asset. The chapter begins by reviewing scholarship on discourse, policy and policy as discourse, foregrounding the work of Fairclough and van Dijk. It then contextualizes and analyses multicultural policies, and multiculturalism as policy, in Australia, drawing on the writings of Ang and Hage. Attention is given to two related diversity discourses – that of the success of Australian multiculturalism, and that of tolerance of diversity being a defining national characteristic. As in Chapter 1, there is an interest in the relationship between the macro (official) and the micro (everyday), leading to a review of research data on Australians' attitudes towards immigration, cultural diversity and multiculturalism. The links between understandings, attitudes, affects and actions are then explored before consideration is given to schools' role in developing capacities for living 'together-in-difference' (Ang, 2003). The chapter concludes with a discussion of research on teachers' orientations towards diversity, and of three 'models of difference' claimed by Boler and Zembylas (2003) to be prevalent in and beyond schools.

Chapter 3 introduces the research location and the two schools studied and details how the research was conducted. Race-critical and critical discourse guidance on methodology, and the tenets and techniques used to analyse the data, are explained. The chapter also reflects on my positionality as a researcher and how this (may have) impacted different stages of the research.

The next three chapters draw on the interview, observational and documentary data collected during visits to the research location to show how multiculturalism is understood, valued and lived in the two school communities. Chapter 4 takes up at a micro level the insights of Chapter 1 regarding macro-level categories and categorization processes, examining how words such as 'culturally diverse' and 'multicultural' are used in everyday exchanges, how community members characterize the ethnic and cultural make-up of their town and the two studied schools, and how different groups are constructed and positioned relative to one another. In doing so it begins to build the case that names and namings are not, respectively, simple identifications and identification acts but rather are integral to the production of new hierarchies of belonging in the town and its schools. Chapter 5 discusses a range of diversity discourses circulating within the schools and the town, paying particular attention to interviewees' perspectives on whether diversity is in fact a strength. Also of interest here is how multicultural policies' positive framing of diversity affects interviewees' construction of their responses, including their ability to articulate experiences, beliefs and emotions that might be construed as negative. Chapter 6 reveals how the understandings and discourses illuminated in the previous two chapters translate into social and educational practices in the studied schools, from the identification of priority areas, structuring of programmes and pedagogical practices to pastoral care. The chapter sheds light on some of the consequences of these practices within and beyond the classroom, and in doing so highlights some of the (potential) barriers to the expressed objectives of multicultural policies. Throughout, emphasis is given to how imaginaries of the rural as well as rural realities (geographic, demographic, social, economic, political) influence individual and institutional orientations towards diversity, and the lives of all residents in this diversifying regional town.

The Conclusion ties together the themes discussed in the previous chapters and reiterates the aims of the book. It also canvasses the implications for educators and educational institutions as the trend towards a more 'plural rural' intensifies (Chakraborti & Garland, 2004). Research must extend beyond data collection, analysis and argument to action (Hylton, 2012). The persistence of racial and ethnic inequalities should in no way deter antiracism efforts; rather, it must strengthen the imperative to question and expose the 'architecture' of categories of and discourses about difference, while attempting to draw the 'politics of recognition close[r] to the politics of structural transformation towards an equal and just society' (Amin, 2010, p. 18). Such ambitions are fundamental to this book.

1

'Our Diversity Is Great' (Part 1)

Diversity as a Multiplicity of 'Cultures'

Introduction

Some years back, at a symposium in Sydney on cultural diversity in the workplace, one of the presentations was accompanied by a slide headed 'Our diversity is great' – 'great' as in substantial (in both the 'large' and 'important' meanings of the word) and 'great' as in 'wonderful', the speaker explained (Taksa, 2013). All of these meanings were prevalent in contemporary discourses about Australia, she noted, and informed workplace activities and practices such as Harmony Day celebrations and images used in corporate communications.

While the slide heading is simple and short, there is much to unpack here, and this task forms the basis of this chapter and the next. In broad terms, this chapter examines the notion that Australia is one of the most culturally diverse nations in the world (Ang, Brand, Noble, & Wilding, 2002; Collins, Reid, Fabiansson, & Healey, 2007) and problematizes two interrelated assumptions about this 'great' diversity – first, that it is evenly distributed geographically and politically; and second, that Australians are therefore all now accustomed to, and reasonably accomplished at, living with diversity. Such a perspective was voiced by the immigration minister in 2011 as he unveiled a new national multicultural policy, *The People of Australia*. 'Australian multiculturalism has worked', the minister declared. 'Different cultures are accepted. Values are recognized. Traditions and beliefs are practised. Foreign languages substitute for English when the right word just can't be found' (Bowen, 2013, Appendix). But as Markus has observed, living with diversity 'is not a destination. We don't get to the destination and say we've done it. It's something we need to work at' (quoted in Chan, 2016). Australia's diversity story is 'everywhere different' (Dunn & McDonald, 2001), always changing and always incomplete (Ang et al., 2006).

At a theoretical level, this chapter problematizes the ways in which diversity is discussed, represented and assessed in official contexts, and in less formal contexts as well – these ways often being quite different (Baumann, 1999). The claim to 'great' diversity is contingent on the idea that 'cultures' can be usefully defined by select domains such as language, religion and ethnicity/race, and groupings (or categories) within those domains; and that cultures themselves can be separated one from another, or categorized, and thus counted and compared. Categories, as Brubaker, Loveman and Stamatov (2004, p.38) explain, 'structure and order the world for us'; they are fundamental to how we perceive ourselves and others, and are perceived *by* others, within social and physical spaces. Accordingly, the chapter opens with an overview of Australian population statistics, looking at recent and historical data, trends and comparisons with other OECD[1] countries. It then examines the history of dominant categories and the nature of categorization processes before theorizing the sociocognitive mechanics of those processes, drawing on the work of Brubaker, Lakoff and Zerubavel. The same logics are extended to rurality and rural spaces – urban/rural being another sociocognitive construct, but one that is more than geographical (Massey, 1992). Here the affectivity of spaces, identities and encounters is considered in the context of debates about affect and emotion; in the context of discourse, the *performativity* of affect/emotion is also highlighted. Throughout the chapter, there is a focus on the relationship between categories and inequalities – or, more accurately, on how categories and categorization processes enable and constrain possibilities of being and belonging (Back, 2012; Fairclough, 2003). Categories, it is argued, can be deceptive, and attention must be paid to how they are deployed.

Deconstructing Diversity

Australia by Numbers

Australia is an immigration nation. Before convicts and settlers from Britain arrived in 1788, the continent had been home to hundreds of Aboriginal nations and language groups for an estimated 60,000 years or more (DFAT, n.d.-a). The Torres Strait Islands, north of the mainland, had similarly been occupied by people of Melanesian origin for thousands of years (DFAT, n.d.-a). The total Aboriginal and Torres Strait Islander population at the time the Europeans arrived is believed to have been between 315,000 and 1 million-plus (ABS, 2010). Today, Australia is home to close to 26 million people – 3.8 per cent (or about 984,000) of whom identify as being of Aboriginal or Torres Strait Islander descent, and 29.1 per cent of whom were born overseas (ABS, 2021a, 2018, 2021b). The 29.1 per cent overseas-born statistic puts Australia well ahead of Canada (23 per cent born overseas), Sweden (19.5 per cent), the United States (13.6 per cent), Germany (16.1 per cent) and the United Kingdom (13.7 per cent), along with the OECD average of 9.5 per cent (OECD, 2023).

Australia's high proportion of overseas-born is no accident but the result of a decade-long policy of nation-building through planned immigration (Collins, 2013). At the end of the Second World War, only one in ten Australians was born overseas – most of them in Britain or Ireland (Mence, Gangell, & Tebb, 2015). Since then, 7 million people have migrated to Australia, with the proportion of overseas-born continuing to rise into the twenty-first century – from 23 per cent in 2001 to 24 per cent in 2006, 27 per cent in 2011 to nearly 30 per cent in 2020 (Markus, 2016; ABS, 2021b). The range of ancestries and languages spoken continues to expand as well, with

Australians identifying with more than 300 ancestries in the 2021 Census, and more than 400 languages spoken at home (ABS, 2022).

Immigration channels have been varied. Currently, 160,000 permanent places are offered annually under Australia's immigration programme – roughly half in the skill stream and the remainder in the family stream (Commonwealth of Australia, 2021). In addition, Australia resettles 13,750 refugees a year through the United Nations High Commissioner for Refugees (UNHCR) programme, with an additional intake of 12,000 refugees from Syria pledged in 2015 (Markus, 2016). Since 1996 Australia has also offered a growing array of temporary visas, with the result that it now has well over 2 million temporary residents (Department of Home Affairs, 2022). Of all the immigrants to Australia in 2019–20, 18 per cent were born in India (the leading country of birth), 13 per cent in China and 7 per cent in the UK (Department of Home Affairs, 2021a). Between 2015 and 2020, immigration to Australia was marked by a shift away from Europe towards regions of Asia; migrant arrivals from the South and Central Asia region were the highest by 2020, followed by those from Oceania and North-east Asia (ABS, 2021b).

Statistics such as these are the basis for Australia's claim to 'great' diversity. But an alternative set of numbers, still using the same domains, presents a different picture. More than half of Australia's overseas-born population still come from English-speaking countries (compared with 5 per cent of immigrants to the US, for example) (ABC FactCheck, 2013), and England remains firmly at the top of 'country of birth' tables (ABS, 2021b). Similarly, while Australians, overall, speak hundreds of languages, 72 per cent of the population speak only English at home – making Australia the third most *mono*lingual country in the OECD (Wesley, 2009). Accordingly, the commentator Alan Jones has argued, 'Australia is not a multicultural society . . . . It is a multiracial monocultural one' (cited in Jakubowicz, 2003). These alternative perspectives highlight that there is no one way of evaluating diversity. Indeed, on a scale that combines ethnic/racial data with a measure of linguistic similarity, Australia is one of the *least* diverse nations (Morin, 2013); a 2002 analysis of ethnic 'fractionalization' (cited in Fisher, 2013) likewise puts Australia near the bottom of global diversity rankings.

What all evaluations of diversity have in common, however, is categories. Categories are central to our seeing and thinking – to rendering the 'blooming, buzzing confusion' of the world around us intelligible (W. James, n.d. [1890]). However, as Brubaker et al. (2004) point out, categories always involve 'more than mere sorting' (p. 38). They provoke expectations, affects and actions; they 'touch people in a variety of ways – they are assigned, they become self-chosen labels . . . . They may be visible or invisible to any other group or individual' (Bowker & Star, 2000, p. 314). Categories, in short, are powerful technologies – central not only to seeing and thinking but to talking, feeling and acting (Brubaker et al., 2004) and, importantly, to the 'play and negotiation of hegemonic practices' (Hall, 1990b, p. 18). As Zerubavel (1993) puts it:

> The way we divide our surroundings . . . determines what we notice and what we ignore. . . . [T]he way we classify people determines whom we trust and whom we fear. . . . [O]nly with [boundaries] do meaningful social entities (families, social classes, nations) emerge out of the flux of human existence. (pp. 1–2)

There are, of course, real differences between human beings – but what differences 'matter' and why, at particular moments in particular encounters in particular places, are realized only in and through language and other semiotic systems (Fairclough, 1993). As Jørgensen and Phillips (2002) write: '[O]ur knowledge and representations of the world are not reflections of the reality "out there", but rather are products of our ways of categorizing the world, or, in discursive analytical terms, products of discourse' (p. 5). Thus, although not real 'things-in-the-world', categories, through their deployment in social practices and relations, have real effects *on* the world (Brubaker et al., 2004).

This book critiques representations of cultural diversity as a smorgasbord of discrete 'cultures', reducible to categories such as ethnic and language background, but contends that the problem with such representations (and the understandings they promote) is not merely that they are simplistic. A bigger problem lies in the way the 'naturalness' of categories obscures the historical, political, social, cultural and organizational processes that have created and naturalized them (Brubaker, 2004; Creagh, 2016b; Santoro, 2014). A further problem lies in the equating of 'culture' and 'difference' (Watkins & Noble, 2021). As Bell and Hartmann (2007) write: 'The language of diversity rests on an assumption that few challenge: "Different from what?"' (p. 908).

. . . and in Words, Images and More Numbers

In light of the point raised by Bell and Hartmann, it is worth spending some time examining how cultural diversity is represented in Australia's multicultural policies. In the years since *The People of Australia* was introduced by the Gillard Labor government in 2011, Australia has had a number of changes of prime minister and government, with multiculturalism receding under successive conservative governments. The exception to this was the 2017 statement, *Multicultural Australia: United, Strong, Successful* (DSS, 2017), issued during Malcolm Turnbull's period in office. The difference between this document and the 2011 policy, however, is the omission of any reference to multiculturalism. The more recent statement gives emphasis to multicultural Australia in a descriptive sense, namely its culturally diverse population. The document highlights the importance of social cohesion and frames support for Australia's cultural diversity with concerns over global terrorism and the need for stronger border protection. In doing so, cultural diversity is cast as a potential threat to Australia's security therein providing only qualified support for a multicultural Australia. With a new Labor government, as of May 2022, a renewed commitment to multiculturalism may be forthcoming. The 2011 document, however, remains policy and so it is worthwhile to consider its focus especially as it offered a (re)commitment to multiculturalism at the time of its release. It begins: 'The Australian Government is unwavering in its commitment to a multicultural Australia. Australia's multicultural composition is at the heart of our national identity and is intrinsic to our history and character' (DSS, 2011, p. 2). This 'character' is represented in the image on the cover of the document.

Here the Australian population is portrayed as 'a multichrome mosaic of monochrome racial, ethnic, or cultural blocs' (Brubaker et al., 2004, p. 45) – a series of faces representing some of the many 'groups' within the nation, such as 'Chinese', 'Indian', 'Aboriginal' and 'Anglo', which together make Australia 'multicultural'. While the emphasis of multicultural policy has varied over the years, the imaginary of a distinct and cohesive Australian society based on a multiplicity of distinct and cohesive cultures has been constant (Cohen, 2001; Watkins & Noble, 2016) – reflected, for example, in the popularity of mosaics as a way of recognizing diversity (Watkins & Noble, 2021). This image also conveys other messages about diversity, and about diversity in Australia. It suggests that diversity is above all a visual phenomenon – about 'race' or 'ethnicity' more than 'culture', or even that culture and ethnicity are essentially the same. The image further suggests that diversity is spread across the country, and that no one 'group' is especially dominant – that in Australia, as the Harmony Day tagline goes, 'everyone belongs' (DSS, n.d.). The idea of Australia as inclusive and cohesive is underlined by the fact that most people in the image are smiling; they look happy.

In a newspaper comment piece for Harmony Day 2016, the minister responsible for multicultural affairs wrote: 'Australia's cultural diversity has been part of the nation's fabric for so long, it is easy to take for granted' (Laundy, 2016, para. 1). It is easy to take for granted, for instance, that the image from the cover of *The People of Australia* is a reasonable representation of the nation's diversity. Equally, it is easy to take for granted that the meanings of words such as 'culture', 'diversity' and 'multiculturalism' – which have long been household terms in Australia (Stratton & Ang, 1994) – are straightforward, and that these words are therefore used in fairly straightforward ways. The same can be said of everyday ways of talking about people's backgrounds and identities. Five decades of multiculturalism have transformed discourses and expectations about immigrants and their identities, and about Australia's identity (Ang, 2014). Before multiculturalism became policy in the early 1970s, migrants were expected to assimilate as quickly as possible, to 'melt into the national pot . . . [but now] they are not expected to melt' (p. 1190). To this end, successive Australian governments have funded programmes and services specifically for immigrants – and, separately, for people of Aboriginal and/or Torres Strait Islander descent. By doing so, governments and their agencies have not only endeavoured to acknowledge and cater to ethnic groups' needs but have played a major role in constituting them *as* groups.

Before examining further the messages conveyed by *The People of Australia* about the national cultural landscape, it is worth considering more closely how diversity is typically measured. As noted above, there is no agreed-upon or consistent way of defining 'culture' or of measuring cultural diversity (AHRC, 2016). 'Culture is ordinary, in every society and in every mind', Williams (2002 [1958], p. 93) has observed – and its ordinariness and everywhereness make it extremely difficult to operationalize. One familiar way in which culture is operationalized is through census categories, which also provide cross-country and historical perspectives on approaches to human differentiation. The Australian Census[2] seeks to quantify cultural diversity by collecting data on four domains: country of birth (of the Census respondent, and also of their parents), ancestry (also described as 'cultural background' and defined as 'not necessarily related to a person's place of birth but . . . an indication of the cultural group that they most closely identify with'), religious affiliation and language spoken at home (ABS, 2022). In addition to the general question about ancestry, the Australian Census asks a separate question about whether respondents are of 'Aboriginal or Torres Strait Islander origin'. By comparison, the Indian Census focuses on religion, caste and tribe; while the US Census eschews questions about religion but is interested in 'race' and 'ethnicity', distinguishing racial groups and origins (White, Black/African American, American Indian/Alaska Native, East/South-east and South Asian, Native Hawaiian and other Pacific Islander) and two ethnic categories (Hispanic/Latino/Spanish and non-Hispanic/Latino/Spanish) (Census of India, 2011; US Census Bureau, 2020).

Census domains and categories change over time as well as from one place to the next, reflecting shifting political, social, administrative and technological priorities and capacities (Jupp, 1995). For example, a review conducted in 2011 to maintain the Australian Standard Classification of Cultural and Ethnic Groups' relevance expanded the categories from 231 to 275 cultural and ethnic groups 'to reflect the changes to Australia's cultural and ethnic profile brought about by changing immigration patterns' (ABS, 2012a).

On the basis of those numbers, one could say Australia was *19 per cent more multicultural* in 2011 than in 2006. While such a statement clearly makes no sense, the enumeration of 'cultural and ethnic groups' highlights that categories and statistics *produce* phenomena and trends as much as they reveal them. As Brubaker et al. (2004) note: '[O]fficial census categories can have the effect of 'making up people' or 'nominating into existence', creating *new kinds of persons for individuals to be*' (p. 34; emphasis added) – not always, they add, with benign intentions or consequences. Equally, censuses can 'expunge' kinds of persons: Starr (1992) cites the example of 'mulattoes', or people of mixed European and African ancestry, who statistically were a distinct group in the United States before being reclassified as Black when the 'one-drop rule' was introduced in the early twentieth century. Censuses 'inculcate the idea that national societies are bounded wholes, composed of discrete, mutually exclusive ethnic, racial or cultural groups' (Brubaker et al., 2004, p. 34). They entrench notions about sameness and difference, about how and where the lines should be drawn. These lines, in turn, guide policy development and political action: 'who is who' paves the way for 'who gets what' (Starr, 1992).

While many people would acknowledge that the 'facts' of birthplace, main language and religion do not point to 'natural' affinities between people, what tends to go underrecognized is what categories – whether 'factual' or not, official or informal, chosen or imposed – *do* in daily life. Categories have consequences (Bowker & Star, 2000) – a reality glossed over by images such as the mosaic map on *The People of Australia*. They are, for instance, foundational to how nations constitute and imagine themselves. Thus, in contemporary political and media discourses, 'multicultural Australia' is a place where an ever-growing number of global languages is spoken and taught. 'Indigenous Australia', by contrast, is country[3] where scores of Indigenous languages have been *lost* since European settlement so that now only twenty to thirty have currency (Racism No Way, 2015; Walsh, 1993).

An Immigrant Nation, a Multicultural Nation ... but Not Always and Everywhere

Australia's identity as a 'multicultural nation' is well established, beyond as well as within its borders. Culturally still aligned with Europe but geographically, economically and increasingly politically tied to Asia, Australia has used its cultural pluralism to raise its profile and prosperity in an ever more interconnected global environment. Yet even if the problematic measures of ethnic, linguistic and religious diversity detailed above are adopted, cultural diversity remains far from ubiquitous in Australia. At a state and territory level, Australian Bureau of Statistics (ABS) data show marked differences in demographic profile. There are likewise significant variations in the distribution and nature of diversity across, and within, regions, towns and suburbs – pointing to variation, too, in people's exposure to ethnic, cultural, linguistic and religious backgrounds different from their own. As noted in the Introduction, immigrants are, overall, more likely to live in the nation's major cities than outside of them: in 2016, 83 per cent of the overseas-born population lived in capital cities compared with 61 per cent of all people in Australia (ABS, 2016).

In NSW, where this study is based, the state capital of Sydney ranks not only as Australia's largest city but as its largest 'EthniCity' (Forrest & Dunn, 2007). More than 40 per cent of its 5.2 million residents were born overseas compared with only 19 per cent born overseas in rural and regional NSW (ABS, 2021a, 2021b). In the state's government schools, 37.2 per cent of all students enrolled in 2021 were classified as LBOTE – but beyond the Newcastle-Sydney-Wollongong coastal corridor, the proportion of LBOTE students was on average 9 per cent, ranging from 8 per cent in the Riverina to 5.8 per cent in north-western NSW (NSW DoE, 2021a). Conversely, in non-metropolitan NSW schools the proportion of students identified as Aboriginal ranged from 10 per cent to 25 per cent, while the proportion of Aboriginal students in metropolitan Sydney schools ranged from just 0.6 per cent to 5.8 per cent (NSW DoE, 2021b). The *mix* of ethnic, cultural and linguistic backgrounds and religious affiliations also varies enormously within and across areas and institutions. The top two languages other than English (LOTE) spoken in Sydney, for example, are Arabic and Indian languages. Sydney West is the area with the largest percentage of LBOTE students, followed by Sydney South-west and Sydney South (NSW DoE, 2021a). Australia may be a 'multicultural nation', as its policies declare, but even on crude measures of diversity it is evident that different geographical areas have very different profiles.

A similar picture emerges in political spheres. As a neighbour of Asia, Australia has been receiving migrants from regional countries for most of the time since it was claimed as a British colony in 1788. The trend has accelerated sharply over the past thirty years, so that six of the top ten settler source countries in 2019–20 were countries from Asia, including India, China, Philippines, Vietnam, Nepal and Pakistan (Department of Home Affairs, 2021b). India and China together accounted for nearly a quarter of arrivals during that period (ABS, 2021b). At the same time, the rise of China and its dominance of Australia's trade tables (DFAT, 2015) have prompted an emphasis on 'Asia literacy', including in the national curriculum (ACARA, 2016a).

The contributions of immigrants to Australia's economic growth have long been recognized, while more recently a diverse workforce has been promoted as providing a competitive edge in the global economy (DSS, 2011) and enhancing problem-solving and creativity (AHRC, 2016; VicHealth, 2013). Despite this, as Hage (2000) points out:

> No matter how much it is maintained that multiculturalism reflects the 'reality' of Australia, the visible and public side of power remains essentially Anglo-White. (p. 190)

In the years since this was written, little has changed. Although an estimated 24 per cent of Australians are from non-European (including Indigenous) backgrounds, they are underrepresented among leaders in business, academe, government and the judiciary (AHRC, 2018). They are likewise underrepresented in the media and popular culture (Screen Australia, 2016) – and even in public forums about multiculturalism (Jakubowicz, 2014). There are, in other words, limits to Australia's claims to 'great' diversity (AHRC, 2016). This alternative discourse receives political, corporate and media recognition occasionally, as indicated by the references above – but only occasionally. 'Black and brown and mixed presence on the street, in stores, in schools, even if not quite at the university, in the boardroom, in the chamber of commerce', writes Goldberg (2006, p. 344). 'Few seem to notice.'

Diversity, then, is unevenly distributed geographically and structurally. Australia, for all its diversity, remains strongly dominated – spatially, politically, economically, intellectually and culturally – by people of Anglo-Celtic descent. The partial truth and contemporary utility of Australia's 'multiculturalism' is what allows this other reality, of its continuing Anglo-ness, to go underacknowledged.

The 'geography of power' sketched above cannot be explained simply by the relative size or length of settlement of different populations. Years/generations since arrival in Australia is certainly one dimension of diversity that impacts on migrants' trajectories. But diversity has myriad dimensions and intersections, including language background, proficiency in English, Indigenous/settler, reasons for migration, visa type and legal status, historical and political relations between groups, visible difference, cultural identification, socio-economic status, gender, age, education, employment, place of residence and so on. The salience of various dimensions is dependent on time, place and sociopolitical context. While categories are socially constructed and categorization processes socially inflected, they are also, clearly, *embodied*. Hence there is a need to consider in more detail humans' perception and experience of the social and material worlds they inhabit.

Categories, Categorization and Schemas

Interest in categorization has long been central to much academic work on culture and ethnicity (Brubaker et al., 2004; DiMaggio, 1997). As Lakoff (1987) notes, the 'classical view' of categories is that they are based on what things have in common – that is, on shared properties. We group things together on that basis, and could not function without the ability to do so. However, as many scholars recognize, that is far from the whole story of how we 'carve up' the world (Zerubavel, 1996). Categorization 'is not a matter to be taken lightly' (Lakoff, 1987, p. 5) – not least because much of it happens beneath the level of consciousness: 'In moving about the world, we automatically categorize people, animals, and physical objects . . . . This sometimes leads to the impression that we just categorize things as they are, that things come in natural kinds' (Lakoff, 1987, p. 6). Accepting that this is not the whole story alters fundamental conceptualizations of the nature of knowledge, truth and the relationship between the material and the social. An example is found in the title of Lakoff's much-cited *Women, Fire, and Dangerous Things* (1987), which in Dyirbal (an Aboriginal language spoken in north-eastern Queensland) are grouped together in the category *balan* – the similarities between them being grounded in a view of the world very different from Western perspectives. The naturalness of categorizing, as a universal and constant cognitive process, cannot be extrapolated to the sociocognitive and discursive *products* of that process – that is, categories – and how categories are deployed at both an official (macro) and everyday (micro) level.

The concept of schemas – borrowed from cognitive psychology – offers a way of explaining how categories are not only constructed but experienced, including why people tend to have strong attachments, both intellectual and affective, to cultural categories and identities (Brubaker, 2004). DiMaggio (1997) and Brubaker et al. (2004) note the historical epistemological and ontological divisions between psychology and sociology but point to growing areas of convergence between the disciplines. One reason sociologists have begun to take more interest in cognitive work is that the understanding of culture as 'values' has ceded to an understanding of culture as 'complex, rule-like structures that constitute resources that can be put to strategic use' (DiMaggio, 1997, p. 265). This shift directs attention to what those structures might look like: how they are formed, how they are organized and how they are activated. Schemas, then, are proposed as knowledge structures that both represent and process information, guiding how we perceive, store, recall, interpret, make predictions about and respond to what is within and around us (Brubaker et al., 2004; DiMaggio, 1997). Brubaker et al. (2004) do not make clear exactly how they conceptualize the relationship between schemas and categories, commenting only that 'there is certainly some overlap' (p. 42). Our ability to distinguish different 'types' of people, for instance, is accompanied by beliefs and expectations about how each 'type' is likely to act. As Brubaker et al. (2004) write:

> Such beliefs and expectations are embodied in persons, encoded in myths, memories, narratives, and discourses, and embedded in institutions and organizational routines. Even when we are not consciously aware of them, they can subtly (or not so subtly) influence our judgments, and even our very perceptions, of objects or persons so categorized, and thereby the way we behave toward them. (p. 38)

Investigating the relationships between perceptions, beliefs and expectations and institutional and individual practices (including discursive practices) is the core work of this book. Indeed, van Dijk (1993) argues that social cognition is 'the necessary theoretical (and empirical) "interface"' between discourse and society (p. 251), mediating between the macro and the micro and between mental processes and actions (p. 257).

Schemas have been conceptualized as hierarchically organized, as Brubaker et al. (2004) explain:

> The top levels, representing core, invariant aspects of concepts, are fixed, but lower levels have 'slots' that need to be filled in by contextual cues, by information revealed in the course of interaction, or by 'default values'. In this respect the concept resonates with the core ethnomethodological idea that all mundane interaction requires participants to 'fill in' unspecified information continuously from their stocks of tacit background knowledge.

The category of 'Aborigine', for example, is embedded in a schema that at the top level may consist of 'original inhabitants' and 'dark-skinned', while lower levels will contain experiential and evaluative information, and corresponding cues to appropriate action. This conceptualization of schemas allows them to be seen as, at the same time, shared (within a social group or across groups) and idiosyncratic. It also allows for modifications (within limits) to schemas, such as 'Aboriginal peoples are dark-skinned, but many people of Aboriginal descent in contemporary Australia are not dark-skinned'.

As well as having schemas for different 'kinds' of people (and objects), we have schemas for concepts, emotions, actions, events and so on. In academe, much attention has been given across disciplines to concepts such as 'culture', 'ethnicity', 'race', 'nationality' and 'religion' and the relationship between them (Baumann, 1999). As nouns, these words suggest entities rather than processes – something one 'is' (i.e. relatively fixed) rather than 'does' (much more fluid and flexible). However, how individuals and groups are identified – and how they identify themselves – may vary significantly depending on the situation, place and time (Brubaker & Cooper, 2000). Notwithstanding the different theoretical, disciplinary and sociopolitical histories of the concepts of 'culture', 'ethnicity' and 'race', the three are viewed here, following Brubaker et al. (2004), as grounded in the same cognitive structures and processes, and as similarly dialogic.

According to Zerubavel (1996), all categorization involves processes of 'lumping' and 'splitting', which entail constructing (as opposed to 'discovering') similarities and differences between phenomena. When we 'lump', we minimize differences among the things we have grouped together (Zerubavel, 1996) – examples being the grouping together in the United States of people of Cuban, Puerto Rican, Mexican, Central or South American origin as 'Latino' or 'Hispanic' (US Census Bureau, 2012); or in Australia of Aboriginal and Torres Strait Islander peoples as a single ethnic and cultural 'unit'. When we 'split', on the other hand, we magnify differences between the groups we have constructed (Park & Judd, 2005). 'In order to perceive a fundamental difference between "us" and "them"', Zerubavel (1996, p. 425) writes, we 'exaggerate in our minds the mental divides separating "different" ethnic, religious, and other social groups from one another'.

Categories, then, do not simply reflect intrinsic properties and affinities. Rather, they are constructed and given currency by a social entity (group, institution, state) in relation to an 'other' entity (person/people, object, action, event); they involve both a 'categorizer' and a 'categorized'. Logically, there is an inherent power imbalance in this process. Jenkins (1994) writes:

> The effective categorization of a group of people by a more powerful 'other' is not... 'just' a matter of classification.... It is necessarily an intervention in that group's social world which will, to an extent and in ways that are a function of the specifics of the situation, alter that world and the experience of living in it. (pp. 217–18)

The idea of categories as interventions is not in wide circulation at an everyday level. Against policies that for many years now have promoted cultural diversity and its benefits, it is easy to overlook or underestimate the power of categories and the capacity of some individuals and groups to categorize others.

Culture, Ethnicity, Race

The interventionary nature of categories is perhaps most recognizable in the concept of race – a form of human differentiation based on phenotypic variables such as eye, nose and body shape, and, above all, skin colour (Miles & Brown, 2003). While physical appearance is an 'obvious' marker of human sameness/difference, in that it is easily observable and reasonably stable over a lifetime (unlike, say, place of residence), what differences are noticed and foregrounded and what meanings are invested in them are social products. As Miles and Brown (2003) explain, 'when the idea of "race" is employed, it is the result of a process of signification whereby certain somatic characteristics are attributed with meaning and are used to organize populations into distinct groups that are defined as "races"' (pp. 88–9). Logically, it follows that the distinctions made and emphasized serve certain social, economic and/or political purposes. Winant (2000) argues that race is a relatively modern construct, one that was integral to the Europe-led development of a world political economy[4]: '[T]he dawn of seaborne empire, the conquest of the Americas, and the rise of the Atlantic slave trade were all key elements in the genealogy of race' (p. 172). Notions of White superiority were used to justify all manner of colonial and industrial practices, from displacement, dispossession and genocide to sterilization, family separation, segregation, language suppression, forced religious conversion, forced labour and slavery, while at the same time creating a sense of common ancestry and interests among those 'allowed' to be White (Koerner, 2011; Leonardo, 2004). Race, in short, was a crucial 'technology of differentiation' (Swanton, 2010) throughout the ages of exploration, colonization and industrialization, including the European 'discovery' and 'settlement' of Australia.

Science and human rights developments combined to discredit biological notions of race (as naturally occurring different races of people, distinguishable by phenotype) through the twentieth century (Amin, 2010; Lentin, 2008). Yet despite widespread acceptance now that races are 'socially imagined rather than biological realities' (Miles

& Brown, 2003, p. 89) – that race is a 'pigment of the imagination' (Rumbaut, quoted in Andersen, 1999, p. 7) – racialized discourses and practices remain pervasive, and powerful (Koerner, 2011; Miles & Brown, 2003). It is this paradox that is central to race-critical scholarship: as Ladson-Billings and Tate (1995) ask, if the concept of race is acknowledged as not 'making sense', why is it still so widely employed?

Other scholars have focused on the post-war turn to 'non-racial' ways of categorizing human differences, such as 'ethnicity' and 'culture' (De Lepervanche, 1980). Lentin (2006) documents how, after the horrors of the religious and ethnic genocides of the Second World War, the United Nations Educational, Scientific and Cultural Organization (UNESCO) gathered a panel of experts to draft a communiqué on race: 'The UNESCO panel, in particular the anthropologists who dominated it, wished to replace "race" as a theory of human difference with "culture", seen as a non-hierarchical, and thus more suitable, means of conceptualizing diversity' (Lentin, 2006, p. 385).

Socially, not only was 'culture' free of the hierarchical relations associated with race (both conceptually and in practice), it was also broader, encompassing language and religion as well as ethnicity, and capable of expanding to other domains such as class, gender, sexuality and (dis)ability. From a theoretical perspective, scholars also embraced 'culture' as allowing for the sort of fluidity and hybridity that characterize many people's identity and identification practices – complexities beyond the scope of 'race' (Ang, 2003; Hall, 1990a). 'Ethnicity', likewise, was taken up as less essentializing and more politically palatable than 'race', and has long been the preferred term in Australia.

'Race', 'culture' and 'ethnicity' are all socially constructed, however, and the distinctions between them are far from clear-cut (Baumann, 1999; Bowker & Star, 2000). In part, this is because they are underpinned by the same sociocognitive structures and processes. For cultural, ethnic and racial categories to be useful in everyday life, as well as in formal contexts, they must have a reasonable degree of definition – that is, of fixed features (Brubaker et al., 2004). Moreover, while the word 'race' may have fallen out of favour in many polities, the concept lives on in stories, artefacts, censuses, laws, institutional structures, curricula, pedagogical practices and so on (Ladson-Billings & Tate, 1995; Winant, 2000): changing the category label, in other words, does not necessarily change the underlying schema. Further, the intellectual and economic imperatives for racialization remain strong. Developed nations continue to depend on sociocultural hierarchies and inequalities for their power and wealth – on the primacy of certain knowledges, structures and practices, the dominance of English being one example, the 'offshoring' of hard labour (rather than indenturing) being another (Leonardo, 2002). At the same time, the ascendancy of a Black man to the White House, the end of apartheid in South Africa, and 'Asian' students' success in schools across Britain, Northern America and Australia (Watkins, Ho, & Butler, 2017) are regularly cited (usually by White people) as evidence that non-Whiteness is no longer a barrier to access, participation and achievement.

Together, these logics raise important questions about the extent to which race may be 'buried but alive' (Goldberg, 2006, p. 334) in twenty-first-century Australia. Cowlishaw (2004b, p. 59) offers a useful example, noting the post-war push by some

Australian scholars to replace 'the Aboriginal race' (the concept of race being seen as 'regressive, fixed and racist') with 'Aboriginal culture' ('culture' being deemed 'progressive, malleable and politically neutral'). These efforts, she writes, had significant impacts on policy and political discourses as well as academic work. However, the new domain 'relied on the same markers and "traditional culture" carried the same symbolic messages of heritability, primitivity and blackness as had "the Aboriginal race"' (Cowlishaw, 2004b, pp. 59–60). At the same time, the multidimensionality and 'malleability' of 'culture', as opposed to the biological determinism of 'race', allow 'cultural diversity' to be promoted as a strength in a way that 'racial diversity' could not. Strengths are usually not problems – and 'race' had become problematic by the mid-twentieth century. This 'turn' and its policy impacts are explored further in the next chapter.

Categorization of Culture/Culture of Categorization

For all the theoretical flexibility and complexity of the concept of culture, 'culture' in practice, as detailed above, is often reduced to a few select and relatively fixed domains. In an age of data, definable domains and categories are crucial, and categories' role in the rise of the 'audit culture' in schools and universities has been a subject of considerable academic interest (Connell, 2009). Globalization has amplified the power of the market, with commodification and standardization processes central to competition and accountability. Governments, Fairclough (2003) writes, 'now take it as a mere fact of life (though a "fact" produced in part by inter-governmental agreements) that all must bow to the emerging logic of a globalizing knowledge-driven economy' (p. 4). The language of commerce and accounting has spread to other fields; indeed, data is arguably the new global language.

States and institutions, like human beings, have to categorize in order to function. Sophisticated categorization systems allow masses of data to be compacted into manageable chunks, and thus facilitate analysis of 'classes' of people, objects, organizations and so on (Lingard, Creagh, & Vass, 2012). Processes of simplification, in other words, are necessary for rendering complexity intelligible (Watkins, 2011). On the other hand, processes of simplification can themselves be complex in both their mechanics and their consequences, and for this reason it is worth examining the categorization processes employed in education. In Australian schools, information is collected about a number of domains including students' language background and Aboriginal and/or Torres Strait Islander heritage. The two main culture-related categories are LBOTE/non-LBOTE and Indigenous/non-Indigenous (Creagh, 2016b). Since 2010, the proportion of LBOTE and Indigenous students at schools – along with a host of other data – has been published on the federal government's My School website, providing 'the most comprehensive data ever on the cultural diversity levels of all schools in Australia' (Ho, 2011).

Yet these categorization processes are far from straightforward. The Australian Curriculum, Assessment and Reporting Authority (ACARA), for example, has published a sixty-one-page document to guide education bureaucrats and schools on how to gather and code the required information. The manual was prepared to standardize reporting of student outcomes by a range of salient 'background variables' (ACARA, 2012).

Accurate data on students' language and ethnic background are important for ensuring schools receive support and services appropriate for their student populations, as part of efforts to tackle educational disadvantage. At the same time, the categories of LBOTE and Indigenous *create* a range of problems, both theoretical and practical. First, there is the construction of 'LBOTE' in opposition to 'non-LBOTE' and 'Indigenous' in opposition to 'non-Indigenous', which leaves the Anglo-Australian majority undefined within the 'non' groups. Not being a category in school data, 'Anglo-Australian' is not only positioned as the norm but also cannot be subject to the same scrutiny as those classified as LBOTE or Indigenous. A second problem is the inability of classification systems to recognize the hybridity that is characteristic of most people's ancestry and many people's lived identities (Lentin, 2006). Children of mixed Indigenous and other heritages, for instance, are required to choose whether to call themselves Indigenous – a not insignificant decision, as discussed in the chapters that follow. Related to this is a third problem: the way in which categories such as Indigenous and LBOTE mask the enormous heterogeneity of the people so classified. The LBOTE label, for example, applies equally to a child with two university-educated parents, one of whom speaks French as a first language, and a recently resettled refugee from Afghanistan whose single-parent mother speaks no English and has never been to school. Thus schools with high-LBOTE populations can be associated with extremely strong academic results, such as Sydney's top-performing James Ruse Agricultural High School (97 per cent LBOTE, selective entry), as well as with results well below average (such as Cabramatta High School, 96 per cent LBOTE, non-selective), depending on a range of other sociocultural measures. Nonetheless, as Lingard et al. (2012) document, for some years LBOTE students, as an overall cohort, have outperformed non-LBOTE students in national literacy and numeracy tests:

> [W]hat we have here is a case of policy recognition with the LBOTE category, but which really amounts to a misrecognition because of the aggregated, 'catch all' character of the LBOTE category. Potentially, this will lead to a lack of redistributive funding to ensure inclusion and equality of educational opportunity. (p. 324)

In other words, the current success of a significant proportion of LBOTE students may lead to a reduction in support and services for the whole cohort, to the added disadvantage of those already struggling at school due to complex social and educational needs.

In contrast to the mixed results for LBOTE students, schools with a high proportion of Indigenous students – most of which are located in rural and regional areas – are overrepresented among schools with weak academic results. Indeed, the proportion of Indigenous students at a school is the most heavily weighted negative variable in the My School national index of school (dis)advantage (Vass, 2014). The Index of Community Socio-Educational Advantage (ICSEA) was created by ACARA 'specifically to enable fair comparison' of students' results in national literacy and numeracy tests, in order to 'identify the difference schools are making to the students attending a particular school' (ACARA, 2015, p. 2). However, demographic data can be used for many purposes. Ho (May, 2011), for example, has analysed My School statistics for secondary schools in metropolitan Sydney and found evidence of 'White flight' – Anglo-Australian students increasingly opting for better-funded and better-resourced private schools, leading to consolidation of LBOTE and Indigenous students in public schools. She concludes: 'If current trends continue, we risk creating highly unbalanced school communities that, rather than reflecting the full diversity of Australian society, instead constitute unhealthy and unnatural bubbles of segregation and isolation' (Ho, 2011).

A final point here is that the current classification structure is not designed to allow that students may be of Aboriginal and/or Torres Strait Islander descent *and* from a language background other than English (Lingard et al., 2012). This is problematic because, while states and schools can detail exactly how many students ticked the 'Aboriginal and/or Torres Strait Islander' box on their enrolment form, they do *not* have accurate data on how many students speak Aboriginal English (recognized as a dialect, or rather dialects); the NSW DoE acknowledges that 'many' of the 50,000 Indigenous students in public schools (NSW DoE, 2014, p. 4) speak a non-standard form of English as their main language. Under the existing system, however, there is a risk such children will not be identified as LBOTE (and so receive appropriate support in learning Standard Australian English), but rather may be assumed to not be good at English or not be paying attention in class.

Together, the examples above illustrate how systems and processes intended to promote equity and inclusion can, under the weight of other factors and interests, have quite contrary effects. Not only does the 'tick-box approach' to categorizing people mandated by the education system have 'no finger on the pulse' of people's lives (Fanshawe & Sriskandarajah, 2010, p. 6) – on the diversity of their experiences, identities, family situations, beliefs, values, motivations, aspirations and so on – but those ticks (or lack of them) can have enormous impacts *on* people's lives. As Swanton (2005) notes: '[C]ategorization and enumeration produce legibility as they cover up the precariousness of identities, and conceal the indeterminacy and contested meanings of [cultural/ ethnic/racial] signifiers' (p. 7). 'LBOTE' and 'Indigenous' render only some people visible and in doing so create a cascade of consequences – educational, economic and social, and not always predictable.

Categories at Work: Classification and Identification, Expectations and Affects

So far this chapter has focused on categorization as a top-down process. Starr (1992) distinguishes between two processes in classification: that of ordering objects into categories and defining the relationship between them; and that of assigning objects to established categories. These powers are typically invested in different governmental bodies (Starr, 1992): the national-level ACARA, for example, determines that information should be gathered on students' gender, socio-economic status and geographic location as well as language background and Indigenous heritage (Creagh, 2016a), and tasks local practitioners and state-based education bureaucrats with collecting and collating that information in accordance with its guidelines. However, even despotic regimes cannot entirely regulate the production and circulation of categories (Brubaker & Cooper, 2000); people have their own ideas about categories and categorization processes – and 'not only ideas, but *strong sentiments*' (Starr, 1992, p. 269; emphasis added). As Fanshawe and Sriskandarajah (2010, p. 8) ask: '[D]o people feel enthralled by their group description or limited by it? Is there a difference when they use it [the description] themselves and when it is used by public bodies to label them?' This section considers categories at work in everyday discourses and practices among different people in different places – or, to put it another way, the relationship between official classification systems on the one hand and localized identifications and identities on the other. Like categorization, identification is processual, but the latter term is used here to distinguish micro-level processes from macro-level (categorization) ones.

One point emphasized by Brubaker (2004) is that categories are not groups, although people whom classification systems put together are often spoken about and treated *as* groups. Rather, categories are, at best, a basis for group-*making*. This distinction shifts interest to what people, individually and collectively, *do* with categories, from 'below' as well as from above – directing attention to 'the "micropolitics" of categories, the ways in which the categorized appropriate, internalize, subvert, evade or transform the categories that are imposed on them' (Brubaker, 2004, p. 170). Jenkins (1994) characterizes groups as essentially internally defined ('groupness' built by people within the group) and categories as externally defined ('groupness' imposed from outside). However, he notes, the distinction is 'primarily analytical. In the complexity of day-to-day social life, each is chronically implicated in the other' (Jenkins, 1994, p. 199). Social identity is forged in the ongoing interplay between categorization and group-making processes (Bowker & Star, 2000; Jenkins, 1994), between being positioned and positioning oneself (Hall, 1990a) or as Baumann (1999), following Charles Taylor, succinctly puts it: 'People . . . come to identify themselves, not in a soliloquy, but in dialogue with others' (p. 117).

One example of this is the production of 'Aboriginal and Torres Strait Islander' as a 'special' and unitary ethnocultural group in Australia. At a macro level, the ABS lists statistics on Aboriginal and Torres Strait Islander people separately from the rest of the Australian population, stating that Indigenous Australians are a 'comparatively small, but highly important, proportion of the total Australian population' (ATSIC, 2012). This is in stark contrast to the situation between 1901 and 1967, when Indigenous Australians were not officially included in the Census because of section 127 of the Australian Constitution, which stated: 'In reckoning the numbers of the people of the Commonwealth, or of a State or other part of the Commonwealth, aboriginal natives shall not be counted' (Museum of Australian Democracy, n.d.). The Constitution's lack of concern with Australia's original inhabitants reflected a widespread belief that the 'natives' were a dying race (Bennett, 2012) – or, in the eyes of some, that they were not 'human being[s] at all' (Tasmanian politician cited in Bennett, 2012). Indigenous Australians did not die out, however, instead gaining political power through the

1960s and 1970s – partly through mobilizing as the group 'Aboriginal and Torres Strait Islanders' even though there was, and is, considerable heterogeneity not only between Aboriginal and Torres Strait Islander peoples but within them (Shnukal, 2001).

At an everyday level, the term 'Black' – historically imposed as a form of racial groupness, boundary-making and domination – has been 'repurposed' by many people of Aboriginal and Torres Strait Islander descent as a form of *cultural* groupness that can serve a range of cultural, social and political interests: an identity, not a classification. There is now a flourishing Blackfella Films production company, for example, and television programmes such as *Black Comedy*, *Black As* and *Living Black* that showcase 'Black' humour (as opposed to 'Black humour'), 'Black' stories and 'Black' talent. Similarly, 'wog', once a term of insult deployed against 'ethnics' (by mostly Anglo-Australians), has been reconstituted by some Australians of southern European and Middle Eastern background as a shared identity and a term of affinity, affection and 'cool' (Panelli et al., 2009; Priest et al., 2016).

In short, categories are created and used in diverse and complex ways, for diverse and complex purposes. Research delving into the contents of people's diversity-related schemas – racial, ethnic and cultural categories, as well as concepts such as 'cultural diversity' and 'multiculturalism' – is discussed at length in the following chapter. For now I note that people's schemas of 'cultural diversity' may or may not include Indigenous Australians:[5] Hickling-Hudson (2003) points out that many Indigenous Australians 'resist being treated as just another culture in the multicultural model of Australian society' (p. 3), asserting their right, as the original and continuing custodians of the lands that are now Australia, to be recognized as a special group. Similarly, if a person is from the dominant cultural category in a nation, they will often not see themselves as included in 'cultural diversity': Australian research with pre-service teachers, for instance, documents Anglo-background students speaking of themselves as 'just normal' (Allard & Santoro, 2004) or not having 'much of an ethnic background' (Mills, 2008), or of people from minority ethnic backgrounds as having 'more' culture than they (the Anglo-Australian students) do (Santoro, 2014).

As the examples above illustrate, categories come to be evaluatively and often affectively 'tinged or charged' (Brubaker & Cooper, 2000, p. 18) by the knowledges and narratives in which they are embedded. Affects may be embedded in category schemas, or triggered, at varying levels of 'feltness', when an experience does not align with an existing schema (DiMaggio, 1997). Ahmed (2008) writes of how, whether consciously or not, we arrive 'at' people, objects, places, events and so on 'with an expectation of how we will be affected by them, which affects how they affect us' (p. 7). We may be disappointed, for example, when objects that we expect to bring us pleasure do not, and this disappointment may 'stick' to the objects that have provoked it. Hence – to paraphrase Ahmed – anyone or anything that creates disappointment (or shock, or frustration) may subsequently be read as *being* disappoint*ing* (or shocking, or frustrating). In other words, our affective experience of an object can alter our schema of the object, in the process transforming from something felt within us into a quality or 'essence' assigned to that object.

Categories and schemas generate expectations and inferences in the interests of efficiency, facilitating rapid interpretation of, and responses to, phenomena (Brubaker et al., 2004). From a sociocognitive perspective, stereotypes fulfil this same purpose – that is, they are part of ordinary cognitive processing, rather than (as they are often characterized) instances of faulty thinking or moral shortcoming (Zerubavel, 1996). Stereotypes are represented mentally in the same way as other categories and, like other categories, they mostly operate below the level of consciousness; this latter attribute, Brubaker et al. (2004) suggest, is why stereotypes are so difficult to shift. In forming stereotypes, we disregard or downplay differences between people we lump together as similar (Zerubavel, 1996) – assuming all 'Africans' are excellent runners, for example, or all 'Asians' are good at maths. Stereotypes mean that when we encounter someone new, we are able to quickly 'sum them up' and anticipate what they might do and say, or how they might make us feel.

While there are clearly downsides and dangers in this kind of thinking, Baumann (1999) cautions against dismissing stereotypes as 'wrong':

> If the people we study come out with theories we find false, we cannot simply rubbish them as 'false ideology' or 'false consciousness.' They form part of the realities we study, and we need to understand how they work, why people use them, and what people want to achieve with them. (pp. 90–1)

Moreover, as Brubaker et al. (2004) emphasize:

> The relevant questions are not only about how people get classified, but about how gestures, utterances, situations, events, states of affairs, actions, and sequences of actions get classified (and thereby interpreted and experienced). The questions, in short, are about seeing the social world and interpreting social experience, not simply about classifying social actors, in ethnic terms. (p. 43)

As these comments highlight, while actions such as topping the class in maths or frequently skipping school are likely to reflect a combination of socio-economic situation, family structure, peer group, gender, cultural background and other factors, they commonly become reduced to a single social domain: of race/ethnicity/culture.

Affects, Emotions, Sentiments

From a sociocognitive perspective, as touched on above, affects as well as actions can be attached to schemas of different racial, ethnic and cultural 'groups'. Not only may we expect certain people to act in certain ways, we also may have expectations about the affective impacts on us of our encounters and exchanges. Affect, feeling and emotion have long been subjects of fascination, contestation and study (Shouse, 2005; Thrift, 2004), although there remains little consensus across or even within disciplines regarding the usage of the terms and distinctions between them. Within education, Watkins (2006) notes, 'affect', 'feeling' and 'emotion' are often (and problematically) used interchangeably. Affect and emotion are of interest in two key respects in this study: first, the affective dimensions of thoughts, memories, beliefs, values, encounters, actions and so on, which may be consciously registered or not; and second, the presence (or absence) of affect/emotion in texts, and the *effects* of that presence or absence. The first, as embodied phenomena, are clearly relevant to the concept of schemas and theorizing about how people perceive, experience and respond to differences. The second sense is quite different and is most relevant in respect of the documentary and interview data used in this study. What I will call 'sentiments' – such as the expression of a view that diversity is 'great' (wonderful) – are discursive practices and have a performative function (J. Butler, 1997). The two come together in one of the significant questions for this book: How do macro-level positive framings of diversity *affect* individuals' expectations about diversity, lived experience of difference and diversity, and the ways in which they (can) talk about their expectations and experiences?

Massumi insists that emotion and affect are not synonymous but rather 'follow different logics and pertain to different orders [of connection]' (1995, p. 88). He distinguishes affect as non- or pre-conscious – 'embodied in purely autonomic reactions' (Massumi, 1995, p. 85) and thus also non-discursive; and emotion as 'the socio-linguistic fixing of the quality of an experience which is from that point onward defined as personal . . . [affect that is] owned and recognized' (Massumi, 1995, p. 88). Analytically, however, such a distinction may be of limited use. Consider, for example, an interview situation: if the interviewee laughs as she says something, she may or may not be conscious of having laughed; the affect or motivation behind the laughter may or may not be identifiable (recognizable) by the interviewer, or even to the interviewee herself; the laughter may be an 'escape' of affect (Massumi, 1995), or it may be feigned (performed) – intended to convey an emotion not actually felt in that instant, as part of the presentation of a particular self.

Other theoretical and empirical work in the field has centred on the number and universality of affects/emotions, their respective embodiments, and the relationship between affect and cognition. Tomkins, for instance, distinguished nine affects (all present at birth but shaped by life experiences): interest-excitement and enjoyment-joy (positive); surprise-startle (neutral); and distress-anguish, anger-rage, fear-terror, shame-humiliation, disgust and what he termed 'dissmell' or dislike of smell (negative) (Tomkins, 1962, 1963). Building on Tomkins's work, Ekman (1992) posited six basic emotions, or what he called 'emotion families' (fear, anger, disgust, sadness, enjoyment and surprise), claiming 'robust, consistent evidence of a distinctive, universal facial expression' for each of the first five (p. 175). However, the experimental evidence underpinning Tomkins's and Ekman's theories has been criticized as flawed, or at least inadequate, by some scholars (Leys, 2011). Matias and Zembylas (2014), meanwhile, raise compelling questions about the *performance* of emotions – suggesting that disgust, for example, may be suppressed and masked by displays of sympathy or caring in situations where the actor believes disgust is or may be socially unacceptable. Given multicultural policies' positive framing of diversity, I am interested in discursive as well as corporeal productions of affect/emotion, and how these mediate diversity-related practices within schools.

Importantly, schemas can have spatial as well as affective and evaluative aspects. Schemas relating to 'Indigenous Australians', for instance, might include associations with the outback, some country towns and Redfern (an inner-city suburb of Sydney with a relatively large Aboriginal population) – but not, say, with company boardrooms or the prime ministerial Lodge (Woods, 2013). Further, being (seen as) 'out of place' in a particular space can have material and social effects (Puwar, 2004b; Valentine, 2010). Writing about a 'very white' academic event she attended, Ahmed (2012) recalls how draining it was, as a 'person of colour' (her words), to be so overrun by Whiteness; conversely, she reports how energized she feels when she is *not* so culturally alone. Thus belonging, too, is a spatialized concept and embodied sensation (energy, ease, contentment): we belong *somewhere* (Noble & Poynting, 2010), often somewhere where there are a lot of people 'like us' in some way significant to us (class, gender, ethnicity, language, age, occupation and so on). In short, 'numbers can be affective' (Ahmed, 2012, p. 36). As survey data presented in the next chapter show, some Australians worry that there are 'too many' immigrants, or that immigrants from certain cultures or countries are less desirable or incapable of 'fitting in'. But as Hage (2000) points out, judgments such as 'too many', while they may have a 'racist' aspect, primarily reflect *'categories of spatial management'* (p. 38; emphasis in original) – attempts by institutions or individuals to define a space as belonging to certain kinds of people, and to regulate the entry of people into that space and the behaviour of people within it. 'Concepts such as "too many" are meaningless unless they assume the existence of a specific territorial space against which the evaluation 'too many' is arrived at', Hage (2000, p. 37) writes. This sets up a consideration of rural spaces and what 'types' of people are imagined to belong in them.

From People to Places – and People *in* Places

If, as social beings, we are always within language and discourse (Hall, 1991), so too are we always, as material entities, within space and place. Our physical surroundings affect us, as we do them; and the way we think of, talk about and represent space also has effects, including affective ones (of which we may or may not be conscious). As Massey (2005) writes:

> We develop ways of incorporating a spatiality into our ways of being in the world, modes of coping with the challenge that the enormous reality of space throws up. Produced through and embedded in practices, from quotidian negotiations to global strategizing, these implicit engagements of space feed back into and sustain wider understandings of the world. (p. 6)

The final section of this chapter links the affective dimensions of numbers and schemas back to the earlier point about the uneven spatial distribution of cultural diversity in Australia – and, crucially, to schemas about rural versus urban spaces. As noted in the Introduction, 'cities', 'towns' and 'villages' are social and historical constructs in the same way nation states and ethnicities are – 'mutually constitutive and dynamic categories, rather than discrete ontological or geographical entities' (McCarthy, 2008, p. 2). Just as with the categorization of humans, the defining and naming of spaces is never innocent; rather, it is an act that continually (re)produces difference and differential power (Edgeworth & Santoro, 2015; Garbutt, 2011). Places become entangled with ideas and images (Appadurai, 1988) – reflected in the association of villages with stability and heritage and cities with change and development, for example, or the supposed superiority of 'city slickers' to their 'country cousins' (Neal, 2002). In other words, spaces are constructed differentially in terms of social, cultural, historical, political and affective attributes as well as physical features.

'Rural', then, is imbued with many meanings beyond 'outside of the city'. In Australia, Ramzan, Pini and Bryant (2009) highlight the pervasiveness and power of 'outback mythology', established through discourses that construct rural and regional areas as 'the opposite of the city, encompassing a pastoral White middle-class elite whose stories are of the taming, conquest and ownership of land or of occasional (and temporary) heroic setbacks in such a pursuit' (p. 438). There is the ring of nostalgia in these narratives – nostalgia for a past when life was 'simpler' and when Europeans were masters of all they surveyed. These long-told colonial narratives present rural Australia as the *real* Australia (Forrest & Dunn, 2013; Jupp & Clyne, 2010) – a 'wilful, lavish land' of 'sweeping plains', 'ragged mountain ranges' and 'stark white ring-barked forest' (Mackellar, 2011 [1908]) in which Aborigines eke out an existence alongside European settlers. Beyond 'Black' and 'White', 'cultural diversity' is unlikely to be part of most Australians' 'rural' schema, notwithstanding contemporary discourses about the 'multicultural nation'. Equally, while multiculturalism may be a cornerstone of modern Australian identity, rural images and narratives are also powerful elements of Australian identity (Holloway, 2007). This connection is evident linguistically in the two main meanings of 'country' in English: 'country' as a nation state, and 'country' as non-metropolitan – the 'countryside' (Atkin, 2003).

The same is true in other culturally diverse nations such as Britain, Canada and the United States. As Williams (2007) writes: 'It is widely accepted that Britain is a multicultural society, except, it appears, in its vast rural expanses where the notion of multiculturalism is all too readily suspended' (p. 741). Cloke (2004) notes that while in terms of geography the urban/rural dichotomy is being broken down, 'the imagined opposition between the *social* significances of urban and rural [is] being maintained and in some ways enhanced' in Britain (p. 21). Thus, in the face of increasing, and increasingly widespread, ethnic and cultural diversity, the countryside continues to be imagined as a repository of 'authentic' Englishness (Sibley, 2006) – an Englishness 'bound up with solid breakfasts and gloomy Sundays, smoky towns and winding roads, green fields and red pillar boxes' (Orwell, quoted in Hunt, 2012), and which is incontestably 'White'. Against such imaginaries, Garland and Chakraborti (2006) found, the arrival in English villages of people who were *not* White often provoked a sense of shock and dislocation among longtime residents. In the United States, Winders (2008) has documented how the arrival of migrants from South America in Nashville unsettled the historical Black/White binary in 'Music City'. With established Nashvillians uncertain where to locate the Latino newcomers racially (were they Black? were they White?), many were 'hesitant and visibly uncomfortable' (p. 258) in interviews when asked about community relations – disoriented in, and by, the changing ethnic, social and cultural landscape.

As Panelli et al. (2009) point out, the contours of rural imaginaries vary substantially between England, the United States and Australia, 'encompassing quaint villages, fields of broad-acre farms, and lushly forested wilderness, as well as pastoral, frontier and outback landscapes' (p. 356). The fact that 'typical' landscapes often feature in popular poems, songs and even national anthems is no accident. Landscapes are one basis for distinguishing one region from another, and hence a basis for identity formation. Since around the time Europeans first came to Australia, Lowenthal (1991) writes, 'national identity has required having a heritage and thinking it unique. Heritage *differentiates*; we treasure most the things that set us apart' (p. 206). Because we 'treasure ... [what] sets us apart', landscape is also a powerful basis for attachment to country. The images quoted above of Australia's 'sweeping plains' and ragged mountains are from one of the nation's best-known poems, *My Country* (Mackellar, 2011 [1908]), in which the poet declares her love for the 'sunburnt country' she was born in over the 'field and coppice' of her ethnic heritage. Rural imaginaries, then, may differ in their imagery but, *through* these differences, be alike in their connection with and importance to national identity.

Another characteristic rural imaginaries share is their construction as spaces where tradition and tranquillity, continuity and connectedness are valued, and which are largely free of the sorts of social and environmental problems associated with big cities (Garland & Chakraborti, 2006) – spaces that afford a 'charmed life' (Baum, 1999, p. 1). Further, the traditions that are valued are overwhelmingly western European in origin, including traditions of permanent settlement, private land ownership and productivity (Prout & Howitt, 2009), and hard work as the basis for success (Atkin, 2003). In short, rural areas are likely to be 'Whiter' culturally as well as ethnically than urban areas.

When rural schemas are monochrome or two-tone, different-looking people who 'turn up' in rural spaces are likely to be perceived and interpreted as truly 'foreign' – in the sense of strange or unfamiliar as well as from another country. They are not 'expected'; they do not fit with the schema. Their out-of-placeness may cause longtime residents to notice them more as they try to reconcile their expectations (based on existing knowledge/past experience) with new information or experiences. As Fiske and Linville (1980) write: 'Within the category of relevant information, incongruent data will be attended more than congruent' (p. 550). This added attention may have effects on the 'attended-to' – a dynamic vividly expressed by Levy, a British writer of Jamaican ancestry:

> In the countryside I am so acutely aware of what I look like, not because people are hostile or unfriendly, but just because you are different. I always get the feeling when I walk into a country pub that everyone is looking at me, whether they are or not. You are glowing with colour. (cited in Cloke, 2004, pp. 17–18)

Numbers, as argued above, can be affective. In country towns, while absolute numbers of new immigrants may be low, in *relative* terms the demographic changes have frequently been substantial (Hugo & Morén-Alegret, 2008; Massey, 2008; Vertovec, 2007) and may be *felt* to be so. 'Visible difference' (from the norm), in other words, may feel more intense.

Another impact of heightened visibility may be that the 'foreigners' are perceived to be more numerous than they actually are. Thus 'a sprinkling of ... black and Asian bodies, especially if they are physically situated together, can be exaggerated', provoking anxieties about 'what will happen to the space if a large number of these "different" bodies are allowed in' (Puwar, 2004b, p. 72). Such perceptions and emotions may arise in rural schools, for example. Schools are enclosed spaces, and the sudden addition of a number of 'different-looking' bodies to a space defined by Whiteness may be unsettling. These dynamics may be one reason the experiences of immigrants who settle in rural and regional areas, and the experiences of members of the receiving community, are often different from settlement and integration trajectories in big cities (Crowley & Lichter, 2009; Popke, 2011). There are marked practical and logistical differences, too: finding suitable or sufficient employment and housing is typically more challenging in regional areas – for any new residents, not only overseas-born migrants (Hugo, 2008); and regional areas do not have the same range of services or specialized migrant services, or networks of people from similar cultural backgrounds, as metropolitan centres (Krivokapic-Skoko & Collins, 2014).

There are some things, then, that regional immigrant destinations have in common, but there are also many differences between them. Hugo (2008) points out that some towns' efforts to welcome and support refugee arrivals contradict stereotypes of rural communities as conservative and socially 'closed'. On the other hand, there have been instances in Australia when refugee arrivals have been overtly rejected – such as the NSW town of Tamworth's refusal in 2006 to resettle a handful of families from Sudan (Edgeworth, 2011; Norrie, 2006). Garland and Chakraborti (2006) also emphasize that 'othering' processes in rural and regional communities are far from homogenous, varying according to the newcomers' ethnicity, religion, gender, visa status, education and profession; spatial factors; the history of the region and current political and economic circumstances; and so on. One of the Tamworth councillors, for instance, attributed the opposition of residents to the refugees from Sudan to fear 'because they [the refugees] are tall and black' (as if that was a logical explanation). A fellow councillor noted that the town had been asked to resettle only five families: 'Five! And we [Tamworth] take 50,000 people for the [annual] country music festival .... [But the people from Sudan are] very tall, very black, and the first time you see them you do go, boing!' (Overington, 2007). Here affective reasons are cited for the locals' opposition (fear and shock or surprise), but there is presumably also an economic aspect: in other words, 50,000 economy-boosting visitors (many of them White) are more appealing than a couple of dozen 'needy' (Black) ones.

In Australia, refugee-resettlement policy has created a tension between schemas of rural spaces as fundamentally 'White' (Forrest & Dunn, 2013) and schemas about the 'culture' of many of the humanitarian entrants – increasingly, people who 'look different', from the Middle East, South-east Asia and northern and western Africa (Hugo, 2008). By looking different – by 'sticking out' – these newcomers may be seen as threatening the very stability, purity and predictability that are integral to popular imaginaries of the rural (Dufty-Jones, 2014). They may challenge the idyll of the 'rural community' as a sanctuary of cohesion and coherence (Baum, 1999) and a stronghold of "'traditional' values and ways of life" (Valentine, 2010, p. 529). They are a visible sign that *things are not the same as they used to be* – an embodiment, literally, of other forces impacting on rural life such as globalization and technologization.

Global flows of people, ideas, capital, commodities and so on continue to intensify, but as Valentine (2008) observes, 'not everyone sees themselves as part of this cosmopolitanism or will choose to participate in interactions with people different from themselves' (p. 326). New arrivals in country towns are, after all, *disruptive* in the sense that their presence alters familiar visual, social and cultural landscapes, thereby effecting 'qualitative changes in the everyday experience of rural space, and in the performance of rural identities' (Popke, 2011, p. 245). These physical and social changes trigger a range of responses. Popke (2011) notes:

> The everyday challenges to taken-for-granted sensibilities have no predetermined outcome; such encounters are equally capable of producing moments of generosity and mutual regard as they are of fomenting defensive postures and hostile dispositions. In order to promote the former, and dissuade the latter, it will be important to consider how these new interactions [between longtime residents and new arrivals] are given meaning. (p. 246)

One factor here may be the extent of an individual's attachment to the (imagined) orderliness and regularity of rural life – to everything being in its place and everyone knowing their place (Lowenthal, 1991). As a child, I remember being puzzled when my mother – who grew up in regional NSW – said things (as she often did) like 'she was a Carter' or 'he's an O'Neill'. I must have understood at some level that these comments were more than mere statements of surnames, but I had no idea what she meant. Now I would identify such namings as a particularly 'rural' practice and understand them as imbued with long histories of localized social and political interactions. In other words, in country towns surnames can speak volumes about where people 'fit' in the community – who they are related to, how long their family has been in the area, where they live, how many hectares they own, where they worship, how they vote, where their children go to school. Just as importantly, in smaller communities an individual's family name can instantly signal whether that person is considered to be, to use a farming phrase, 'of good stock' – 'well bred' in the sense of brought up with 'good' values and manners: someone who can be trusted. In a South Australian study, Baum (1999) found that for people born and raised in rural areas, the intimacy of social life was 'perhaps the single most defining feature of their experiences of community in the country' (p. 2). New settlers in an area, whether overseas-born migrants or not, may temporarily undermine this cherished intimacy and connectedness. Not only are the newcomers' faces unfamiliar but their names have no local history and hence no local meaning, leaving oldtimers to turn to other forms of identification such as (apparent) ethnicity. As long as a person can be identified as 'African' or 'Afghan', for example, she can be 'placed': the identifier can then rely on his 'African' or 'Afghan' schema to fill in other 'essential' information about that individual.

As for Indigenous Australians, the legacy of colonization means that they, too, may be seen – or feel as if they are seen – as 'not belonging' even when their forebears have lived in an area for centuries, if not millennia. In an ethnographic study of relations in the NSW country town of Bourke, Cowlishaw (2006) documents how the 3,500 residents tend to separate along Black/White lines even though many have Indigenous *and* European ancestry; with a third of the town's population identifying as Murri (a local Aboriginal designation), one elderly Murri resident commented: 'They [the "Whites"] look at you as if you shouldn't be here' (p. 435).

Cowlishaw provides an insight into the perspective of many of the town's Anglo-Australian residents, writing:

> The local Whites' pragmatic, empirical knowledge of Aborigines exists in opposition to the city's romantic view of them. Urban elite idealizations have allegedly led to the suffering of hard-working good [White] citizens whose property, security and decency have been undermined [by local Murris' actual or suspected petty crime and public disorder]. (Cowlishaw, 2006, p. 433)

Moreover, Cowlishaw (2006) reports: 'Besides feeling themselves to be victims of the bad behaviour of blackfellas, White people [in Bourke] are hurt by being dubbed racists for voicing what they believe to be unmediated accounts of their experiences' (p. 433). Thus 'justified' White resentments about damage to property may be amplified by White resentments about *unjustified* (undeserved) damage to reputation – that is, concerns about being perceived as 'racist' when in fact they have good cause to be annoyed.

Worth highlighting again is the effects of the historically and politically grounded, and bureaucratically perpetuated, separation between 'Indigenous' Australians and 'ethnic' Australians, and their simultaneous positioning as 'cultural others' in relation to Anglo-Australians. One consequence of this is that 'the Whites relating to Aboriginal people appear as totally unaffected by multiculturalism, while the "Anglos" relating to the "ethnics" appear as if they have no Aboriginal question about which to worry' (Hage, 2000, p. 24). For institutions (including schools) committed to multiculturalism, such fissures remain problematic, but also largely unacknowledged.

Conclusion

All systems of human categorization are moral as well as social and political constructs (Bowker & Star, 2000). Public discourses about ethnic and cultural issues thrive on 'moral and political binaries [such as White/Black and Anglo/ethnic], creating a façade of unified positions, a series of left/right orthodoxies that caricature the complexity of racialized relationships being lived out across the nation' (Cowlishaw, 2006, p. 431). One concern of this book is to investigate the categories used in interviews and everyday talk to identify individuals and groups in a regional town – who is named, how, by whom and in what contexts – and how people identify themselves. Naming, as a discursive practice, produces as well as reflects subjects and the differences between them (Fairclough, 2003; Kohli & Solorzano, 2012). Difference is also produced through silence and absence (Boler & Zembylas, 2003); the book is therefore equally concerned with who is *not* named and spoken about – whose presence is denied, or perhaps so 'normal' that it need not be named at all.

This is the first layer of what is considered here: how macro-level discourses and classification systems shape popular understandings of diversity, and how people in a mostly White regional locale describe themselves and others, and *in relation to* others. To uncover the impacts of these positionings, however, it is necessary to go beyond namings and names to a second layer – that of affects and attitudes, which may or may not be overtly expressed. Of central interest is how official positivity towards diversity is echoed, appropriated, challenged and resisted in how people talk about and respond to diversity. As Williams (2002 [1958], p. 93) has argued, '[a] culture has two aspects: the known meanings and directions, which its members are trained to; [and] the new observations and meanings, which are offered and tested'. Chapter 2 explores these two aspects, and the relationship between them, with regard to discourses about the *qualitative* 'greatness' of Australia's diversity.

2

'Our Diversity Is Great' (Part 2)

Policies, Discourses and Public Opinion

Introduction

The previous chapter focused on Australia's status as a 'multicultural nation', based on the diversity of cultural and ethnic origins, language backgrounds and religious affiliations of Australia's citizens as captured in Census and other demographic surveys. As that chapter began to suggest, however, 'diversity . . . is not what it used to be' (Vertovec, 2007, p. 1024). It is not only different in degree but different in nature: more complex, more dynamic and more widespread, as people, ideas, practices, systems, resources, products and so on circulate around the globe with unprecedented force and speed, causing ethnic and cultural origins to be refracted through an expanding array of variables (Vertovec, 2007; 2023). This is recognized in *The People of Australia* multicultural policy when it states that 'Australia will continue to have an ever evolving and ever diversifying population' (DSS, 2011, p. 6).

The starting point for this chapter is that Australian multicultural policies do not simply state the fact of the nation's cultural diversity. Perhaps because there *are* now 'no exits . . . from the multicultural world', as McCarthy (2003, p. 133) asserts, the policies go further, embodying and exhorting a particular perspective on, and orientation towards, cultural diversity. *The People of Australia* begins, for instance, by acknowledging the 'amazing breadth and diversity of Australian society' and repeatedly draws attention to the 'benefits and potential' (DSS, 2011, p. 2), both economic and cultural, inherent in that multiplicity.

In short, Australians are told, diversity is 'great' – good for everyone, and good for the nation as a whole. Whereas the previous chapter focused on Australia's diversity being 'great' in degree by examining the categories used to quantify it, this chapter focuses on the alleged *qualitative* 'greatness' of that diversity. The interest here is not in research purporting to investigate whether diversity is, in fact, a social and/or economic asset – such as US and British studies by Putnam (2007) and Letki (2007) on the impacts of increased ethnic diversity on social cohesion. Rather, the interest is in *discourses* about the merits (or otherwise) of diversity, as captured in policy documents, political speeches, media commentary and research data. This exploration of discourses begins with a discussion of critical discourse theories and consideration of policies as discourses. This paves the way for further contextualization and analysis of diversity-related policies in Australia, including state-level multicultural education and Aboriginal education policies. The chapter then reviews quantitative and qualitative studies on Australians' attitudes towards immigration, cultural diversity and multiculturalism, with a particular interest in participants' orientations towards and discourses about diversity compared with official discourses. Finally, consideration is given to studies on *teachers*' attitudes towards diversity, given teachers' influence in shaping young people's perceptions and experiences of cultural differences. Two questions guide the discussions throughout: First, *why* do Australian multicultural policies frame diversity as a strength – what, and whose, purposes might this framing serve; and second, how does, or might, this positive framing affect everyday talk about and responses to cultural diversity? As Ang (1994) observed almost three decades ago:

> So often do we hear official spokespersons make the claim that Australia as a nation has discarded its shameful racist past and embraced the values of cultural pluralism and tolerance that we are compelled to wonder what is at stake in the repetitive and insistent, ritualistic enunciation of such a rosy and 'politically correct' image. (p. 139)

The rhetoric remains insistent, making the question of 'what is at stake' even more important as the population continues to grow and diversify.

Discourse, Policy, Policy as Discourse

Language and discourse are integral to the human experience and have been objects of study for centuries. While much scholarship has focused on the mechanics of language – discourse as a linguistic concept – Foucault (1972 [1969]) shifted attention to discourse as a system of knowledge generation and circulation. Here discourse is conceived of as language *in action* (Danaher, Schirato, & Webb, 2000) – the product of rules that delimit what can and cannot be said (what is 'meaningful', 'true', even moral), and by whom, at a particular time under a particular sociopolitical regime (Hall, 1997; Jørgensen & Phillips, 2002). Discourses, in other words, do not (simply) identify phenomena but *constitute* them, and in so doing conceal the (f)act of their construction (Foucault, 1972 [1969]). 'Discourse may seem of little account', Foucault wrote, 'but the prohibitions to which it is subject reveal soon enough its links with desire and power' (quoted in Maguire & Ball, 1994, p. 6).

Such a perspective influenced Fairclough's approach to discourse analysis and his development through the 1990s of critical discourse analysis (CDA) – although within CDA there are also multiple approaches, including van Dijk's more sociocognitive orientation. Fairclough describes its aims as:

> to systematically explore often opaque relationships of causality and determination between (a) discursive practices, events, and texts, and (b) wider societal and cultural structures, relations, and processes; to investigate how such practices,

events, and texts arise out of and are shaped by relations of power and struggles over power; and to explore how the opacity of these relationships between discourse and society is itself a factor securing power and hegemony. (Fairclough, 1995, pp. 132–3)

As with Foucauldian analyses, CDA emphasizes the importance of the *con*text of texts – what they 'arise out of' – to the meanings that are made of them and hence their cognitive, social and political effects and consequences (Fairclough, 2003). Central to CDA is a concern with 'continuity and change' (Fairclough, 2003, p. 3) – how language (re)produces, and occasionally unsettles, systems of power and differential advantage. Following Foucault, Fairclough (2003) explains that discourses are not simply representations of the world, they are also 'projective, imaginaries, representing possible worlds which are different from the actual world, and tied in to projects to change the world in particular directions' (p. 124).

Policies, as texts, can be usefully subjected to CDA, with analysis focusing not only on a policy's linguistic features but on its links with other policies and discourses, present and past – their intertextuality and interdiscursivity (Ball, 1993; Fairclough, 2003). In the case of *The People of Australia*, one might ask questions such as: What are the national and global contexts of this policy? How does it relate to other national policies on matters such as immigration, trade and security, and discourses about national identity, values and so on? What *actions* does the policy's positive framing of diversity suggest and, conversely, disallow? How are the policy's objectives ranked, explained and connected? And what continuities and changes are implicit in all of the above? These questions underpin the discussion of *The People of Australia* and other diversity-related policies that follow.

First, however, it is worth considering more closely what policies are and what they are intended to do. Policies take many forms, but are commonly understood as texts that set out a position and/or guidelines for action in relation to a significant issue or problem. That is, they provide a representation of some phenomenon and seek to promote a particular (re)orientation towards it among particular audiences. At a national level, policies are likely to relate to (perceived) national interests and their protection or optimization. A positive framing of cultural diversity, for example, may be seen as related to an interest in maintaining a harmonious and productive society as international migration broadens and intensifies. Policy, however, is never simply about 'rational decision making and planning' (Bacchi, 2000, p. 50). Rather than necessary governmental or institutional responses to existing conditions and issues, policies can also be read as 'a discourse in which both problems and solutions are created' (Goodwin, 1996, p. 67). In other words, the very (f)act of having policies on diversity helps to construct diversity as a (potential) problem, even as the policies' purpose is to minimize the potential drawbacks associated with diversity in order to maximize potential gains.

In this context the ordering in *The People of Australia* of its four multicultural principles (DSS, 2011, p. 5) bears examination. The first principle promotes the celebration and valuing of diversity within a cohesive, harmonious and democratic society. The second emphasizes the values of fairness and inclusivity, and the importance of strong access and equity programmes for immigrants. Third is an appreciation of the wide-ranging economic benefits that diversity has brought and continues to bring. The final principle complements the first and second in its commitment to advancing intercultural understanding and reducing racism and discrimination. Only in this last principle – after the 'celebrating', 'valuing' and 'embracing' – is there tacit acknowledgment that cultural differences and how people respond to them are potentially a *threat* to social cohesion, and hence to national unity and prosperity (Kalantzis, 1988; Salter & Maxwell, 2016). 'Multiculturalism is our shared future and is central to our national interest', the policy declares (DSS, 2011, p. 6). In this lies the critical challenge for multiculturalism: the tensions between the inevitability and economic desirability of cultural diversity, the democratic ideals of fairness and equality, and the realities and legacies of long histories of social exclusions and oppressions (Hartmann, 2015).

A final point here is the relationship between discourse and dominance. Van Dijk (1993) draws attention to the roles of repetition and consensus in hegemony, noting that 'dominance may be enacted and reproduced by subtle, routine, everyday forms of text and talk that appear "natural" and quite "acceptable"' (p. 254). Hegemony depends not only on the discourses of the powerful but on the *take-up of those discourses by the less-powerful*, leading to their normalization. Thus it is vital to investigate not only official multicultural policies but what ordinary Australians say, and feel, about them – the ways in which policies-as-discourses (Bacchi, 2000) are 'actually received, and responded to, by audiences' (Condor, 2000, p. 179). Such data are critical to understanding the effects, and effectiveness, of multiculturalism on the ground (Jakubowicz & Ho, 2013b). Also important are the international and national contexts of current policies.

Before turning to these topics, some further explanation is needed of the organization of multicultural policies and initiatives in Australia. At the federal level, *The People of Australia* is the most recent in a series of national multicultural policies spanning almost fifty years. Unlike Canada, Australia does not have a national Multiculturalism Act, but in reality much policy work is done at the state and local government levels (Dunn et al., 2001; Koleth, 2010). NSW *does* have a Multicultural Act, the Multicultural NSW Act 2000, and 'was the first state in Australia and the second in the world to introduce a deliberate policy that welcomes cultural and linguistic diversity as a social and economic advantage' (Multicultural NSW, n.d.-b). This Act, as noted in the Introduction, begins by establishing a particular orientation towards diversity ('. . . regarded as a strength and an asset'), and the multicultural principles it subsequently sets out provide the framework for the NSW DoE's *Multicultural Education Policy* (NSW DoE, 2016c, 3.2, 3.3)[1]. Another policy of relevance to this study is the NSW DoE's *Aboriginal Education and Training Policy*, developed in partnership with Aboriginal organizations and communities in response to a statewide 2004 review of Aboriginal education (NSW DoE, 2016a). The state education department's first Aboriginal education policy was published in 1982, its focus being on 'involving Aboriginal communities and students in education, enhancing Aboriginal students [sic] self-esteem and cultural identity, and teaching all students about Aboriginal societies past and present' (BOSTES, 2010). The policy came a decade after the overturning of a long-standing right of public school principals to remove Aboriginal children from their schools or refuse them entry (BOSTES, 2010). In contrast to *The People of Australia* and earlier education policies, both current NSW DoE policies foreground equity rather than cultural recognition, acknowledging educational institutions' particular importance in shaping how cultural differences are perceived and attended to, which in turn can substantially affect students' educational and social outcomes. Both the *Multicultural Education* and *Aboriginal Education and Training* policies are also underpinned by the NSW DoE's *Anti-racism Policy*, which commits to 'the elimination of all forms of racial discrimination in NSW Government schools' (NSW DoE, 2016b). However, schools do not exist in a vacuum: as Ball (1993) reminds us, 'policies enter existing patterns of inequality, eg the structure of local markets, local class relations [and] "impact" or are taken up differently as a result' (pp. 11–12). While specific education policies may be designed to reduce inequalities, they are at the same time 'affected, inflected and deflected' (Ball, 1993, p. 12) by other policies, discourses, structures, practices and so on that will mediate their effects.

Multiculturalism: The Sales Pitch and the Small Print[2]

If multiculturalism is 'at the heart of our national identity' and 'our shared future' (DSS, 2011, p. 2, p.6), it is crucial that ordinary Australians support it. From this perspective *The People of Australia* can be seen as a promotional document – one designed not only to set out values, principles and initiatives but to 'sell' the public on them as well. Certainly it has some of the characteristics of promotional materials (Taylor, 2004): attractive, uncluttered layout; use of colour; the front-cover mosaic image (discussed in Chapter 1) and high-quality photographs inside (smiling people of different ethnicities); a foreword by the prime minister ('I am a migrant . . .' – DSS, 2011) along with messages from immigration officials; and a confident, engaging 'voice'. Following Foucault, Fairclough and van Dijk, I draw attention to the heightened importance of language as a technology of governance in modern societies. Noting governments' increasing use of promotional genres in their communications with their publics, Fairclough (2001) argues that this has become 'a crucial element in producing change', adding: 'And part of what genres do is manage perception, shape the way people "see" [a phenomenon or issue] . . . and promote new discourses' about that phenomenon or issue (p. 254).

So how *do* Australians 'see' themselves, their country and their future? A 2013 study commissioned by the Special Broadcasting Service (SBS)[3] found that 'all Australians believe one thing is certain, the growth of multiculturalism' (SBS, 2014). The attractive simplicity of this finding, however, is immediately complicated by the use of the word 'multiculturalism'; what the researchers appear to mean is 'growth of cultural diversity'. This example highlights the often-confused application of the word 'multiculturalism' and its adjectival offshoot, 'multicultural' – a situation that demands careful reading of policy documents and research data alike. Hage (2008) has argued that multiculturalism 'is not the existence of communalized ethnic groups, nor is it cultural diversity or cultural plurality as such. Rather, it is a very specific mode of perceiving, experiencing and evaluating both the existence of communalized cultural difference and the inability of the state to nationalize this difference' (p. 492). As already touched upon, there are tensions between 'multicultural' as a description of 'how things are' (Goldberg, 2006, p. 358) – that is, ethnically and culturally diverse – and 'multiculturalism' as a *prescription* for 'how things are to be done' (Goldberg, 2006) – that is, for managing that diversity (Salter & Maxwell, 2016). As Kalantzis (1988) points out, that there is felt to be a need for such prescription implies diversity is, at the least, challenging. Nonetheless, ordinary Australians do not necessarily make the distinctions between cultural diversity, cultural plurality and multiculturalism – or between culture, ethnicity and race, or nationhood, ethnicity and religion (Lentin, 2006) – that academics do when thinking and talking about these phenomena. The meanings and implications of multiculturalism are 'diffuse, amorphous and multifaceted', Hartmann (2015) notes, and, not surprisingly, 'contested and controversial . . . . it means different things in different contexts' (p. 623).

International and National Contexts

Political developments and discourses since the September 2001 terrorism incidents in the United States have made promoting multiculturalism as the basis for a *shared* future more complicated. In 2005, the UK Commission of Racial Equality chairman, Trevor Phillips, famously warned that Britain was 'sleepwalking' into ethnic and cultural segregation (*The Guardian*, 2005). Six years later, the nation's prime minister, David Cameron, made public his loss of faith in state multiculturalism (BBC, 2011). Around the same time, the German chancellor, Angela Merkel, declared that *multikulti* – 'the approach [to build] a multicultural [society] and to live side-by-side and to enjoy each other' – had 'failed, utterly failed'[4] (quoted in BBC, 2010).

It was against the backdrop of this 'death of multiculturalism' discourse (Modood, 2014) that *The People of Australia* policy was released in February 2011, accompanied by a speech by the immigration minister entitled 'The Genius of Australian Multiculturalism'.[5] The minister began:

> It appears to be fashionable around the world at the moment to declare multiculturalism dead or to blame it for crime and terrorism . . . . Around the world, particularly since September 11 2001, the question has been asked: does multiculturalism strengthen a society or weaken it? My argument tonight is that multiculturalism has, without a doubt, strengthened Australian society. But it is a unique, Australian multiculturalism, built differently to other models.

The speech was used, in short, to draw a line between 'Australian multiculturalism' and other 'brands' (such as the English and German models) – to acknowledge concerns about diversity and its impacts, but to reassure Australians that *this* nation's multicultural future remained not only viable but vibrant. Three elements were identified as pivotal to the 'genius' of Australian multiculturalism: respect for Australian values, a citizen-centred multiculturalism and political bipartisanship.

Domestically, the policy was part of the then Labor government's (2007–13) efforts to position itself as more socially progressive than the conservative Coalition government that had preceded it (1996–2007). A priority for the new Labor government was a national apology by the prime minister, Kevin Rudd, to Australia's Indigenous peoples (Australian Government, n.d.) – something Rudd's predecessor, John Howard, had refused. *The People of Australia* came three years after the apology, and was symbolically significant 'if only for the willingness to re-embrace the term "multiculturalism", which had been in danger of disappearing altogether from official discourse' (Ho, 2013, p. 40). Before becoming prime minister, Howard had publicly declared his opposition to the word 'multiculturalism', and under his government the policy, while never abandoned, was sharply downgraded (Ho, 2013).

Towards the end of the 'genius of Australian multiculturalism' speech, the minister also contrasted the culturally diverse Australia of today with the Anglocentric Australia of the 1970s and earlier, saying: 'We now live in a nation shaped by migration: one with broader horizons, open and tolerant. . . . We recognize and celebrate different cultural heritages but insist that our future is common, is shared.' This is a key aspect of the multiculturalism sales pitch for both domestic and international audiences: Australia is culturally diverse, as are many other nation states, but *its* diversity is not divisive. It is, on the contrary, a defining strength – or, in the language of marketing, a unique selling point.

Immigration has been critical to Australian nation-building for seventy years – contributing not only to population growth but to a general prosperity that has made it easier for immigrants to establish themselves financially, thereby facilitating their social integration (Colic-Peisker & Robertson, 2015). Aided by an unprecedented twenty-five years of national economic growth, Australians are presented as better at living 'together-in-difference' (Ang, 2003) than other countries' citizens. Indeed, a later prime minister, Malcolm Turnbull, has repeatedly claimed: 'This is the most successful multicultural society in the world' (Davey, 2017). In addition, the diversity of Australia's population has been presented as making the country a superior global citizen: 'We better understand the world and better understand our region', the immigration minister declared in 2011. As Ang (2014) observes:

> Australia today prides itself explicitly as a multicultural nation that has been extremely successful in integrating migrants from all over the world. This inclusionary national self-definition has been put forward as an enormous break from the exclusionary policy of 'White Australia',[6] which imposed a strictly homogenizing and assimilationist national image on the citizenry. (p. 1186)

The Small Print

Notwithstanding the 'pride' in Australia's successful metamorphosis into a 'multicultural nation', 'diversity' remains diversity within limits; this is the 'small print' of Australian multiculturalism. Diversity is constructed as a strength provided immigrants are committed to an Australia in which English is the common language (the fourth principle of the Multicultural NSW Act 2000, for example); provided, as the former prime minister Tony Abbott said at the launch of the 2013 election campaign, they 'come here to join us, not to change us' (Abbott, 2013); and provided, above all, it has broad and substantial benefits for business, trade and the overall economy.

In spite of this small print – or perhaps because of it – a second aspect of the multiculturalism 'sales pitch', as noted by Ang (2014), is that current policy is far removed from historical policies such as assimilation (the 1950s and 1960s) and racial exclusion (the first half of the twentieth century). Even at a commonsense level, it is clear that policymakers, try as they might, cannot separate new policies from old so decisively: new laws and documents may replace previous ones, but the effects of past iterations linger in institutional structures and practices, and in everyday understandings, discourses and interactions. Social relations in twenty-first-century Australia are marked by tolerance *and* prejudice, harmony *and* racism, inclusion *and* inequality. These contradictions show up consistently in both quantitative and qualitative research on diversity and diversity-related phenomena.

In terms of wider political and social effects, the contrasting of multiculturalism with pre-1970s policies – particularly the White Australia policy – has been the subject of much analysis and debate. Even when multiculturalism was still in its infancy, De Lepervanche (1980) summed up the issue when she asked: '[W]hy is ethnic diversity celebrated today when the past was very different? [In] what way is [the] shift in the culturally acceptable related to structural changes in Australian society?' (pp. 25, 26). The White Australia policy was intrinsic to progress towards and then actual federation in 1901 (Markus, 2003) – designed in part to enhance a sense of ethnic and cultural unity, of mutual belonging to and investment in a new commonwealth. Although explicitly discriminatory and rooted in a belief in European racial and cultural superiority, the White Australia policy was also underwritten by a desire for a version of social justice (Markus, 2014a): keeping cheap (non-European) labour out was central to the quest to free the (White, Christian) 'working man' from the shackles of second-class citizenship he had endured in Britain. Politically, economically and socially, the aim was to be like Britain, only better and fairer.

The social justice agenda did not extend to Indigenous Australians, in part because it was assumed they would soon die out. That the Aborigines did *not* become 'extinct', as expected, was a key factor in the unravelling of the White Australia policy in the 1940s and 1950s – other factors being the difficulty of preventing mixing between Anglo and Indigenous Australians, and of keeping out all non-European migrants; the need, given Australia's geographical location, to nurture diplomatic and trade relations with Asian neighbours; and international concern with human rights in the aftermath of the Second World War – both reflected in and heightened by 1948's *Universal Declaration of Human Rights*, in which Australia played a leading role (AHRC, n.d.-b; Markus, 2003). As migration flows increased and trade opened up in the post-war decades, mass immigration and cultural diversity came to be seen not as a threat but as a fillip to growth, prosperity and global political presence.

Nonetheless, approaches to regulating migrant inflows and managing the resultant ethnic and cultural diversity have gone through several phases since the establishment in 1945 of Australia's first immigration department. During the 1950s and early 1960s, as the White Australia policy became increasingly untenable (Bulbeck, 2004), the political, social and cultural environment remained strongly assimilationist. The assumption was that adapting to a new country was reasonably straightforward, requiring only effort (on the part of the immigrants) and time (Koleth, 2010). There was also a view that the new arrivals were lucky to be in Australia and should not expect 'special treatment' in the form of language learning, translation or other migrant-specific services (Collins, 1993). By the mid-1960s, however, there was a growing recognition that resettlement was a challenging and protracted process, and that targeted assistance for migrants could in fact yield substantial social and economic dividends. Indeed, both 'old' and 'new' Australians had come to see – if from different perspectives – that for people who were not Caucasian in appearance or whose first language was not English, 'becoming same... [was] an impossible project' (Ang, 2014, p. 1190). Allowing migrants to retain certain aspects of their 'ethnic' selves therefore seemed the best way forward. At the same time, there was a greater insistence on the part of 'new' Australians as their numbers grew that their becoming Australian should not necessarily require that they 'extinguish' (as far as possible) their pre-arrival selves. With these shifts came a move towards a policy of integration – a transitional phase between assimilation and the introduction of multiculturalism in the 1970s (Ho, 2013).

The term 'a multi-cultural society' was first used in an official Australian policy statement in 1973 in a speech delivered by the immigration minister of the day, Al Grassby (Labor) (Koleth, 2010). Two years later, when the Liberals came to power, Prime Minister Malcolm Fraser endorsed and consolidated the concept. The year 1975 also saw the enactment of the Racial Discrimination Act, making it unlawful to discriminate against anyone on the basis of their racial, ethnic, cultural or national background or immigration status. A 1977 submission by the Fraser-appointed Australian Ethnic Affairs Council proposed social cohesion, cultural maintenance and equality of opportunity as the core principles of the fledgling policy (Koleth, 2010).

Notwithstanding the various shifts in policy emphasis and prominence since then, Hage (2008) makes an important point when he writes that proponents of multiculturalism have often portrayed its introduction as 'a moral choice: because they [political leaders] "thought" it was good in opposition to the policy of 'assimilation', now deemed racist and bad' (p. 491). In reality, it was not so much a choice as a product of social pressures: '[I]t was not because of multiculturalism that people strived to maintain their cultures; rather, it was because people were striving to maintain their cultures that multiculturalism was needed' (Hage, 2008, p. 491).

Virtues and Strategies

In short, official policy over the course of the twentieth century moved from trying to stamp out non-Anglo identities and practices (assimilation) to 'allowing' them (integration) to actively encouraging them (multiculturalism). This is the well-known narrative of Australia's journey from intolerance to tolerance of diversity – a journey in which schools were always seen as the pace-setters, the 'crucibles'[7] of a new ethos. Schools are potent social, political and cultural sites – places 'where the state, as nation builder and maker of national identity, can play its most deliberate, systematic, and sustained socialising role' (Kalantzis, 1989, p. 3), particularly as schooling is compulsory for all Australian children between the ages of six and at least fifteen[8] (ACARA, 2013).

In addition to the agency of immigrants in engineering Australia's turn to multiculturalism, what is missing from the discourse of the nation's 'transformation' is the impact of contemporary geopolitical developments. Australia's resettling of refugees from Vietnam during 1976–81 – after the fall of Saigon in 1975, and soon after Australia's official adoption of multicultural policy – was framed as guided by compassion and humanitarian obligations, but was at least as much a capitulation to intensifying pressure from Australia's South-east Asian neighbours (Betts, 2001; Kalantzis, 1989). Other data also undermine the presentation of the turn to multiculturalism as a 'mere benevolent choice' made by 'enlightened' (White) Australian leaders (Hage, 2000, p. 101). Opinion poll data from the time, for example, show a steady rise in antipathy towards Vietnamese 'boat people' (asylum seekers who arrived by sea, without visas) as their numbers swelled between 1977 and 1979, with saturation media coverage fanning fears of an 'Asian invasion' (Betts, 2001).

The 1975–83 Fraser government, generally lauded today for its openness and tolerance, succeeded in making 'a virtue of necessity' (Betts, 2001, p. 36). However, as Hage (2000) argues, tolerance is a strategy, not a virtue. In twenty-first-century Australia, it is a strategy that serves at least two important functions. The first relates to processes of government and governance and how tolerance contains within it the capacity of people with power *not* to tolerate people with less power. The 'enormous break' (Ang, 2014) from the exclusionary past thus is merely a difference of threshold:

> If the nationalist practices of exclusion emphasise a capacity to remove the other from national space [as was the case under the White Australia policy], the nationalist practices of tolerance emphasise a capacity to position [others] in specific places so that they can be valued and tolerated. (Hage, 2000, pp. 94–5)

Such a strategy has been effectively deployed to deny or limit Aboriginal sovereignty and agency: the success of Indigenous land claims, for instance, remains dependent on the determinations of British-based bureaucratic and legal systems (Povinelli, 1998; Ramzan et al., 2009), while Aboriginal policies and programmes are often still embedded in White paternalism (Kirk, 2006). One outcome of this 'benevolence' is what Back (2012) terms 'new hierarchies of belonging', wherein 'the fantasy of white restoration is replaced by a racial reordering, a differential inclusion that is selective and conflict-ridden' (p. 140), and under which the benefits of multiculturalism accrue more to some individuals and groups than to others (Bloemraad & Wright, 2014).

Indeed, Bell (1979) argued that major policy shifts occur only when there is interest convergence – when the dominant group(s) as well as minority groups benefit, or believe they will benefit. Writing about the landmark *Brown v Board of Education* ruling that racial segregation in US public schools was unconstitutional, Bell contends that the Supreme Court's 1954 decision

> cannot be understood without some consideration of the decision's value to whites, not simply those concerned about the immorality of racial inequality, but

also those whites in policymaking positions able to see the economic and political advances at home and abroad that would follow abandonment of segregation. (p. 524)

Bell goes on to list some of those advances while also pointing out that at a local level, integrated education has been embraced by many White parents because of the value they see in it – socially, culturally and academically – for their children. The pragmatics of policy and practice reform are muted, and thereby neutered, by the morality-based discourses (emphasizing tolerance and respect) that are constructed around them. The White Australia policy and multiculturalism have been similarly beneficial to the nation's Anglo majority in the crucial role each has played in the evolution of Australia's distinctive identity (Stratton & Ang, 1994): the former in bolstering support for federation – a 'shared future' of the times – and the beginning of a decoupling from Britain, and the latter in bolstering support for a greater openness to and engagement with a globalizing world. Each has also served the industrial and economic imperatives of the times: for example, labour protection in the early years of federation, and labour mobility a century later.

The second, and related, function of 'tolerance' – or rather of the promotion of Australians' idea of themselves as especially tolerant people – is the 'whitewashing' of Australia's history. Broadcaster and social commentator Phillip Adams, writing about nationwide consultations he and others were involved in in the lead-up to the 2001 centenary of federation celebrations, reports that his first question to everyone he met was: 'What's best about Australians?' The invariable answer, pronounced with pride, was 'the T-word. Our tolerance' (Adams, 2015). Nelson (2015, p. 348) similarly reports that participants in her study articulated tolerance as 'almost a cultural trait of Australians'. Most Australians would not associate themselves or their country with the now-condemned practices of apartheid or slavery. Yet the White Australia policy was in force for much longer than apartheid (policy in South Africa from 1948 until 1994); and before and into the early years of the White Australia policy Australia had its own form of slavery in 'blackbirding', the forced or induced relocation of 50,000 South Sea Islanders to Queensland in the late nineteenth century to labour in the cane fields (Sparrow, 2015). Such histories, and their continuing legacies of differential advantage, are glossed over in official celebrations of harmony, cohesion and respect.

While there is little doubt that new settlers in Australia would rather be embraced and valued than ostracized and despised – or not allowed in in the first place – tolerance, as Hage (2000) notes, does not touch social and institutional power structures. In fact, the very discourse of tolerance – whether produced in political, policy or media spheres – is argued to be critical to *protecting* existing power structures. Writing about the Netherlands – renowned for its liberalism – van Dijk (1992) notes that when tolerance is constructed as a national virtue, it becomes 'much more difficult for minority groups to challenge remaining inequalities, to take unified action and to gain credibility and support among the (white) dominant group. Indeed, they may be seen as oversensitive, exaggerating or overdemanding' (p. 96). In other words, 'they' may be seen as a problem because they, with their complaints, are testing the tolerance of a tolerant nation.

In the Australian context, Nelson (2015) has found celebratory initiatives to be the most common and popular way of valuing and embracing diversity in local communities (including schools – Watkins and Noble, 2019). Such initiatives typically involve a gathering of people from diverse backgrounds for an enjoyable event, such as a picnic or a concert. However, as Phillips (2004) has commented about practices in Britain:

> Too many institutions have seized one half of the integration equation – recognition of difference – while ignoring the other half: equality.

'Australian Multiculturalism': Public Opinion

So far this chapter has focused on multiculturalism from a 'top-down' perspective – that is, on policy, political and media discourses. As van Dijk (1993) notes, also important to how multiculturalism plays out are 'bottom-up relations of resistance, compliance and acceptance' (p. 250). These can be partially gauged by examining data on Australians' opinions about immigration, cultural diversity and multiculturalism. As one example of the relationship between official discourses and public opinion, a 2014 online poll asking readers if they agreed that people should not migrate to Australia 'unless you want to join our team' (as then-prime minister Abbott had said) attracted more than 9,000 responses – 60 per cent of them in the affirmative (Cox, 2014). Similarly, a 2012 parliamentary inquiry was reportedly 'swamped' with submissions claiming that 'multiculturalism has failed, that Muslims are to blame, that they threaten democracy in Australia and refuse to assimilate' (Shepherd, 2012). These responses suggest that the daily reality of living with diversity may not be as 'happy' (Ahmed, 2008) as political rhetoric claims.

Dozens of formal studies have been conducted as Australian multiculturalism has developed over the past fifty years, together illuminating the complex and contradictory nature of people's understandings of and discourses about immigration, cultural diversity and multiculturalism. As Hage (2000, p. 241) notes, Australia's policy of non-discriminatory immigration evolved in disregard of public opinion at the time and has been the subject of constant polling and debate ever since.

A Statistical Snapshot

Extensive quantitative research has been conducted in Australia and internationally to measure and compare attitudes towards immigration, cultural diversity and multiculturalism. Research by the US-based Pew Research Centre has highlighted marked differences between Americans and Europeans, for example, in their attitudes towards cultural diversity: while 58 per cent of Americans in a 2016 poll agreed that increased diversity made their country a better place to live, the highest level of agreement among European countries was 36 per cent in Sweden, ranging down to 10 per cent in Greece. The dominant view in most European countries was that diversity was neither a positive nor a negative in terms of its effect on citizens' lives (Wike et al., 2016).

On attitudes towards immigration, Australia ranks as one of only a handful of countries where immigration is regarded favourably by a majority of the population (Markus, 2015). However, the polls also reveal considerable volatility in Australians' attitudes towards immigration levels over the past five decades (Goot & Watson, 2005; Markus, 2021). Although the overall trend has been towards endorsement of intake levels – the proportion of Australians who think immigration levels are too high has halved to 35–40 per cent since the early 1990s – unemployment levels and the political prominence of issues such as asylum seekers have been shown to strongly impact poll results (Markus, 2015). Further, the national *Mapping Social Cohesion (MSC)* surveys (2009–21) have found little correlation between the degree of public support for immigration levels and actual changes in intakes (Markus, 2021). In other words, the data suggest that economic factors and political discourses have more influence on public perceptions about immigration than immigrant numbers.

Opinion regarding the *benefits* of immigration, by contrast, has shown remarkable stability. In the recent *MSC* report, Markus (2021) notes increasing levels of agreement with statements such as 'immigrants improve Australian society by bringing new ideas and cultures', 'multiculturalism has been good for Australia' and 'accepting immigrants from many different countries makes Australia stronger' – in other words, that the diversity that results from immigration is good for the nation. Commenting on earlier findings, he writes: '[W]hen the issue of cultural diversity is raised in the abstract and most general terms, the level of agreement [that it is a positive] reaches the range 70-90 per cent' (Markus, 2010, p. 83). A nationwide survey by Ang et al. (2002) found a somewhat lower proportion of respondents – 59 per cent – agreeing that cultural diversity was a 'strength to Australian society' (p. 19); this was lower than the level of support for immigration (64 per cent) but higher than support for multiculturalism (52 per cent).

Stronger support for multiculturalism is evident in the 2018–21 *MSC* surveys, which show 83–86 per cent of respondents agreeing that 'multiculturalism has been good for Australia' (Markus, 2021). In regard to *what* is good about multiculturalism, the perceived economic advantages are on par with the social. As for whether multiculturalism should be a one- or two-way process, the largest proportion of respondents to the 2015–18 *MSC* surveys – 60–66 per cent – agreed that both Australians and new immigrants should accommodate each other (Markus, 2018).

When respondents are asked about specific government assistance for immigrants, however, support levels decline dramatically. In response to the statement that 'ethnic minorities should be given government assistance to preserve their customs and traditions', polls in 2018, 2019, 2020 and 2021 found levels of agreement ranged from 31per cent to 39 per cent (Markus, 2021). Another series of polls (1993–2006), of mostly Anglo-background Australians in a Melbourne suburb, reveal overwhelming support for the view that policy should be directed towards helping immigrants fit into Australian society as quickly as possible, and less than 5 per cent support for government assistance for cultural maintenance even during the early years of resettlement (Markus, 2010). This is despite government funding for cultural maintenance having been a core principle of Australian multiculturalism since its inception. Further, in the 2021 *MSC* report, the only diversity-related measure to achieve a high strong negative (17 per cent) compared to strong positive (7 per cent) was in response to a statement in favour of integration, based on a concern that many immigrants are not integrating into Australian life. When presented with the proposition that 'ethnic minorities should be given Australian government assistance to maintain their customs and traditions', the number of those with strong negative views was greater than those with strong positive views (Markus, 2021).

Taken together, these different studies indicate that while most Australians profess to endorse the policy of multiculturalism, their conceptualization of multiculturalism in practice (notably in the case of Anglo-Australians) aligns more closely with pre-1970s assimilation policies (Forrest & Dunn, 2010). Overall, the research suggests that Australians see cultural diversity as inevitable and perhaps broadly advantageous (especially economically) but also a potential threat to social cohesion, particularly if immigrants are encouraged and supported to maintain their language and other forms of cultural expression. Tolerance is endorsed; welfare, by and large, is not (Bulbeck, 2004). In terms of the impacts of increasing cultural diversity on Australian society into the future, Markus (2015) suggests that a more useful statistic may be the proportions of Australians who are *strongly* positive about and *strongly* negative about immigration, diversity and multiculturalism – the argument being that they are the people, given the strength of their opinions, who are more likely to sway others. The 2021 *MSC* survey found that, overall, the proportion holding strong negative views has decreased since 2018 across seven of eight diversity-related measures, ranging from 1 per cent to 10 per cent compared with the proportion of strong positive views (6–24 per cent). This negative proportion has been consistent across recent large-scale surveys, including Scanlon Foundation surveys (Markus, 2014a) and the *Challenging Racism* project (Dunn et al., 2008). In the latter case, the researchers write of this cohort: 'They believe that some races are naturally inferior or superior, and they believe in the need to keep groups separated' (Dunn et al., 2008, p. 2).

Words Matter

As alluded to, the way in which questions about immigration, diversity and multiculturalism are framed can have a significant effect on responses (Goot & Watson, 2005; NMAC, 1999). The National Multicultural Advisory Council (NMAC), for instance, reported that questions about 'multiculturalism' provoked much more polarized responses than questions containing the word 'multicultural' – reflecting, in part, differences in understandings of what the policy entailed, whom it applied to and whom it benefited. Another example comes from market research conducted for the Howard government in the late 1990s, which cast a surprising light on the term 'cultural diversity'. As noted in the previous chapter, 'cultural diversity' is commonly presented as an inclusive and neutral term. However, the market research – intended to inform an antiracism campaign and written up by Eureka Research but never officially published – contains a strong caution about the use of 'cultural diversity'. Noting that the immigration department had 'vigorously promoted' diversity as one of Australia's strengths, the Eureka report concludes:

> The focus group discussions showed that this term [cultural diversity] will not be an effective means of promoting the benefits of having many cultures within Australia. Usage of this term assumes that diversity is, and is perceived as, a positive by the majority of the community. In reality, when reacting to possible campaign themes and titles, 'diversity' was often opposed . . . because it was seen as emphasizing the differences between people rather than the similarities. In a social climate where assimilation is preferred by many, the discussions indicated that cultural diversity is perceived as a divisive rather than unifying description of our society. It is therefore not a term we would recommend for usage either in an anti-racism or pro-harmony campaign. (Eureka Research, 1998b, p. 45)

In a separate report on the qualitative phase of the study, the researchers described messages such as 'unity in diversity' as ineffective because they were too intellectual and/or not believed. What the research pointed to was the need for an emotional rather than a rational approach to countering racism – a message that encouraged people to feel good about themselves and about the communities in which they lived and worked (Eureka Research, 1998a). Research conducted by Irving Saulwick and Associates around the same time also identified a desire among Australians for unity and harmony, and fears that multiculturalism might promote separateness rather than togetherness (NMAC, 1999).

The upshot of the Eureka and Saulwick research was the Living in Harmony campaign. In launching the campaign in 1998, the immigration minister, Philip Ruddock, highlighted and praised Australians' 'instinct for acceptance and goodwill' (DIMIA, 1998, p. 1). Although it was billed as an 'anti-racism education and awareness campaign', Living in Harmony was focused more on helping Australians to 'recognise the truth' (DIMIA, 1998, p. 1) of their country's multicultural success than on talking explicitly about or systematically tackling racism. Consistent with this orientation, the United Nations International Day for the Elimination of Racial Discrimination on 21 March became Harmony Day (Nelson, 2015) – 'a day of cultural respect for everyone who calls Australia home' (Harmony Day, n.d.). Schools have been particularly important in promoting Harmony Day and its messages about celebrating diversity (Mansouri & Percival Wood, 2007).

With the release of *The People of Australia*, 'racism' and 'antiracism' received renewed emphasis (Ho, 2013), but they have since receded again in favour of the 'multicultural success' narrative. In his Australia Day 2017 address, for instance, Prime Minister Malcolm Turnbull highlighted the nation's 'great achievement' of '[h]armony in the midst of extraordinary diversity', and 'the solidarity, the mutual respect [and] the mateship' that bind Australians together (cited in Thomsen, 2017).

Hierarchy of Differences: Immigrants' Background

The above has given an overview of attitudes towards immigration, multiculturalism and cultural diversity. The vast majority of Australians endorse or do not object to the openness of current immigration policy, with 16 per cent believing that some 'groups' of people should be excluded due to their religion or ethnicity (Markus, 2021). Despite the picture of broad support, however, it is clear that some immigrants command more 'respect' than others – or, to put it the opposite way, that 'some others are more other than others' (Appadurai, 1986, p. 357). 'In all countries of immigration there is a hierarchy of ethnic preference, which informs attitudes to newcomers', Markus (2013, p. 37) writes. In the 2021 *MSC* survey, when Australian respondents were asked whether they had positive, neutral or negative feelings towards immigrants from a range of source countries, 6 per cent reported negative feelings towards immigrants from Europe compared with 46 per cent expressing negative sentiment towards immigrants from Sudan. In between were immigrants from India (27 per cent), Lebanon (38 per cent), Iraq (42 per cent) and China (43 per cent) (Markus, 2021). Highlighting the influence of method on results, however, a 2014 study of third-generation Australians found that 44 per cent of respondents to an online survey expressed negative attitudes towards Muslims, but that this proportion fell to 28 per cent when the same survey was administered by an interviewer (Markus, 2016). This difference was attributed to 'social desirability bias', or the tendency of respondents to give answers in face-to-face situations that do not contravene perceived social norms (such as tolerance and acceptance).

On immigrants' visa status (the basis on which they were granted residency in Australia), the 2018 *Essential Report* found majority support for specific immigrant categories: entry on short-term student visas was accepted at present levels (or higher) by 58 per cent, short-term working holiday visas by 54 per cent; permanent family reunion by 52 per cent, and skilled working visa by 51 per cent (Essential Research, 2018).

While the title of this section is 'immigrants' background', it is important to consider also where Indigenous Australians sit in the hierarchy. Reflecting the cleavage in research, policy and practice between 'Aboriginal issues' and 'migrant issues', it is difficult to find studies that address this. The Eureka studies conducted for the Howard government found that respondents' views about Indigenous Australians were 'more extreme' (Eureka Research, 1998b, p. 41) than their views about immigrants, with 40 per cent of respondents agreeing that Aborigines were 'lazy'. In studies conducted in Perth, Western Australia, Pedersen et al. (2005) found high levels of false beliefs about Indigenous Australians, including that 'Aborigines are more likely to drink alcohol than non-Aborigines' and that 'being Aboriginal entitles you to more social security benefits'. Overall, almost half the respondents voiced negative attitudes towards Indigenous people. Finally, in a South Australian study, Bulbeck (2004) found that although a strong majority of respondents were positive about Australia's cultural diversity, only 55 per cent supported a national apology to Aboriginal and Torres Strait Islander people for mistreatment and only 59 per cent supported Indigenous land rights. Bulbeck (2004) writes:

> Very few respondents understood any of these issues [concerning welfare for immigrants and redress for Indigenous Australians] in terms of structural inequality, that some groups in society are systematically disadvantaged in relation

to other groups.... Indeed egalitarianism was invoked to deny land rights because they were constructed as 'special measures' given to continually complaining Aboriginal people who already receive more than a fair share of welfare. (351, 354)

In other words, the discourse of egalitarianism as intrinsic to Australian identity, together with a more generalized discourse about meritocracy, was used by many people in Bulbeck's study to construct equity measures as 'unfair'. Here we see how the 'virtues' of egalitarianism and meritocracy can, like tolerance, become strategies for maintaining relations of power.

Further Complexity: Respondents' Background

As well as differences in attitudes depending on immigrants' background, studies reveal differences depending on *respondents'* background. There is broad consensus in the literature that respondents' level of education is a significant variable, with years of formal education strongly correlated with support for cultural diversity and multiculturalism (Forrest & Dunn, 2010; Goot & Watson, 2005; Markus, 2010). This is important in relation to the attitudes of teachers, as tertiary-educated professionals, towards cultural diversity and multiculturalism, which are examined shortly. Overall, younger Australians are more positive about diversity and multiculturalism than older Australians (Ang et al., 2002; Markus, 2010), although Forrest and Dunn (2010) found 'unexpected variations' in attitudes across age groups depending on the demographics of where respondents lived (p. 97). The data on other variables including political affiliation and English-speaking/NES are more mixed. Ang et al. (2002), for example, found that significantly more immigrants agreed that cultural diversity was a strength than did longtime Australians. While this might be expected, the researchers also uncovered 'remarkable' (their word) differences in support for diversity *between* ethnic minorities. Dunn, et al. (2010) – noting the paucity of research on Indigenous perspectives on cultural diversity and multiculturalism – found that Indigenous Australians' attitudes were not substantially different from non-Indigenous Australians': that is, there was strong support for diversity but considerable concern about ethnic minorities 'sticking to their old ways'. Interestingly, Dunn et al. (2010) also found a strong belief in race among Indigenous respondents. Although 'race' is no longer widely used in Australia, the authors emphasize the continuing salience of the concept for people who have been, and often still are, defined in racial terms: '"Race" is a reality of life for people of colour, for those who are racialized, but it can also be a source for community organisation, political mobilisation, identity and pride' (Dunn et al., 2010, p. 24). Goot and Watson (2005), meanwhile, suggest that social conservatives hold more negative views about immigration but stress that where people live is important, with people who live in the inner city less likely to say they think immigration should be reduced than those who live in rural and outer metropolitan areas.

Geographical variance in attitudes towards diversity is, of course, of great import here given the focus on rurality and regional schools. Again, the data are somewhat mixed. Markus (2018) found that negative attitudes regarding multiculturalism were nearly twice as prevalent outside of capital cities (16 per cent of respondents strongly disagreed or disagreed with the statement, 'Multiculturalism has been good for Australia', compared with 9 per cent of respondents in capital cities). An earlier study of selected regional areas (Markus, 2014b) also found large differences between metropolitan and non-metropolitan centres. Ang et al. (2002) found that although people living in rural and regional Australia tended to be less positive overall about immigration, multiculturalism and cultural diversity, 'on one well-known indicator of cultural diversity, the enjoyment of cultural variety of food, regional Australia scores almost as highly as capital city residents!' (p. 21).

Taken as a whole, the research presents most Australians as reasonably comfortable (and, relative to most other countries, very comfortable) with diversity. Although there is ambivalence (or at least a lack of understanding) about what multiculturalism means in practice, quantitative studies show that multiculturalism enjoys consistently high in-principle support across demographics. Markus (2013) concludes that multiculturalism 'is established as a strong and supported "brand", one that resonates with the Australian people' (p. 3). Based on focus-group data, Ang et al. (2006) reached a similar assessment: 'It is important to stress that . . . multiculturalism is seen as a particularly Australian experience. . . . [It] was perceived [by the focus-group participants] as a defining characteristic of Australian society, and most felt strongly attached to it' (pp. 17, 18). It seems, in short, that 'Australian multiculturalism' *is* perceived as different, and better – a national 'brand' that has widespread loyalty. The ideas of 'resonance' and 'attachment' also point to the affective dimension of attitudes: what people believe is often not something they merely 'know' but something they 'feel', as argued in the previous chapter.

At the same time, the data highlight the complex intersections of factors such as age, education, employment status, ethnocultural background, cultural mix in an area, localized community relations, political discourses and so on that produce *differences* in attitudes. As noted in Chapter 1, factors such as ethnicity and geographic region are themselves context-dependent: as social constructs, they vary both temporally and spatially. Notwithstanding Australians' broad acceptance, even embrace, of cultural diversity, an important point is Forrest and Dunn's (2010) finding of *no* instances where minimal ethnocultural diversity in an area was associated with positive attitudes towards cultural differences and multiculturalism:

> So while it is possible for the experience of living with diversity to generate negative and/or positive attitudes towards diversity, there is no evidence that the lack of such a context will have productive results. [The presence of diversity] is therefore critical to attitudes, but the effect will depend on the history and context of cross-cultural relations in given areas, or, in the absence of diversity, on attitudes learned from elsewhere, such as the mass media, and the cultural and socioeconomic resources and capacities in those places. (p. 99)

Here Forrest and Dunn (2010) emphasize the potentially heightened influence of the media on attitudes in low-diversity communities (such as most rural and regional areas), along with localized social, cultural and economic factors. Beyond these, resources and capacities are also crucial in determining how attitudes translate into actions.

A final point here concerns immigrants' and longtime Australians' own perceptions of Australians. One question in the *Australians Today* survey asked recent arrivals to rank, in order, a list of thirteen statements about what they most liked about life in their new country. At the top of the list were 'Australian way of life/lifestyle', 'freedom/ democracy' and 'standard of living'. However, an image that many Australians have of themselves, as 'kind and friendly people', was ranked last by these respondents, regardless of their country of origin (Markus, 2015). This contrasts with results from the federal immigration department's longitudinal surveys in the 1990s in which Australians' kindness and friendliness was ranked highly among things recent arrivals liked about their new country (Markus, 2015). At a public forum to discuss the survey findings, Markus (2014a) observed that overall, the data indicated that longtime Australians, in their personal relations with immigrants, had become more 'standoffish' (his word), although 'their talk [about immigrants and diversity] remains strongly positive'. In other words, expressed attitudes towards immigrants remain upbeat, but there is some suggestion of a decline in affection and purposeful engagement.

Understandings, Affects, Attitudes and Actions

The link between attitudes and actions has long been a subject of debate, within and beyond academic circles. If a person expresses a negative attitude towards 'Asians', for instance, that reveals little about how likely the person is to *act* negatively towards Asians, how often, in what ways, in what contexts and so on – let alone whom they classify as 'Asians'. Indeed, despite the evidence of persistent racial and ethnic prejudice in Australia, there has been remarkably little social conflict under multiculturalism – less interethnic violence, for example, than in less culturally diverse European countries. Even in the Forrest and Dunn South Australian study, where rural residents were generally less positive about multiculturalism and some aspects of cultural diversity than residents of Adelaide, the capital city, there were 'noticeably lower levels of *experience* of racist behaviour by ethnic minority group members than the analysis of attitudes might have suggested' (Forrest & Dunn, 2013, p. 8). The forms of racism that were experienced most often – and much more frequently by immigrants from non-English-speaking backgrounds (who are likely to look as well as sound 'different') – were everyday instances of mistrust and disrespect in social interactions rather than overt institutional discrimination.

Other research confirms that experiences of racism vary in form, severity and frequency depending on an array of spatial and social factors, including the ethnocultural background of the person targeted. Drawing on data from 10,500 online and print surveys and 51 focus groups, the *Australians Today* project (Markus, 2016) found that immigrants from South Sudan reported the highest levels of discrimination, with more than three-quarters (77 per cent) saying they had experienced discrimination in the past twelve months. As in the Forrest and Dunn (2013) study, immigrants from non-English-speaking backgrounds reported higher levels of discrimination than those from English-speaking backgrounds, although Indigenous Australians also reported very high levels at 59 per cent. The most common forms of discrimination were found to be verbal abuse and other 'small' acts of social exclusion, followed by workplace/employment discrimination, property damage and physical assault (Markus, 2016). Separately, almost three in ten respondents to the 2014 and 2015 *MSC* surveys reported experiencing discrimination at least once a month (Markus, 2015).

It is, of course, impossible for researchers to judge how truthfully people answer questions about their attitudes and actions. Forrest and Dunn (2007), for example, speculate that more highly educated people may be more likely to identify questions as 'a test of their "racism"' and accordingly answer in ways they see as demonstrating 'progressive attitudes' (p. 703). In a paper on Australians' images of their country and perceptions of how it had changed over the years, Brett and Moran (2011) report that they were 'struck' by how regularly their interviewees followed up any doubts about diversity with a moderating statement or example – 'as if, having expressed an anxiety about the possible negative consequences of an ethnically diverse population, the respondent was now at pains to calm and contain it' (p. 199). The 1998 Eureka market research reports, on the other hand, highlight a degree of backlash against what is perceived as 'political correctness': some participants in the focus groups expressed not only negative feelings about immigration, multiculturalism and government assistance for Indigenous Australians but resentment at not being 'allowed' to voice their views for fear of being seen as racist (which they did not regard themselves as being) (1998b).

If individuals or institutions do want to conceal or minimize their negative affects, attitudes and/or actions towards an 'other', international research points to an abundance of strategies for doing so, and hence avoiding censure. In a UK study, Valentine (2010) found that participants (all White British adults) regularly framed negative attitudes towards minority groups as 'justified by rational explanations' (p. 526), thereby ensuring that their articulation of prejudices did not compromise their identity (in their own and others' eyes) as tolerant and fair-minded people. Similarly, individuals may deny, downplay or excuse negative attitudes or acts towards cultural 'others' in order to appear compliant with the law or social norms and affirm their fundamental decency (van Dijk, 1992). Maintaining a certain (self) image, Ahmed (2008) argues, is important to sustaining 'good feeling' about oneself. As already argued, diversity discourses can also be used by nations and institutions to manage their image. 'Diversity' can appear as quite 'cool', in the sense of both fashionable and non-emotive (Ahmed, 2012), but that is part of the problem: if diversity discussions and initiatives sidestep 'scary issues, such as power and inequality' (Ahmed, 2012, p. 66), it is unlikely they will achieve their purported social justice objectives. A central aim of CDA and race-critical scholars, then, is to draw attention to the ways in which such failures may occur not in spite of, but partly *because of*, the language used in policy and political discourses; to how policies-as-discourses frame social entities, relations and norms, and how this in turn affects possibilities for action (Bacchi, 2000; Fairclough, 2001) and, ultimately, policy outcomes.

Even if we, individually and institutionally, believe that successful multiculturalism involves more than acceptance and appreciation of cultural 'others', our possibilities for action may be limited by our *capacities* to act – by resources, knowledge, skills and so on. People who have grown up and still live in areas where there is relatively little cultural heterogeneity – as is the case for many rural residents – are likely to have a more limited 'living together-in-difference' (Ang, 2003) action repertoire than most urban dwellers; moreover, they will be less *practised* in their actions (unaccustomed, for example, to using translating and interpreting services). At a macro level, building capacity for harmonious living in increasingly diverse and complex societies requires significant investment in research, community development and education. In recognition of this, governments over the decades have established and funded various diversity-related agencies and programmes, including the Living in Harmony and the more recent Racism. It Stops with Me initiatives and community grants programmes (AHRC, n.d.-c; Multicultural NSW, n.d.-a).

As mentioned earlier, schools have also always been central to Australia's multicultural mission. In 2008, the infrastructure for a national curriculum (to supplement and/or guide state-based curricula) was established. One of the general capabilities embedded in the draft curriculum – now finalized and being implemented in schools across the nation – is 'intercultural understanding'. Schools are tasked with developing this capability in students so that they are 'equipped . . . for living and working together in an interconnected world' (ACARA, n.d.). Among other things, intercultural understanding is said to involve all students, from kindergarten through to Year 12, in 'learning about and engaging with diverse cultures in ways that recognize commonalities and differences, create connections with others and cultivate mutual respect' (ACARA, n.d.). Given teachers' front-line role in implementing education policies and curricula, it is therefore important to review some of the literature on their perceptions of cultural differences and attitudes towards diversity and multiculturalism.

Back to School: What Teachers Think about Diversity and Multiculturalism

Much research has been undertaken on teachers' understandings, attitudes and practices, as well as the affectivity of teaching and learning, from many different theoretical perspectives. As Mansouri and Jenkins (2010) write: 'Teachers are very influential . . . not only in their role as classroom educators but as role-models for appropriate and positive inter-personal behaviour . . . . Teachers' interpersonal [*sic*] behaviour includes their response to issues of diversity and their approach to students with diverse cultural backgrounds' (p. 94). In the *Australians Today* study, a notable finding from the focus groups was the strong positive effect school principals could have on community relations in high-diversity, low-socio-economic areas (Markus, 2016). In Australia, as in many other Western countries, the teaching force is significantly 'Whiter' than the general population: of Anglo-Celtic heritage, middle-class and disproportionately female (Allard & Santoro, 2008). Thus teacher education and training programmes are in turn important in shaping (trainee) teachers' understandings of cultural diversity, multiculturalism and intercultural understanding (Mansouri & Jenkins, 2010).

In a statewide survey of NSW public school staff, Watkins et al. (2013) found high levels of agreement among respondents with statements such as 'It is a good thing for schools to have students from different cultures' (93 per cent) and 'It is the responsibility of schools to cater for the needs of students from diverse cultural and linguistic backgrounds' (89 per cent) – indicating a 'shared and consistent professional ethos amongst teachers' towards diversity even if views differed on the best way to cater for it (Watkins et al., 2013, p. 43). In contrast to the general population, however, respondents were much less likely to say that racism was a problem in Australia, and even less likely to see it as a problem in schools. A nationwide study by Mansouri and Jenkins (2010) suggests that racism *is* a substantial problem in Australian schools, leading Watkins et al. (2013) to propose that teachers may have downplayed its significance in their survey responses – possibly reflecting efforts at impression management. Less than half of the respondents (48 per cent) reported having had pre-service training in aspects of multicultural education such as teaching a culturally inclusive curriculum, promoting positive community relations and combating racism, while only 28 per cent said they had received pre-service in training in EAL/D (English as an Additional Language or Dialect) teaching. Most worrying in the researchers' eyes was that only 15 per cent of respondents had apparently undertaken any professional learning in any aspect of multicultural education (Watkins et al., 2013).

Levels of teacher education and training may be cause for concern, then, but concerns have also been raised about the quality and/or effectiveness of teacher education programmes (Connell, 2009; Mills, 2008; Watkins & Noble, 2016). Santoro (2014), for example, provides an analysis of pre-service teachers' accounts of a trip to India they had taken as part of their course. The purpose of the trip was to promote a deeper understanding of 'culture' and 'difference', in order to better prepare the students (all Anglo-Australian and from rural or regional towns) to teach in culturally diverse classrooms. Instead, the students tended to construct the Indian people they encountered as either 'exotic' or 'lacking' – objects of admiration or pity. Rather than facilitating critical reflection on ethnicity, identity and cultural practices, the trip appeared to (re)produce colonial-era understandings of and orientations towards ethnic and cultural 'others', as evident in the students' discourses of benevolence and charity (Santoro, 2014). An interesting point in Santoro's conclusion, in light of Fairclough's observations about the increasing use of promotional genres, is the way in which the trip was presented: 'Flyers [for] the trip . . . resembled tourism materials that exoticized India and Indians . . . . [There were also] photos of female pre-service teachers from previous trips dressed in salwar kameez and surrounded by large groups of Indian children shoddily dressed and clearly poor' (Santoro, 2014, p. 442). In the face of dominant ways of seeing and talking about diversity and difference, it is perhaps little wonder that the trip, as a learning experience, fell short of its objectives.

Three Approaches to Difference

The Santoro (2014) case study is, of course, only one of thousands of studies into teacher education, but I use it here to point to the difficulty inherent in trying to change attitudes and practices. Engaging in critical inquiry, for instance, 'often means asking students to radically reevaluate their worldviews' (Boler & Zembylas, 2003, p. 111), involving processes that are challenging not only cognitively but emotionally. In the absence of such 'labour', Boler and Zembylas (2003) contend, approaches to difference in schools tend to fall into three types (or what they call models): the natural response/biological model, the celebration/tolerance model and the denial/sameness model. They see these models as reflecting broader political and popular discourses about difference and diversity, and producing tendencies to either overemphasize (celebration/tolerance and natural response/biological) or underemphasize (denial/sameness) ethnic and cultural differences. Each model is also theorized as connected with a particular affective orientation (or what the authors call 'emotional stance') towards difference.

The natural response/biological model, for example, is connected with fear, explaining 'fear of differences as a natural emotion . . . a fundamental feature of being human' (Boler & Zembylas, 2003, p. 113). This approach can be linked to theories of evolution and also now-discredited biological notions of race (Amin, 2010; Hesse, 2007) – a 'commonsense' view that human beings have evolved to be fearful of people 'different' from them, just as other animals have evolved to 'fight or flee' species different from them. The celebration/tolerance model, by contrast, represents a positive orientation towards difference and diversity, as promoted in Australian multicultural policies. It is, in other words, an 'enlightened' approach to difference – but one that nonetheless obscures the fact that only *some* differences are celebrated while others are merely tolerated, and others still not tolerated at all. Finally, the denial/sameness model reflects a view that differences are unimportant – that '[w]e are all the same underneath the skin' (Boler & Zembylas, 2003, p. 113), and thus should be treated the same. Like the celebration/tolerance model, the sameness approach can be seen as an advance on previous 'racist' conceptualizations of difference. In practice, however, it can provide a rationale for failing to take or maintain action against racism and inequality. In other words, the denial/sameness model, by making claims to equality (our common humanity, for example), can mask the continued vitality of social divisions and hierarchies. In its focus on the future – 'can we just move on?' (Boler & Zembylas, 2003, p. 114) – it disavows the still-material legacies of colonialism and other systems of oppression, and in so doing helps carry those legacies forward.

Conclusion

A key purpose of this chapter has been to grapple with the question of why Australian multicultural policies frame cultural diversity as a strength. In attempting to answer this question I have drawn in particular on critical discourse scholarship. According to CDA, discourse is only one form of social practice but an increasingly powerful one in modern societies, and one whose power depends in part on the frequent opacity of its relationships with other social practices (Fairclough, 2003). Australia is, as our politicians claim, strikingly conflict-free for such a diverse society. However, the discourses of tolerance and multicultural success can perform other functions, including masking the continuing power of Anglo-Australians to tolerate and position immigrant and Indigenous Australians. The extent to which official discourses can 'legitimate control, or otherwise naturalize the social order' (van Dijk, 1993, p. 254) depends also on how those discourses are taken up – echoed, challenged, resisted – by the media and ordinary Australians. While Australians are unusually (by international standards) positively oriented towards diversity and multiculturalism in the abstract, they are often significantly less enthusiastic about specific aspects of these phenomena, particularly equity measures. These may be constructed as 'unfair', and 'unAustralian'.

Given the centrality of schools to the multicultural project, teachers' orientations towards diversity and multiculturalism, and their capacities to meet the challenges of teaching in increasingly diverse classrooms, are crucial. The Australian education system, like other Western systems, is steeped in colonialism: 'Not only are institutions shaped along colonial lines, but dominant epistemologies carry implicit Western assumptions with little or no opportunity for students to explore other epistemological frames' (Mansouri & Percival Wood, 2007, p. 51). This has begun to change and is intended to change further under Australia's national curriculum. Nonetheless, the discursive and material practices within schools will remain critical to the outcomes of these developments, in rural and regional areas just as much as in metropolitan centres.

3

Ends and Means

Researching Diversity in Regional Schools and Communities

Introduction

This chapter discusses the approach to research that has informed this book. In the preceding chapters I have drawn on the work of scholars from a range of disciplines to examine not only the socially constructed nature of categories but how categorization processes work and some of the impacts of categorization – key focuses in the chapters that follow. As shown in Chapters 1 and 2, the varied meanings and usages of diversity-related terms, and tensions between and within public policies, contribute to obscuring *how multiculturalism 'happens'* in educational institutions, workplaces, clubs and other 'spaces of association' (Amin, 2002; Jakubowicz & Ho, 2013b). My focus here is to shed light on how public discourses and policies are taken up by particular people in particular places at particular times and, importantly, with what effects. The intent is to look at what James (2004 [1907]) lists as 'first things' – 'principles, "categories", supposed necessities' – and then *beyond* them to 'last things, fruits [and] consequences' (lecture 2); or, as James also expresses it, to bring out of words, numbers, images and ideas their 'practical cash-value' – their worth in the (social) world. To do this, I draw on diverse sources of data and different ways of analysing them – an eclecticism that is captured by Thomas (1995 [1979]), who remarks:

> We pass the word around; we ponder how the case is put by different people; we read the poetry; we meditate over the literature; we play the music; we change our minds; we reach an understanding.

This reflects an understanding of the research process as 'more cyclical than linear' (Mackenzie & Knipe, 2006), and much broader than is often acknowledged.

In investigating how multiculturalism is understood, valued and lived by members of school communities in a regional town, I draw on both quantitative and qualitative data. While the field of inquiry points to a focus on meanings (and meaning-making), values and experiences, numerical data are seen as also demanding close scrutiny. As Barnes and Hannah (2001) argue:

> Numbers are woven into the very fabric of modernity . . . . [They] create worlds embedded within wider social projects turning on authority and control . . . . For this reason, statistics are much too important to be left only to the statisticians. How and why they are constructed, by whom and about whom, how they are used and mobilized, and to what ends and for whose interests are critical social scientific questions. (pp. 379–80)

Philosophically, ethically and practically, a constant question for this book has been *cui bono*, or who benefits – from this research, this policy, this programme, this pedagogy, this positioning and so on. From the outset, another guiding question has been perhaps the ultimate 'last thing': What might the research informing this book achieve?

Mertens (2009) suggests that before even considering undertaking research, researchers should ask themselves:

> 'Who am I and what do I value; what's of importance to me; what are the beliefs that I hold?' and allow that . . . process of thinking and self-examination to be what guides you to the next step of 'what's my research interest and how should I go about approaching it?'. (1:10–1:30)

This chapter, then, begins with some answers to Merten's questions – an account of how this project came about and my position as researcher – before introducing the research location and sites and detailing aspects of the research process. Throughout, attention is given to the imbrications of rurality and cosmopolitanism, local and global, past and present, and how they combine to produce a distinctive multiculturalism in the studied town and high schools. The chapter also reflects on some of the dilemmas, problems and missed opportunities encountered along the way.

From early on, there was an intrigue about the reasons behind multicultural policies' framing of diversity as 'a strength and an asset'. I wondered what the research evidence was for the claim; what, and whose, purpose this framing served; and what the implications were for how 'ordinary Australians' perceived, experienced and responded to cultural differences. These early questions were underlined by a conversation I had with a colleague who had recently moved to Sydney from the regional town in which she had lived all her life. She recounted how struck she was at first by Sydney's cultural diversity – and how 'guilty' she felt about noticing. What she was 'noticing' was the high proportion – relative to her home town – of visibly different (that is, non-Anglo-looking) and audibly different (non-English-speaking) people on the streets. She had had little direct experience of cultural diversity and had no strong view on whether diversity was 'good' or not. However, she did know – thanks to community celebrations, media headlines and political speeches – that she was *supposed* to think it was good. Consequently, her initial unease about the new diversity she was encountering was compounded by her discomfort about her discomfort. The perspectives and experiences reported by my colleague raised a range of theoretical, methodological and logistical questions, including the central question of where the research could most fruitfully be located.

The Research Location

The Town and Its Surrounds

As noted in Chapter 1, concepts such as 'city', 'town' and 'village' – along with categories such as urban/rural or, in Australia, metropolitan/ regional/rural/remote – are socially, culturally, historically and politically inflected. The distinctions, or boundaries, between these theoretically distinct spaces are often contested and difficult to map (Tsolidis, 2016). As with other categories, everyday usage of such terms can differ significantly from official usage. Under the ABS's Australian Statistical Geography Standard, for instance, 'urban' is divided into 'major urban' (centres with a population of 100,000 or more) and 'other urban' (1000–99,999 people), with all other areas classified as 'rural' (ABS 2021c). In everyday usage, however, most of these 'other urban' centres would be thought of as regional or rural settlements, and spoken of as 'country towns'.

The area on which the research for this book focuses may variously be spoken of as a city, a regional centre, a (large) (country) (coastal) town, or other terms, depending on the context, the perspective of the speaker and the audience. According to ABS data and classifications, it is a mid-sized 'other urban' centre. With a population of about 50,000 it ranks among Australia's thirty largest 'cities', but in this book I refer to it as a town or regional centre, in keeping with common and local practice. With two-thirds of Australians living in the nation's capital cities, as noted previously, the relatively small number of substantial non-metropolitan settlements means that a few details can make it easy to identify places, and institutions and people within them. For this reason, I have chosen to call the town 'Easthaven', and have tried not to include identifying features while still presenting relevant and meaningful information about the place and its people. In the following profile of Easthaven, therefore, most information sources are unable to be specified because they would or might identify the town. Sources include ABS data, local government and business websites, newspaper and magazine articles, reports written or published by council and other local institutions, and several academic papers about the area.

In a 2013 policy brief on population changes in regional Australia, Hugo, Feist and Tan (2013) note a common view that there are 'two regional Australias': growing coastal settlements and declining inland settlements. However, the picture is more complex than that. A coastal drift has been under way for some time, with the proportion of Australians living within 50 kilometres of the coast rising from 80 per cent to 85 per cent between 1991 and 2016 (Hugo et al., 2013; Commonwealth of Australia, 2017), but the mining boom and 'tree change' movement (typically families moving out of capital cities) have brought new people to other non-metropolitan areas as well in recent years (Hugo et al., 2013). In Easthaven, population growth has been strong for the past four decades. Its population grew by 6 per cent between the 2011 and 2016 national censuses, and is forecast to grow by a further 34 per cent by 2041. The growth has been fuelled by relatively affordable housing; an escalating flow of retirees; the area's status as an education hub; its attractive climate and coastal environment, and related popularity as a holiday destination; and government programmes channelling more immigrants (including refugees) to regional areas, among other factors. Additionally, the Covid-

19 pandemic has influenced migration into regional areas. The Centre for Population predicted a net shift in migration away from capital cities in favour of regional areas in 2020–21, due to factors such as the ability to work remotely, economic uncertainty and market conditions as well as restrictions on international borders. Recent data confirm a net shift in favour of regional areas, though this is also driven by an increase in the numbers of people choosing to stay in regional areas, rather than leave for capital cities (Commonwealth of Australia, 2020).

Easthaven is actively marketed by local government and business as well as by tourism bodies as a 'haven' for city 'escapees' and holidaymakers alike – a city that offers a full range of cosmopolitan conveniences and cultural attractions while retaining the charm and congeniality of a country town. It is characterized as 'friendly', 'laid-back' and 'relaxed', and at the same time 'vibrant', 'dynamic' and 'exciting' (all adjectives taken from local websites), with an abundance of interesting shops, restaurants and cafes. Physically, the area is described as 'uncrowded', 'unpolluted' and 'stunningly beautiful'. A promotional video for the town showcases a carefree, active lifestyle – footage of people surfing, sailing, fishing and practising martial arts. These scenes and descriptors present 'happy, healthy and problem-free images of rural life safely nestling with both a close social community and a contiguous natural environment', thereby (re)producing a localized 'rural idyll' (Cloke & Milbourne, 1992, p. 359) – a place where no one needs to lock their house and everyone is greeted by name in the street.

Statistical data, however, suggest a less 'picturesque' narrative about the town and its people. Although Easthaven by some measures is flourishing, it faces significant social problems, some of which have been exacerbated by its growth. Of NSW's 128 local government areas at the time of the 2021 national Census, the one in which Easthaven is situated ranked in the bottom half on the ABS's 2016 Index of Relative Socio-Economic Disadvantage. At a national level, Easthaven was one of the lowest-ranked in a 2012 survey of Australia's most 'liveable' cities due to its particularly high unemployment (above 5.3 per cent, compared with a 2021 NSW figure of 4.9 per cent), poor health statistics and relatively high crime rates.

In other respects, Easthaven aligns closely with the general ways in which regional centres in NSW diverge from NSW as a whole. There is widespread underemployment, median household weekly income is 30 per cent below the state average (and also slightly below the average for regional NSW), tertiary qualifications are less common (13 per cent of Easthaveners have a degree compared with 20 per cent for all of NSW), and the proportion of single-parent families is well above average. In common with many other regional areas, reported levels of domestic violence in Easthaven are higher than in metropolitan areas (Mitchell, 2011); the town is struggling with a growing 'ice' (crystal methamphetamine) problem (Duff, 2015), in addition to long-term high levels of drug and alcohol abuse; and its schools and students are markedly disadvantaged on a range of measures compared with the majority of their urban counterparts (Davie, 2015).

In line with many other regional areas, the proportion of people who identify as Aboriginal and/or Torres Strait Islander is markedly higher in Easthaven, at more than 4 per cent, than it is for NSW as a whole (2.5 per cent; see Table 3.1 for a statistical snapshot of Easthaven). As Prout and Howitt (2009) note, Indigenous Australians

Table 3.1 Selected Population Statistics from the 2021 Census

Data measure	'Easthaven' (%)	NSW (%)	Australia (%)
Proportion of people who identify as Indigenous	5.8	3.4	3.2
Proportion of people born in Australia	78.4	65.4	66.9
Proportion of people with both parents born in Australia	63.7	43.7	45.9
Proportion of people who describe their ancestry as Australian, English, Scottish or Irish[1]	102	75.2	81
Proportion of people who speak only English at home	84.8	67.6	72
Households where a non-English language is used	9.8	29	24.8
Percentage change from 2011 Census in number of NESB people from a non-English-speaking background	+87		
Percentage change from 2011 Census in number of people born overseas	+39		

are more dispersed than the rest of the population – inhabiting 'the full spectrum of geographical and . . . settlement structures' (p.398) – and are relatively more likely to live in non-metropolitan areas. The proportion of Easthaveners who speak a language other than English at home, on the other hand, is sharply below the NSW figure of 19 per cent at about 5 per cent, consistent with the regional average. Historically, the region's population has been a mix of Indigenous and predominantly European heritages (English, Scottish, Irish, New Zealander, American, German, Dutch, Italian, Indian and White South African still lead the list). For several decades Easthaven has also taken in small numbers of refugees, beginning with refugees from Vietnam in the 1970s, then Central America in the 1980s and Bosnia in the 1990s.

However, the nature and degree of its diversity have changed dramatically since the early 2000s with the arrival of scores of families from Africa, Burma and the Middle East. The first of these refugees were from Sudan, but they were soon joined by families from Liberia, Eritrea, Togo, Burundi, Benin, Sierra Leone, Nigeria, the Democratic Republic of Congo, Ethiopia, Ghana and more; multiple ethnic minorities in Burma; and, most recently, several Middle Eastern states. Today, over 20 per cent of Easthaven's population were born overseas, and over 14 per cent have at least one parent who was born overseas in a non-English-speaking country (ABS, 2022). Over the five years to 2016, the number of Easthaveners from a language background other than English surged by 40 per cent, while the number of overseas-born jumped by almost 15 per cent. As Easthaven's reputation as a 'multicultural' centre has grown, it has increasingly become a site of secondary migration (immigrants moving from other parts of Australia) and a destination for international students as well. Even so, these recent arrivals together account for only about 1 per cent of the total population. The key point here is that while the absolute number of new immigrants remains low in Easthaven, in *relative* terms the demographic changes have been substantial, amounting to a significant 'diversification of diversity' (Vertovec, 2007, p. 1025). The changes have also been rapid.

An interesting 2009 university study (unpublished) exploring Easthaveners' perceptions of their community found they saw it as characterised socially by high unemployment, economic disadvantage and cliquishness; geographically by beaches, tourism and sport; and ethnically by Sudanese, Indian and Aboriginal 'groups'. The authors note the discrepancy between the discursive foregrounding of 'Sudanese', 'Indians' and 'Aborigines' and the social and cultural reality of overwhelming Anglo-Australian dominance. The study further found that 'Sudanese' was the word used to identify *all* African-background settlers in the town, who were primarily described in terms of their colour ('black') and height ('tall'). The validity and significance of these findings are taken up in the following chapter.

As that study suggests, tourism is a major industry in Easthaven. Like many other settlements along the NSW coast, the town was founded in the mid-1800s on timber cutting before turning to dairying and agriculture in the twentieth century when the forests had all been felled. Now hospitality and tourism drive the local economy, along with agriculture and manufacturing. However, the region's timber-cutting past lives on in its landscapes, transformed and 'tamed' into countryside more reminiscent of pastoral England (Garbutt, 2011). The area's primary-industries roots remain reflected, too, in its politics, where at both a state and federal level, it is represented by members of the Nationals, the self-described 'party for regional Australia' (The Nationals, n.d.).

The Lie of the Land: Another View of Easthaven

The account of Easthaven given above reflects typical Western constructions of a 'place', based on where it is in relation to other towns or cities, its physical features, how many people live there and what it produces. Today, thanks to technologies such as Google Earth, it is possible to virtually visit distant places, including taking a 'bird's-eye' tour of them. Such a perspective on Easthaven and its surrounds reveals swaths of green (farmland, bushland, landscaped gardens, lawns, playing fields), neat rows of buildings, criss-crossing roads, the blues of the ocean and swimming pools, the whites of surf breaks and fine-sand beaches – in large part, a picture of 'ordered, owned, occupied and productive' space (Prout & Howitt, 2009, p. 396). Although I had never visited Easthaven before beginning the fieldwork for this study, the town looked much as I had expected it to look, based on images I had seen in the media and my familiarity with other country-coastal towns in Australia. I was also broadly familiar with the history sketched above from school lessons on the settlement and development of eastern Australia.

In researching the area, however, I came across another history, and another geography – perspectives that remain largely unknown and unacknowledged in Australia (Garbutt, 2009; Prout & Howitt, 2009). An alternative story of Easthaven is of an Indigenous nation whose 'country' has been the local lands and waters for thousands of years. From the mid-1800s on, this becomes a story of dispossession as European settlers took over and cleared the land, and of depopulation due to disease, starvation and violence. Some Aboriginal people were forcibly removed from their ancestral lands to out-of-area missions and reserves. Some children were forcibly removed from their families. Aboriginal children could be removed from NSW public schools if any non-Aboriginal parent complained about their presence at the school (see Chapter 2), leading to the establishment of 'Aboriginal schools' and the implementation of a downgraded curriculum for students at these schools (Cadzow, n.d.). At the same time, it is a story of resistance by and the creativity and resilience of the Aboriginal population. This is quite a different discourse about Easthaven to the dominant one of a carefree coastal retreat. The latter is, of course, more contemporary, and well aligned with the town's growth and 'cosmopolitan' ambitions. However, the legacies of the lesser-known history remain strong, including in educational institutions.

In this context, it is important to note the very different meaning of 'country/countries' in Aboriginal English to the (Standard Australian English) ways in which I have used the term so far in this book. In Aboriginal languages, including Aboriginal English, 'country' is used to 'convey the ontology of connection which underlies many Aboriginal peoples' situated and multidirectional relationships with specific lands -seas-waterways-animals-plants-atmospheric events and so on' (Panelli et al., 2009). Thus 'country' is incorporated in relationships and responsibilities (spiritual, familial, environmental) rather than laws (national sovereignty, property rights) or in opposition to 'the city' (Panelli et al., 2009, p. 358). Understandings of and relations with a place are established by *paying attention* to it (Hokari, 2012) – not by asking questions and searching for information but by being still, looking and listening, waiting for knowledge to come to you, and then sharing your findings (orally, pictorially or through your body movements) with others. In addition:

> You have the obligation of maintaining your living country as your country has the obligation of looking after you. When you move around your country, you should always be aware that you are surrounded by your home, which is full of life. You are not the owner of your home, but a part of it. (Hokari, 2012, pp. 101–2)

Here there is a much stronger sense of spatial-as-social/social-as-spatial (Massey, 1992) than in dominant Western ontology. Indeed, lands and their peoples are believed to be inalienable, which is why land cannot be 'owned' and why the Europeans could so easily claim the 'land belonged to no one' (that is, was *terra nullius*) when they arrived in the eighteenth century.

Politically, Aboriginal and Torres Strait Islander conceptualizations of land-people/spatial-social, along with their pre-European inhabitation of Australia, have begun to be recognized in the practice of 'acknowledgment of country'. Performed at the beginning of events, meetings, school assemblies and so on, acknowledgement of country is 'a way that all people can show respect for Aboriginal cultures and heritage and the ongoing relationship the traditional custodians have with the land' (NSW DoE, n.d.). Even while this practice becomes increasingly common, however, it is also regularly challenged as irrelevant, tokenistic or even racist (Kowal, 2015).

In a co-authored paper (Ramzan et al., 2009), Bebe Ramzan, from the Anangu Pitjantjatjara Yankunytjatjara Lands in South Australia, reveals how hegemonic discourses about 'the country' (rural and regional spaces) typically render Indigenous residents either invisible or 'problematic'. A complementary perspective on the impacts of such discourses comes from Prout and Howitt (2009), who argue:

> [E]nduring settler imaginings about the nature of Australian rurality – discovered, claimed, tamed, settled, transformed and economically productive – have authorised those whose presence they legitimise to write, order and dominate space.... [In this writing the Indigenous is narrated] as authentic only in historical [or] 'wilderness' spaces; and as defined by dispossession and loss. (p. 397)

In the face of such narratives, attempts by Indigenous Australians to exercise their rights and responsibilities in relation to their historical lands have been perceived as a threat to the 'triumphalist imaginaries of colonial nationalist geographies' (Howitt & McLean, 2015, p. 140). Geography is as cultural as history, and intimately entwined with it. Space is intrinsically political – 'full of power and symbolism, a complex web of relations of domination and subordination' (Massey, 1992, p. 81). Significantly, as Gulson and Symes (2007, p. 99) point out, the 'language of [social] exclusion is, by and large, spatial; who's in, who's out, at the heart, on the margins'. Spaces, places, positionings and so on always have a history, a past – a past that is also always present through particular human practices in particular locations.

Why Easthaven?

Easthaven was chosen as the location for this research because of the features and dynamics described above – because of its long Indigenous history, its dominant European-settler history and its more recent immigrant and refugee-resettlement histories, and the impacts of all these on social, cultural and political life in the town and its schools. As a nexus of urbanity and rurality, Easthaven is a place where colonial narratives about the virtues of ethnic and cultural Whiteness entangle with contemporary narratives about the virtues of ethnic and cultural heterogeneity. Like many other regional centres, it is a place with substantial wealth as well as entrenched poverty, with traditional ANZAC (Australian and New Zealand Army Corps in the First World War) memorials as well as new commemorations of diverse cultural holidays and events, and with heavily promoted tourist attractions as well as hidden or demolished Aboriginal sacred sites.

In choosing Easthaven, and while collecting, analysing and writing about my data, I tried to be (and remain) mindful of my subjectivities as an Anglo-background, inner-city-dwelling, middle-class, middle-aged, no-children, private-school-educated, never-unemployed Australian woman – and to reflect on their impacts on how I 'saw' (and see) Easthaven, how I interacted with Easthaveners, how I understood those interactions then and understand them now, what and who I have included – and left out – and so on (Santoro & Smyth, 2010). Such considerations are rooted in even more basic epistemological and ontological questions including:

> who can be a knower, what can be known, what constitutes knowledge, sources of evidence for constructing knowledge, what constitutes truth, how truth is to be verified, how evidence becomes truth, how valid inferences are to be drawn, the role of belief in evidence. (Nakata, 2007, p. 8)

Importantly, the same questions – about what constitutes knowledge and evidence, and what becomes 'truth' – are fundamental not only to how research is conceived but how education is conceived. In the same way that what happens in educational institutions such as schools extends well beyond the neutral transmission of knowledge (or transmission of neutral knowledge) from teacher to student, the research process and the data it produces must be recognized as more than simple 'knowledge building'. The data are generated in social interactions with the consequence that the 'sheer doing of fieldwork, especially ethnographic fieldwork, performs functions other than those ascribed by the researcher' (Shaw et al., 2006, p. 273). While 'do no harm' has become a core principle of research ethics (Lewis, 2003), there is also the issue of *cui bono* – to whom the good? Various researchers and commentators (Nakata, 2007; Santoro & Smyth, 2010) have highlighted the failure of most studies involving Indigenous peoples to work to the advantage of those people. Shaw et al. (2006), for example, note how Indigenous communities 'have repeatedly seen anthropologists and other scholars arrive, take and leave, building their careers on the contributions of Indigenous knowledges while giving nothing in return' (p. 273) – a pattern that led L. T. Smith (1999) to characterize 'research' as 'one of the dirtiest words in the Indigenous world's vocabulary' (p. 1). Santoro and Smyth (2010), meanwhile, have suggested strategies that can militate against the 'potentially exploitative effects' (p. 497) on marginalized groups or individuals of investigation by researchers from the dominant culture. These issues are explored further later in the chapter.

How Easthaven Was Chosen

In searching for a non-metropolitan setting (or settings), I began by scouring ABS, My School and NSW DoE data on regional centres and schools. Decisions such as whether to focus on one town or several; how many schools to include in the research; and whether the schools should be primary, secondary or both were made gradually as I read into the field and checked school profiles. Like other reasonable-sized regional centres, Easthaven has two government high schools as well as several private schools. The decision to include both of the public high schools in the project was based on an interest in the 'microcultures of place' (Amin, 2002) – a curiosity about how factors such as school histories, physical environments, catchment areas, student demographics, educational priorities, leadership styles and so on might affect the interpretation and enactment of multicultural policies within different schools. Schools are seen here as mini-societies in which people mix and negotiate meanings and practices every day, and in which local influences and discourses entangle with macro (national/global) ones to produce the distinctive 'grain' of a place (Amin, 2002, p. 967). The intentions, then, were to provide an in-depth account and analysis of the discursive and material practices within each school, to illuminate commonalities and points of difference between them, and to consider the extent to which practices within the schools might be (reasonably) specific to Easthaven or reflective of more general regional orientations and dynamics.

As sites of everyday and extended contact (both formal and informal), schools are places where important 'habits of practice' are developed (Amin, 2002, p. 976). It is through the repetition (of categories, discourses, encounters) they both afford and inculcate that schools become significant shapers of our social worlds – of habitual ways of seeing, thinking, talking, feeling and acting, and also ways of not-seeing, not-thinking, not-talking and so on. Routine practices are also 'the central site of identity and attitude formation' (Amin, 2002, p. 967). High school, coinciding as it does with the teenage years, is a time/space in which such processes are particularly intense, as students 'engage actively in . . . renegotiating their individual and collective identities among their peers' (Forman, 2001, p. 35). Schools can have pronounced effects here through the range of identities presented, promoted and (perhaps tacitly) discouraged through their staff selection, curriculum choices and pedagogic practices. At the same time, as the emphasis on academic outcomes and preparing for the final year Higher School Certificate (HSC) examinations grows throughout the adolescent years, relatively less time is often given to groupwork and exploring alternative perspectives on topics. As a NSW DoE employee involved in multicultural education commented during a pre-fieldwork interview:

> In primary school, there's such an opportunity to explore cross-curricular themes and issues . . . . Kids are encouraged to explore their identity, 'who am I?', and are typically very open to that. But in high school they might get embarrassed, for example if their parents don't speak English.

These factors were core reasons that high schools rather than primary schools were chosen as the sites for the research.

Several other factors also pointed to high schools as optimal sites for the study. First, there is some evidence that racist incidents are more common in high schools than in primary schools (Cahill, 1996), and during the senior years of high school (Mansouri et al., 2009) – although little is available in the way of comparative data. While not directly bearing on experiences of racism, Watkins et al. (2013) found that a higher proportion of secondary school teachers (58 per cent) saw racism as a problem in schools than did primary school teachers (45 per cent), and that teachers in regional schools were more likely to report racism as a problem than teachers in Sydney schools. A study by Mansouri and Jenkins (2010) showed school was the main place young people encountered racism, with seven out of ten high school students reporting having experienced some form of racist behaviour. Significantly, the majority of those who reported having been subjected to racism said they had not taken any action, and that the impacts of the racism included feelings of anger, frustration and social exclusion (Mansouri et al., 2009). Second, differences in cultural identities, values and practices between immigrant parents and their children may be more likely to cause intra-family conflict as the children grow towards adulthood: for students from refugee families from Africa, for instance, adolescence in Australia will typically involve quite different roles and activities than it would have in their country of origin (Reiner, 2010). Similarly, cultural differences may create or exacerbate tensions between parents and schools: in a study in Melbourne, girls from refugee families from Somalia reported that parental pressure to marry young was their biggest obstacle to continuing their education (Reiner, 2010). Third, proficiency in English matters more at the secondary level as students are required to understand and use increasingly academic and specialist language (Brown, Miller, & Mitchell, 2006). While primary school teachers teach across the curriculum, secondary teachers have traditionally been seen as – and viewed themselves as – subject-matter experts, with literacy work seen as the work of English and ESL teachers (Wilkinson & Langat, 2012). This can contribute to growing gaps in academic achievement between different cohorts over the high school years (Uptin, Wright, & Harwood, 2013). Finally, students' career aspirations – and the 'fit' between these aspirations and their abilities, and their teachers' and families' expectations – become increasingly important as students move towards leaving school. There may be significant tensions, albeit not always made explicit, between students' ideas about their future and other people's ideas (Pini et al., 2010).

I wrote to the principals of Easthaven's two state high schools to seek an indication of their interest in participating in the research. The initial response of both principals was that there was already 'too much going on' at their schools for them to contemplate participating in a research project. After being assured that the research would not be disruptive to school routines nor demand too much of his and his teachers' time, the principal of Hillview High agreed to discuss the project with his staff, subsequently indicating Hillview's willingness to be involved. The first response from Seaview High's principal was to suggest that Hillview High would be a better location for my research because it 'has a more developed multicultural program and more ESL teachers due to significant ESL (especially refugee) enrolments'. I was already aware of this from the My School data and a comment by an acquaintance that Hillview High was commonly referred to locally as 'the refugee school' or 'the black school'. Even so, the Seaview principal's response reinforced that there could be interesting differences between the schools in their diversity-related perspectives, programmes and practices and Seaview High's principal eventually agreed to be involved.

Data Collection

In seeking insights into how multiculturalism was understood, valued and practised at Seaview High and Hillview High, the study was constructed around a combination of interviews and focus groups, ethnographic observation and existing texts. Semi-structured interviews were seen as affording the best opportunity to explore personal perspectives and experiences – and the logics and affects associated with them – across a range of topics. Ethnographic observation provided a window to people's interactions and practices (in the classroom, at school assemblies and at meetings as well as in less formal settings such as the school grounds). Existing texts such as enrolment data, school annual reports and newsletters, policy statements, websites, newspaper articles, student writings and artworks and other visual artefacts such as murals, posters and signage provided an alternative window on the values and practices of both individuals and institutions. Drawing on these diverse sources allowed a comparison of what schools said they did (e.g. in their annual reports and the interviews for this project), what they actually did (observation of practices and interactions) and what they were required to do (e.g. NSW DoE policies and procedures) – a multilayered, multidimensional picture of how policies were interpreted and enacted in everyday decision-making and interaction.

Another aspect of building this picture was seeking multiple perspectives on cultural diversity and multiculturalism – not only the perspectives of school leaders and teachers (crucial given their positions of authority and influence within schools) but those of students, parents and members of the broader Easthaven community. Schools, while physically bounded, are not socially bounded: every day, students – and staff – bring their home lives and histories into the school, and incorporate their school experiences into their broader lives and identities. Complex, not necessarily explicit, hierarchies exist within schools, as they do within other social groups. Accordingly, one-to-one interviews were chosen for all adult participants for the confidentiality they allowed as well as the scope for exploring perceptions and meanings. In contrast, focus groups were chosen for students to provide peer support (to mitigate researcher/researched differences) as well as insights into how the students related to each other and each other's perspectives and experiences (Drury et al., 2014). The focus groups were also structured to allow exploration of potential differences between junior (Year 7, aged 12/13 years) and senior (mostly Year 11, aged 16/17 years) students in understandings, attitudes, peer relationships and so on. Topics varied according to the category of interviewee (principal, parent etc.) but included questions about interviewees' background; their characterization and experience of the school; the school's multicultural education and Aboriginal education agendas; their understandings of 'culture', 'multiculturalism' and 'intercultural understanding'; social mixing and social cohesion within the school and in the broader community; and whether they agreed that diversity was a strength, as stated by multicultural policies. Altogether, forty-eight interviews and focus groups were conducted, involving a total of sixty-five participants or 'voices'. Table 3.2 sets out the sample.

The fieldwork schedule was based around school and community events including Parents and Citizens (P&C) meetings, council meetings, parent-teacher evenings, school assemblies, Harmony Day (March), Refugee Week (June) and NAIDOC Week (July) celebrations, cultural performances and community events. Participants were recruited through a variety of methods – initially, through information sheets distributed by the principal at each school and later through the school's ESL teachers

Table 3.2 Research Sample

	Number of interviews	
Group	Seaview High	Hillview High
Principal	1	1
Deputy principals	2	2
Staff	6	6
Students	3 focus groups (10 students in total)	3 focus groups (12 students in total)
Parents	5	4
Community members		16

and Aboriginal support staff and by speaking at P&C meetings. The aim was to ensure, as far as possible, a mix of cultural and linguistic backgrounds, ages, genders, levels of experience (in the case of teachers) and roles (teachers and community members) across all groups. All interviews and focus groups with school leaders, staff, students and parents were held on school premises; interviews with community members were held in workplaces and cafes. These community members – recruited through direct approach (people met at community events, for instance) and snowball techniques – included a police officer, a council employee, a nurse, two TAFE[2] employees, a recent graduate from Hillview High and ten people who worked in refugee support services in various capacities, including counselling, interpreting, English language instruction and community development.

Having introduced the research location, Easthaven, I now want to give a more detailed picture of the main research sites within that location – that is, Hillview High and Seaview High. First, though, it is worth examining where Easthaveners saw their town on the rural-urban continuum. Given Easthaven's reasonable size as a regional settlement, along with residents' varied life histories and reasons for living in the area, it was not surprising to find a range of perspectives. Three interviewees – all Hillview High parents, all Anglo-Australian – provide an overview. To Graham, Easthaven was 'a city in name only' and a place where, like other rural and regional centres, it was important to know people – particularly in terms of getting a job. Erica said she had moved to Easthaven when she was pregnant 'because it was not too big and not too small'. The third parent, Caryn, said she had settled in the town as a 'lifestyle choice' but found it 'very parochial'. Interestingly, no one characterized Easthaven as 'close-knit', a word often used in connection with rural and regional communities (Garland & Chakraborti, 2006). Interviewees were more likely to talk of the town as cliquey, socially and politically conservative (a couple of interviewees mentioned widespread homophobia, for instance) and highly stratified. Status was presented as tightly tied to broad and deep community connections based on property ownership and generational history in the area (Bryant & Pini, 2009). Notwithstanding its well-promoted 'cosmopolitanism', most interviewees appeared to see Easthaven as still markedly more rural than urban. This was particularly true in respect of two dimensions of community life: the region's high levels of poverty and its 'second-class' (compared with major cities') facilities and services.

The Schools

While there were significant differences between the schools, from location and layout through to leadership and local reputation, one thing they had in common was below-average ICSEA scores – that is, below-average levels of socio-educational advantage in their respective communities. These scores reflected the overall socio-economic profile of Easthaven sketched earlier. Moreover, the executive at both schools reported that the socio-economic situation of their student populations had deteriorated over the past two or three decades, in part due to the establishment of several private schools, which tended to attract the more affluent families in the area (reflected in above-average ICSEA scores for these schools). A second characteristic Seaview High and Hillview

High shared – and which was typical of public schools throughout the region – was that the average age of their staff was over fifty, many had worked at their respective schools for decades, and the vast majority were Anglo-Australian and monolingual. In this last respect they were aligned with the general trend in the teaching workforce in Australia (and in countries such as the United States and Britain) (Allard & Santoro, 2004; McKenzie & Scheurich, 2008).

However, the elevated average age of teachers (Lamb et al., 2014), and, somewhat relatedly, the breadth and depth of community connection in these Easthaven schools, is a point of difference with most metropolitan schools. Quite a few of the teachers had been students at the schools themselves and many were well acquainted with the local families, often having taught the parents of the children they were now teaching. This pattern was beginning to change as staff retired and new recruitment strategies were implemented, but it remained an influential factor in the dominant understandings, values and practices at the schools.

Seaview High

The centrally located Seaview High is Easthaven's original state high school. From its grounds, the visitor can glimpse the ocean and nearby marina and hear the clink of masts and the cry of seagulls. The site is overbuilt – all brick and concrete, indicating how much the town and the school have grown since the school opened its doors. In part reflecting its age, Seaview High has a traditional look and feel. The foyer, for instance, features a royal-blue-and-cream-colour scheme, high ceilings, an old fireplace and glass cabinets full of trophies and certificates. According to Brody, a teacher, the liking for tradition suggested by these artefacts was more than superficial. In fact, he said the school was one of the most traditional he had come across. He described it as a 'multicultural backwater', 'very right-wing', but it was also 'a school in change . . . with a shifting demographic'.

Notwithstanding the unfolding demographic changes, most Easthaveners expressed a view that Seaview High was the 'classier' of Easthaven's two state high schools. It was certainly the larger school in terms of enrolments, with about 900 students. The principal, Sally, said places had been significantly oversubscribed: 'We're supposed to be capped at 850, because of our site, because we can't expand. But it [demand for places] is huge this year and I've turned away a lot of people.' The school had a Gifted and Talented programme and some very high-achieving students – giving it, 'almost a private-school feel'. At the same time, it had many students who struggled:

> They either have economic poverty or they have social – it's not even poverty, but it's a deficit. So they're living with one parent, or their experiences don't go beyond [Easthaven]. Their vocab is limited. Their ways of dealing with conflict are restricted. (Sally, principal)

Six per cent of Seaview High's students were classified as LBOTE; of those, only about one-third (fewer than twenty in total) were from refugee backgrounds and had significant language learning needs. Roughly the same proportion of students – 6 per cent – identified as Aboriginal.

All of the senior executives were new to the school. Sally had been at Seaview High for less than three years and the two deputy principals, Stephanie and William, had been there less than two years. All of them had come to Seaview from other schools in the region, however, so were not new in that sense. A key priority was building 'Asia literacy' at the school. To this end, Seaview High had secured a couple of Mandarin instructors, set up a 'Mandarin classroom' and instigated teacher exchange programmes. Sally (formerly a language teacher) explained that the Mandarin programme was about broadening regional students' horizons, acknowledging 'Australia's place in Asia' and choosing a 'realistic' (in terms of affordability) destination for future study trips. The focus on Mandarin was not a reflection of student demographics (there were only two students of Chinese heritage at the school) but about encouraging a more global orientation among Seaview High students. The new leadership team had sought to modernize the school in other ways, including transforming pedagogical practice. Both Sally and Stephanie commented on how 'behind' they had found pedagogy when they moved to Easthaven from Sydney – primarily reflecting the fact that the majority of teachers in the region were in their fifties and sixties and had been at the local schools for at least twenty years. For example, there was reportedly a lot of 'siloing':

> Teachers had their domain and expertise. They had their relationships with the class, and you taught that class for forty minutes and it didn't matter what was happening to that child in the next forty minutes. It was all compartmentalized. (Sally, principal)

Introducing a more collaborative and process-focused ethos had therefore been another major aspect of the senior executive's reform agenda, along with achieving a better gender and age mix among staff. In terms of cultural diversity, only two teachers out of more than seventy reportedly had a language background other than English. The school had the equivalent of one full-time ESL teacher, and two support staff for Aboriginal students.

In addition to non-Western histories, literatures, cultural practices and so on covered in the core curriculum (Kindergarten to Year 10), Aboriginal and multicultural perspectives and programmes at Seaview High included:

- Aboriginal Studies: This was available as a subject in the senior years although, according to the Year 11 students I interviewed, no one was studying it in their year.
- Special events: An annual Multicultural Day for Year 8 students (as discussed in the Introduction). Harmony Day did not feature as an event – it had 'taken off' as a community event, one teacher said, but there were no specific activities associated with it at the school. Assemblies always began with acknowledgement of country by an Aboriginal student, and the school marked NAIDOC Week and Reconciliation Week.
- LOTE: Mandarin was the main language taught. Principal Sally commented that sustaining more than one LOTE was 'really hard in a country school', with

student demand for LOTE electives (in the middle and senior years) generally low.
- Other programmes: The school ran an intensive swimming course for ESL students – because 'you can't live in [Easthaven] ... they need it for access to the curriculum, almost, because of excursions and activities' (Sally). It also offered various mentoring and cultural programs for Aboriginal students.

In sum, Seaview High was a school that was, to use the language of commerce, 'under new management'. It had, as it had long had, a mix of relatively affluent and very poor families. LBOTE and Aboriginal enrolments at the school had risen sharply over the past few years, but overall numbers in these cohorts remained small. Both in terms of student behaviour and academic performance, Seaview High was said to be well regarded in the broader community, with its favourable reputation reflected in the strong demand for places.

Hillview High

Hillview High is Easthaven's other state high school. Located on the western outskirts, it was built some forty years after Seaview High as the town expanded inland. It occupies a much larger site than Seaview – one surrounded by green playing fields, trees and, further away, low hills; the sounds are of birds calling and cows mooing. The pathway to the reception office is flanked by well-maintained gardens. Inside the reception area, the visitor finds a couple of corkboards, worn black lounges, plants and a screen featuring the word 'Welcome' handwritten in a dozen or so languages.

Enrolments were about 650. Many of the students were from disadvantaged backgrounds, making the school eligible for additional government funds under the now-defunct Priority Schools Funding Program (Australian Policy Online, 2009). The principal, Neil, described Hillview High as having 'some extremely low socioeconomic kids ... very difficult-to-manage kids and difficult-to-manage parents'. Deputy principal Reg explained: 'We're inland from the coast and the coastal strip is where the dearer houses are, on the waterfront' – whereas Hillview High's catchment area had high levels of public housing, unemployment, substance abuse and family violence. About 18 per cent of the students at the school identified as Aboriginal, while 13 per cent were 'ESL' (the term always used in the school) – by far the largest proportion of any school in the region and, it is worth reiterating, quite extraordinary for a non-metropolitan school. In contrast to Seaview High, almost all of Hillview's LBOTE students were from refugee backgrounds – two-thirds of them from Africa. To meet the needs of its non-Anglo-background families, the school had the equivalent of three full-time ESL teachers (one of the largest ESL units outside Sydney, according to Reg), and a full-time Aboriginal education officer (AEO) and four other aides/tutors to assist Aboriginal students. It also had a Support Unit for students with intellectual and/or physical disabilities.

Neil had been at Hillview High for three years, as had one of his deputies, Vince; the other deputy, Reg, had been there since the 1980s. The rest of the staff Neil described as 'overall, White Anglo-Saxon'; a few had 'European backgrounds . . . [but generally speaking] your traditional white Australian upbringing, quite conservative'. As at Seaview High, many of the teachers had been at the school for a long time, with a sizeable proportion having started as young teachers when Hillview High opened and stayed there ever since. In other words, at both Seaview High and Hillview High there were significant differences between the age, level of socio-educational advantage, ethnic and cultural background, family structure and so on of the teachers and the children they were teaching – a disjunction common both in Australia and internationally (Allard & Santoro, 2004). Vince explained:

> A lot of teachers are more affluent, they've all gone to university, they're all pretty smart and intelligent people. And they don't understand the community they're dealing with. . . . They don't know what it's like to leave home without having had breakfast, they don't know what it's like to leave home without having the basic necessities. With Aboriginal kids in particular, they [the teachers] don't understand there's a cultural difference, that kids don't live with parents. Once the kids leave the school gate, there's no such thing as homework, there's no such thing as study. They don't go home to parents who have had success in education, in learning. They don't go home to a stable home life.

Vince was highly critical of many of his colleagues' perceived lack of effort to engage with such differences in family structure, support levels and experiences of education. Describing Hillview High as 'very dysfunctional', he characterized the school as lacking direction and suffering from the legacy of 'poor leadership' and protracted instability in the senior executive. The interviews I conducted with Neil, Vince and Reg pointed to continuing issues in leadership, given their very different backgrounds, perspectives and approaches, including cultural diversity both generally and within their school. This was a contrast to Seaview High, where the senior executive appeared to be much more closely aligned in their values, priorities and practices. At the same time, throughout the fieldwork I found Hillview High much more open: staff were more helpful in organizing interviews and focus groups, more generous in the time they were prepared to spend with me and more relaxed about my sitting in on classes, meetings and other school activities. This was consistent with a strong ethos of caring at the school: many times I observed students assisting and including students with disabilities, for example. This ethos was highlighted by all the Hillview High parents I interviewed, who used words such as 'welcoming', 'inclusive' and 'tight-knit' to describe the school.

Aboriginal and multicultural perspectives and programmes at the school included:

- Aboriginal Studies: All students had to take this subject in Year 7, and it had recently been introduced as a subject in the senior years as well.
- Special events: Harmony Day, Refugee Week, Reconciliation Week and NAIDOC Week were all major events in the school calendar. Acknowledgment of country by Aboriginal students (sometimes in the local Aboriginal language) was part of every assembly and event. African drumming performances – by a mixed group of students – were also a regular feature of school and community events.

- LOTE: The main language other than English taught at the school was German but, as at Seaview High, student interest in LOTE electives was reported to be low. There was, however, an intention to include the local Aboriginal language in the curriculum.
- Personalized learning plans (PLPs): The school had begun designing PLPs for all of its (self-identified) Aboriginal students, with the aim of improving school attendance, academic achievement and parental involvement in their child's education.
- Other programmes: The school ran a breakfast club for disadvantaged students; a homework club for ESL students; and various Aboriginal peer support, leadership and cultural programmes.

In sum, Hillview High has always been the smaller school. It began life as a solid middle-class educational option, but as catchment areas changed, coastal property prices soared and private schools entered the market, it had become a school of predominantly low socio-economic students and families. In the early 2000s it also became the first school in the area to take refugee families from Africa rising to almost one in three of its students being from a refugee background or of Aboriginal descent, compared with less than one in twelve at Seaview High. There was little evidence at Hillview High of an emphasis on developing 'global citizens' (as at Seaview High); rather, the emphasis appeared to be on building students' sense of pride and self-worth and providing a welcoming, safe and stable environment. As one teacher commented: 'I know the perception of the school in the community can be sometimes that it's a bit rough. And I think there's an element of tough kids here, but there's also plenty of nice kids.'

Staff at both schools said there were relatively few conflicts between students from different cultural backgrounds but that neither, overall, were there strong connections. At Seaview High, deputy principal Stephanie said:

> We don't have very many conflicts. I think we're still at the stage where the kids stick together a fair bit . . . . If you walk out into the playground you'll see the African kids are sitting together, the Indigenous kids are sitting together.

Similarly at Hillview High, principal Neil said students got on 'pretty well' but 'I don't think it's to the stage where you could walk around the school and just see an even blend of kids'. There was more mixing in the junior years, he said, but with 'the older kids, it tends to be African kids, Aboriginal kids and White kids [in separate groups]'. This description is consistent with what I observed in the playground during breaks. For Neil, this state of affairs was reflective of broader community relations in Easthaven, which he characterized as 'harmonious but . . . a little bit fragmented'.

The 'fragmented' nature of Easthaven society seems to have been a factor, in different respects, in parents' choice of school. For some, Seaview High was more attractive because it was more 'Anglo', had a larger proportion of well-off families, catered better for academically gifted students and had fewer 'behavioural issues' (to use one parent's words) than Hillview High. Hillview High, on the other hand, was seen as providing more opportunities for interaction between people from different socio-economic and cultural backgrounds, encouraging students to develop their strengths whatever they might be and offering a more relaxed physical as well as social and academic environment ('space and greenery' as opposed to the 'concrete jungle' of Seaview High, as one parent put it).

For other parents, the choice was between public and private. Fleur, a parent at Hillview High, explained:

> We possibly could have afforded to send them [her children] to a private school, but I wanted them to have the experience of living and studying within a public school where they were going to have interaction with all sorts of people from all levels of society, and to learn to be able to integrate and have that ability to – you know, I don't want them to think that they are better than anyone else.

A similar reason was given by Seaview High parent Hope:

> I went through public education myself and I think it's really important to be able to relate to all levels of society. . . . There's still an opportunity to experience the whole of society [at public schools], where I feel like at [name of private school] you obviously only experienced a very small cross-section.

School choice is a complex and often controversial issue, encompassing parents' aspirations for their children, their values around education and community, and how they (wish to) position themselves in relation to others in the community. In a study of school choice in a regional town in Victoria, Australia, Tsolidis (2016) highlights the influence of factors such as family history with a school, hearsay and public perception, and the politics of catchment areas. She argues that choices are more 'visible' in regional communities because of their relatively small size and limited range of educational options, and 'the consequences of decisions taken and talked about also reverberate more noisily' (p. 36). Accordingly, some interviewees in Tsolidis's study had heightened concerns about the confidentiality of their comments, affecting what they were prepared to say on the record. Reflecting Tsolidis's portrayal of 'a highly networked community with clear boundaries between 'us' and "them"' (p. 36), Hope, the Seaview High parent quoted above, said:

> I'm looking at my children's peer group and their parents and – I hope I'm not identified by this [*laughs*], but really I don't socialize [with them]. And some of the parents, I'm – just, like, their attitudes towards drugs, alcohol, cultural diversity – it's a fairly interesting mix, this area.

From the outset, confidentiality presented as an important consideration. If Easthaven was given its real name, the two schools would be immediately identifiable, as would many of the participants in the research. Choosing to give the town and participants pseudonyms was not only an ethical issue, however (i.e. about protecting participants' privacy and social and professional standing), but about trying to maximize the quality of the data by creating a space for candour in the interviews. As an 'outsider' to Easthaven, I was astonished by the apparent frankness I encountered from the very first interviews – for example: 'A funny story – we shouldn't record it, but we will [chuckle] because it's all anonymous . . .' (deputy principal). I was struck, too, by participants' eagerness to share stories and illustrations, which they would often explicitly introduce as such – for instance, 'I have another story for you', 'Here's one you might like' and 'I'll give you an example' (the 'you' in these phrases pointing also to the interviewees' awareness of audience). Phrases such as 'I remember once when I was . . .' and 'I had this lady one time . . .' were used to preface stories as well. Once, after a teacher and I had finished the interview and the recorder had been turned off, the teacher suddenly remembered a story he wanted to share and asked that I turn the recorder back on to capture it.

The formulation and exchange of stories is fundamental to the construction of social reality, according to discourse and race-critical theories. Stories 'serve as interpretive structures by which we impose order on experience and it on us' (Ladson-Billings and Tate, 1995, p. 57). They emphasize the importance of 'voice' – revealed through poetry, analogies, parables, chronicles, alternative histories and more – in exposing and countering hegemonic discourses and practices. Through repetition, the stories of the dominant group become 'commonsense'; in becoming so, they are less likely to be questioned and, in turn, more likely to remain in force (Ladson-Billings, 2005). Following principles of critical research (Jørgensen & Phillips, 2002;), this study seeks to challenge the logics of hegemonic discourses while also creating space for alternative voices and stories.

Data Analysis

In line with discourse theories, interviews are treated in this study not (only) as representations of interviewees' lived realities (beliefs, practices, experiences, affects and so on) but as *discourses about* their lived realities (Fairclough, 2003). They are discourses developed *for* an 'audience' (the interviewer most immediately), whether consciously or not, and in dialogical interaction *with* the interviewer-as-audience. As such, they produce social texts that have potentially multiple motivations as well as multiple meanings. The meanings produced during and after my interactions with Easthaveners must be acknowledged as inevitably, and always, shaped by my position as an outsider to the schools and the town, and as a middle-class, Anglo-background female researcher (Santoro & Smyth, 2010). At the same time, the performativity of any interview situation must be recognized – that is, the extent to which different beliefs, practices, experiences, affects, expectations, intentions and interests may be foregrounded, minimized or suppressed in order to present certain 'selves'. Just as I endeavoured to present myself as attentive and non-judgemental, for example, interviewees might have tried (consciously or not) to respond to my questions in ways they thought would show them to have particular values and attributes – such as being positive about cultural diversity and being open and accepting (van Dijk, 1992). This performativity was evident to different extents across the interviews – for instance, in phrases such as 'That's terrible, isn't it, that

I don't even know' and 'I feel I rambled a bit' from Seaview principal Sally, pointing to a consciousness of her leadership position; and in other interviewees' frequent checking questions ('Has that answered your question?'; 'Does that make sense?').

Of more interest given the concerns of this study were phrases such as 'I shouldn't say, and this is stereotyping...', 'I don't mean this the wrong way...' and 'I don't want to sound nasty' – seemingly innocuous phrases that nonetheless did important work in delineating what could and could not be said, and how. Research by van Dijk (1992) found that even blatantly racist texts typically included disclaimers or qualifications to racist comments, suggesting the texts' producers were well aware they might be perceived as contravening social norms of tolerance and civility. The researcher, then, must be alert – during the interview, in transcribing and in analysing transcribed text to inconsistencies, contradictions, equivocations, qualifications, clarifications, repetitions, explanations, justifications and sentiments (articulated emotions), as well as potential indicators of affect. As McLeod and Yates (2003) note:

> Analyses of research interviews usually focus on the words from transcripts. But attention to emotional response and levels of affect – evident through tone of voice, animated or bored or indifferent looks and body language, willingness to say much, and grounded as well in knowledge of the biography of the interviewee over time – captures an important dimension of the subjective investment in national and racial discourses. (p. 36)

In listening to and transcribing the interview recordings, I therefore sought to capture pauses, emphases, laughter, sighs and so on, as well as what I could remember of gestures and facial expressions. While interviews were mostly transcribed as fully as possible, not every 'you know' and '..., like, ...' (for instance) was included, and on a few occasions blocks of speech that seemed irrelevant (such as a long story about a change in colour of the school shirt) were left untranscribed. As Jørgensen and Phillips (2002) point out, transcription is already theory in action because of the editorial decisions made throughout the process.

Through multiple and careful readings of the interview transcripts, themes and subthemes were identified along with dominant categorization patterns, associated discourses and stories, indications of affect, gaps and repetitions, and assumptions, explanations, rationales, qualifications and tensions. In addition to vocabulary, attention was paid to grammatical and syntactical textual features highlighted by Fairclough (2003), including impersonalization, intransitivity and collocations. Analysis of the use of pronouns was also germane to understanding how groups were constructed and ordered in Easthaven and its schools (Fairclough, 2003). CDA can be used in different ways to different ends; here, it was taken up as 'a resource which can be used in combination with others for researching change in contemporary social life' (Fairclough, 2001, p. 229), rather than as a basis for rigorous and systematic linguistic analysis.

As explained in Chapter 1, affect is of interest in this study. The distinction was made between affects and emotions as 'felt' in the body (albeit at different levels of consciousness) and what I call sentiments – that is, 'emotion' words ('happy', 'worried' etc.) deployed in discourses. Sentiments allow a speaker to orient themselves (and others) in a particular way in relation to other discourses, events, actions and so on. A useful illustration is this excerpt from an interview with Hillview High parent Caryn. Commenting on the level of social inclusion in Easthaven, she said:

> I'm astonished by some of the things I hear people say [about the recently arrived refugee families]. I think [*chuckles*]: 'How is that a problem?' For instance, my hairdresser is shocked that the African men gather in the mall in the early evenings. I think it's lovely.

Here both affect (chuckle, word emphasis) and sentiment ('astonished', 'shocked', 'lovely') are evident. The 'truth' and intensity of the affects and emotions implied and articulated are not directly knowable. However, the performative function of the sentiments expressed is clear, as the interviewee seeks to contrast her orientation towards the refugee families with the (perceived) orientation of her hairdresser and others in the community.

It must be acknowledged here as well that interviews are not only dialogical; they are also affective, both during and potentially after the event. Several moments of awareness of this stood out and are recorded in my field notes. On my part, there were feelings of immediate connection and affinity with several interviewees; feelings of discomfort or uncertainty with others; and feelings of excitement, particularly during my first two interviews when I felt I was already obtaining some immensely rich data. As for the interviewees, some (all parents) appeared slightly nervous, while others (usually school staff) were quite distracted during the interview. Twice, at the end of an interview (and to my great surprise), the interviewee gave me a hug. In doing so, one commented on how valuable it had been to reflect; the other thanked me for undertaking research on the region, adding: 'It's so important, and finally someone is looking at what's happening here.' Lastly, one of the ESL teachers recounted that after a focus group with Year 11 ESL students, there had been 'very lively conversation' among the students throughout the following class. Such moments are important reminders that interviews are far more than opportunities for 'data collection'.

Writing is 'as much about the creation of effects and affects as it is about representation' (Swanton, 2010, p. 2337). The account of Easthaven, and Easthaveners, presented here is necessarily partial, in the sense of both incomplete and subjective. As Santoro and Smyth (2010) reflect, how possible is it to really understand and represent the perspectives of those with whom one may have little in common, and with whom one has spent at most a couple of hours? Time constraints meant that not only were my engagements with individuals mostly one-off and relatively brief but it was difficult to connect with some of the people whom I might have most wanted to reach, such as parents of Indigenous, refugee and other LBOTE students (Santoro & Smyth, 2010). Through local elders and a school staff member, I did manage to schedule one interview with a parent of a student who identified as Indigenous, but the appointment was not kept. Because I was primarily recruiting through the schools, I had the same problem the schools had: how to involve parents who could speak little English, who had had negative experiences themselves at school and wanted minimal contact with the education system, who were too busy or who simply might prefer not to participate in an interview. Their voices, regardless of ethnic or cultural background, are regrettably absent from this account.

With some recognized gaps in the data, the writing does attempt to include as many voices as possible, and to allow them to 'name their reality' (Ladson-Billings & Tate, 1995) by making extensive use of their own words and stories. This emphasis on 'voice' is a feature of race-critical scholarship, the premise being that creating space for less-dominant voices to communicate their experiences and perspectives is a 'first step on the road to social justice' (Ladson-Billings & Tate, 1995). Nonetheless, I acknowledge that my own voice is constant even when others are speaking, in the presentation of their words as 'packets of meaning' (Warren & Vincent, 2001, p. 47): ultimately, it is my account of their accounts. Further, simply including the voices of people from minority groups is not enough. From a critical research perspective, the power to research comes with a responsibility to contribute to 'pragmatic strategies for material social transformation' (Ladson-Billings, 1998, p. 11). In other words, the question raised in the introduction to this chapter – what might the research achieve? – is never an afterthought but rather is pivotal to the methodology. By utilizing techniques such as critical reflection, counter-storytelling and discourse analysis and adopting a praxis orientation, my hope was, and is, to avoid 'hit and run' research (Warren & Vincent, 2001) – to try to ensure instead that it is *for*, rather than (merely) on, those who are marginalized in 'multicultural Australia'.

Conclusion

Policy documents and poems, observations and artworks, interviews and casual conversations, academic texts and newspaper articles have all informed my attempts to reach an understanding of Easthaven as a space/place where the material meshes with the social, the global and national with the local, urbanity with rurality. This approach is consistent with the pragmatism advocated by critical discourse and race-critical scholars, to whom 'good' research is research that is relevant (i.e. addresses a social problem) and ultimately contributes to effecting change (i.e. solving the problem) (Dixson & Rousseau, 2005; van Dijk, 1993). Chapter 6 and the Conclusion of this book focus, respectively, on potentially problematic school and social practices, and how they might be reimagined and redesigned to increase inclusion and equity.

A final point concerns how my position vis-à-vis Easthaven and its residents changed over the course of the fieldwork. On my first field trip to Easthaven, I knew only two people (they worked in the town and lived nearby). When I returned to Easthaven after a few months, I was already being recognized and greeted in the street and at community events. By my final field trip, I was being invited to people's houses for dinner. To some extent, then, my position as 'outsider-researcher' had been modified: as Santoro and Smyth (2010) note, the researcher's position in relation to that of the (other) research participants cannot be reduced to a simple 'insider/outsider' binary. 'We are all insiders and outsiders in different ways and settings', writes Shah (2004, p. 556) – and our status and subject position change as the research progresses. In another important respect, however, my status did not change: I remained a middle-class White woman, and in that sense 'familiar' to the majority of Easthaveners. While being invited to people's homes may accord with imaginaries of country towns as friendly and welcoming, it was not, as I learnt, a privilege extended to everybody, whether or not they were 'locals'. This idea of the 'racing of space' became a central theme as the book developed and is discussed at length in the chapters that follow.

4

'Sprinkles of Everything'

Names, Namings and Numbers

Introduction

Race, ethnicity, culture. Each of these has been a powerful way of polities grouping people, and people grouping themselves, over decades – in short, of 'seeing' and 'being' distinctive cultural entities. In Australia, as noted, the word 'race' was largely superseded by 'ethnicity' in the post-war period and 'ethnicity', in turn, has been largely superseded by 'culture'. While the Community Relations Commission and Principles of Multiculturalism Act 2000 refers to different 'linguistic, religious, racial and ethnic backgrounds' (NSW Government, 2015a), for example, the Act's 2014 successor, the Multicultural NSW Act 2000, replaces 'racial and ethnic backgrounds' with 'ancestral backgrounds'. The words 'race' and 'racial' continue to be used in some other official documents and discourses, however, as well as in media and popular discourses (Hartmann, 2015; Lentin, 2008).

The focus of this chapter is the categories that Easthaveners, particularly those involved with the town's two public high schools, use in talking about their community and themselves. What dimensions of difference do they foreground, and how? Changes in official terminology notwithstanding, does race, for instance, remain current either as an actual term or as a concept? In drawing attention to the causes and effects of shifts in terminology, I pursue three avenues of investigation proposed by De Lepervanche (1980) more than four decades ago but which remain relevant today. The first is the distinctions people make between themselves and others by invoking 'descent, blood, race, religion, language, ethnic background, or some attribute that asserts roots, origins, sameness of one kind against difference in others'; and how these 'attributes' may then be given explanatory power in terms of a person's or group's (perceived) status, beliefs, values and/or practices (De Lepervanche, 1980, p. 32). Such concerns are the focus of this chapter, which uses the ideas presented in Chapter 1 to interrogate how diversity-related terms are routinely employed in Easthaven; how and where category boundaries are drawn (and contested); and what characteristics, motivations, agency and 'worth' people ascribe to different groups – in other words, what peoples' observations, opinions and stories suggest about their ethnocultural schemas. These insights are important to understanding their evaluations of diversity's merits (or otherwise).

The second area of investigation builds on this to identify 'various historical instances in which race and ethnicity have emerged, and how both are linked to structural relations of dominance and subjection' (De Lepervanche, 1980, p. 33) – widening the focus, in short, from concepts and categories to discourses and relations of power. The third area involves tracing how ethnocultural categories, categorization processes and discourses translate into social practices, particularly educational practices, and hence their (likely) sociopolitical effects. These latter areas of inquiry are developed, respectively, in Chapters 5 and 6.

This chapter begins by presenting participants' perspectives on whether regional Easthaven is culturally diverse. It then details who is named – and who is not named – in discussions about who lives in the town and who attends the schools; *how* different groups and individuals are named, and name themselves; and the extent to, and ways in which, dominant 'ethnic' labels are contested and resisted. The latter part of the chapter examines more closely identification and identity strategies in relation to particular 'groups' within the school and broader communities. Throughout, consideration is given to how the categories and categorization logics utilized by interviewees impact on, or may impact on, students' sense of belonging, identity and academic achievement – the argument being that 'difference' is created, not simply reflected, in our everyday articulations and silences (Colvin, 2017), and that these constructed differences are intrinsic to the distribution, validation and regulation of power within communities.

Easthaven: Culturally Diverse or Not?

As discussed previously, the contemporary ubiquity of terms such as 'culturally diverse' and 'multicultural' does not mean that they are used in consistent ways between and within organizations and communities, or even by the same individual. Given the significant demographic changes in Easthaven over the past ten to fifteen years, a key question was: *Did* Easthaveners see their town as culturally diverse? The perspectives of members of the broader Easthaven community are important here for contextualizing the discourses and practices within the schools that are the primary focus of this study: the 'borders' between school and home, home and community and community and school are, after all, always porous.

As detailed in Chapter 3, compared with figures for Australia as a whole and – particularly compared with most of Australia's large cities – regional Easthaven does not rate as very diverse. However, recent population changes mean that the town now has 'sprinkles of everything' (as one interviewee put it), even if the numbers remain low. The local council declares itself 'proud' of this growing ethnic, cultural and linguistic diversity and has actively promoted its 'multicultural' credentials. To delve into Easthaveners' understandings of diversity, then, a valid starting point appeared to be not only finding out whether they judged their home town to be culturally diverse or not but how they benchmarked their judgments – were they, for instance, comparing Easthaven's population today with how it used to be twenty, thirty, fifty years ago, or were they comparing the town with cities such as Sydney and/or other places they might have lived in (or even just heard about)? In short, were their frames of reference local and historical, national/international and contemporary, and/or rural versus urban?

Attesting to both the imprecision of diversity-related terms and the critical influence of personal histories and reference points on perceptions, Easthaveners' characterizations of their town showed substantial variance. Claire, a local council employee involved in multicultural planning, said the area had 'really changed' over the eighteen years she had lived there and was now 'quite diverse . . . we've got about fifty nationalities'. Hillview High deputy principal Reg echoed this assessment, saying the school had been very 'White Australian' when he started teaching there in the 1980s – but 'now it's very multicultural. We've got – I wouldn't like to guess at how many nationalities. There'd be lots of them.' Many of the interviewees similarly characterized Easthaven as reasonably or very 'diverse' or 'multicultural' – mostly, in the case of longtime residents, in relation to how it used to be. Citing earlier influxes of immigrants from Italy and India, another interviewee compared the town with other non-metropolitan centres, saying it had always been 'fairly diverse for a regional area'.

Even these simple observations about Easthaven's diversity point to complex understandings and usages of diversity-related terms. First, '(culturally) diverse' and 'multicultural' were often used interchangeably by interviewees although, as noted in Chapters 1 and 2, the terms are not equivalent. Second, there is an understanding of 'cultural diversity' as inhering in a certain number of 'nationalities' – for instance, 'fifty' or 'lots', as opposed to two or three. Third, 'nationality' is not, of course, 'culture' (Baumann, 1999), and what Claire and Reg meant by 'nationality' is unclear: to take just one example, how might they have classified Celine, a Seaview High student who was born in Burundi to parents from different tribes, grew up in a refugee camp in Uganda, speaks French, Swahili, Kirundi and English, and has been an Australian citizen for several years? Fourth, there are the pronouns: '*we*'ve got [*x* number of] nationalities' and 'there'd be lots of *them*'. Again, exactly who the 'we' here is unclear – it could be the town, the school or the community of longtime Easthaveners – but the people from 'other' nationalities (the vast majority of whom would, in fact, be Australian by citizenship) are outside of the central 'we', in the distal space of 'them'. Finally, and relatedly, it is likely that 'we' is people of Anglo-Celtic descent – people whom diversity discourses typically position as outside of diversity. As the AHRC (2016, p. 5) notes: 'A reference to "culturally diverse" backgrounds is frequently a shorthand for "non-Anglo-Celtic" ones, though it can more specifically refer to those that are "non-European".'

In the eyes of Seaview High parent Catriona, Easthaven is *not* very diverse but rather 'vanilla'. Whereas other residents focused on the growing number of people from non-European backgrounds in the region, Catriona focused on its continuing 'White' essence:

> Because it's not a big enough mixing pot, you don't have the shops and the restaurants and all the – Those other sort of cornerstones that reflect your ethnic diversity in Sydney, you don't really have that here yet. And so it [diversity] is still seen sometimes as being a little bit special, a little bit 'out there', rather than just being seen as a norm.

Here Catriona foregrounds the lived reality of diversity in Easthaven, emphasizing the low numbers of other-than-Anglo relative to Anglo-background people in the town. Accordingly, she says, people and practices of non-Anglo and non-Indigenous origin are still a bit 'out there' in the eyes of longtime Easthaveners. Catriona's views are perhaps also informed by the leadership structures at Seaview High, where the school executive, P&C (of which she is a member), Student Representative Council (SRC) and Gifted and Talented streams are almost exclusively Anglo domains – hence her description of Easthaven as 'still very much a vanilla aristocracy'.

Catriona's observations about cultural and ethnic dominance were echoed forcefully by Hope, another Anglo-background, middle-class parent at Seaview High. Hope did not see even Australia, let alone Easthaven, as diverse or multicultural, describing Australia as 'actually the *whitest* country in the world, it is *amazing* . . . even now we're still taking mainly Irish, Scottish, British [immigrants]'. Some minutes later, she returned to this theme, saying:

> I think in Australia we're in such a privileged position to think that we actually have diversity, because we don't. Like we just discussed, 85 per cent of our culture is English-American culture[1]. And we have the 'nice' parts of multiculturalism because the [non-Anglo-background] groups are so small they have no political power, they have no clout, you know. So you just collect the food and maybe the dance, the theatre, all the nice, pretty cultural parts.

Hope described the diversity in Easthaven as '*very* small . . . quite different to living in Sydney' (where she had grown up). What is interesting is that Hope, within the one interview, used 'diversity' to refer to country of origin, power relations, customs and artefacts, and beliefs and values. She contrasted the sociocultural situation in Australia with that in Cuba, where she and her family had spent some time. Cultural diversity there was 'huge', she said, adding: 'It was the only society I've ever been to where I felt that everybody was treated equally, and you would see a Black person in a role of authority just as equally as you'd see a White person sweeping the streets.'

These comments suggest that for Hope, cultural diversity is entwined with social justice, so that a truly 'diverse' society is one in which a person's status and opportunities are not delimited by their ethnic or cultural background. In this latter quote 'White' becomes a marker of skin colour (in contrast to 'Black'), whereas in the former quote 'White' is associated more with cultural heritage and hegemony. This distinction accords with that proposed by Leonardo (2002), wherein 'whiteness' is a worldview (re)produced through a 'collection of everyday strategies' (p. 32), particularly discourse, while 'white people' is a socially constructed category or identity, typically (albeit variably) based on skin colour. I will follow this distinction in attempting to illuminate the practice(s) of Whiteness in Easthaven.

For reasons very different to Hope's, another interviewee, Hillview High deputy principal Vince, also questioned Australia's diversity along with Australians' 'multicultural' competence:

> I think it's because we're so isolated here. You go to Europe . . . most people speak three languages, four languages. And you cross a border and you have got a

different culture – whereas here, it's just all Australian. . . . We don't know what multicultural is in Australia . . . we just give it lip service. We don't understand it and we probably never will.

Vince, whose parents were born in Italy, links Australians' alleged lack of understanding of multiculturalism to low rates of multilingualism (he himself speaks three languages), a lack of routine exposure to and engagement with cultural differences, and physical separation from the rest of the world. These primarily historical and geographical factors, in Vince's opinion, will remain largely insurmountable barriers to Australia's moving beyond 'lip service' to multiculturalism.

The idea of routine interaction between people from different backgrounds as key to 'true' multiculturalism was echoed by Thomas, a Year 11, Anglo-Australian student at Hillview High. At the end of the focus group in which he participated, Thomas – who had lived all his life in Easthaven – indicated there was something he still wanted to say, continuing: 'Australia is a *not* multicultural country [*sic*]. [*Laughter and exclamations of "What?" from other students*] Everyone thinks it is but it isn't, 'cause you don't see any people mingling together.' For this student, 'mingling' – everyday mixing between people from different ethnic and cultural backgrounds – is a hallmark of multiculturalism, and one that he has not personally observed and experienced. Hence while Australia may be multi-*ethnic*, growing up in Easthaven has led him to dispute the assumption that Australia is multi*cultural*. What is particularly interesting in this exchange is the other students' reaction to Thomas's somewhat hesitantly offered view on multiculturalism. Their laughter and exclamations of 'What?' indicate bemusement at, even perhaps a ridiculing of, his unorthodox perspective. The 'truth' of Australia's multiculturalism is so ingrained that it is seldom questioned, and any questioning of it may disrupt nationalistic schemas and provoke unexpected affects – dynamics that are examined in detail in the next chapter.

For the majority of interviewees, then, cultural diversity and 'multicultural' were about the presence of (increasing numbers of) people of non-Anglo and non-Indigenous background in their town. One experience I had during an early visit to Easthaven proved illuminating in this regard, and confirms the AHRC comment above about the usage of 'culturally diverse'. As part of my fieldwork, I attended a P&C meeting at each school. At both meetings I had an opportunity to talk about the research project and promote it to parents, emphasizing that I was seeking to interview people from a range of backgrounds including Anglo-Australian. At the Seaview High meeting the dozen or so parents present showed considerable interest in the project, asking questions and offering to mention it in their communications. However, nobody contacted me over the next few days. When I returned to Easthaven some weeks later, I met one of the P&C members in the street. She asked how the research was going; I told her I was having difficulty recruiting enough Seaview High parents and was surprised not to have been contacted by any of the P&C attendees, given their apparent interest in the project. 'Oh', she said, 'we all thought you only wanted to interview culturally *diverse* people!' The P&C members, all Anglo-Australians, evidently took it for granted that 'diverse' meant 'other' than them.

'Culturally and linguistically diverse' (CALD) has become widely used in government and community agencies, preferred as a broader term than 'non-English-speaking-background' (NESB) as well as one free of the Anglocentrism of '*non-English*-speaking' (Piller, 2016). Logically, 'CALD' includes everyone – but in practice, it still applies to immigrants whose ethnic, cultural and/or linguistic background is not Anglo-Celtic. By exempting people with an Anglo-Celtic heritage from being 'diverse', Piller (2016) argues, '"diversity" becomes a euphemism for "linguistically and racially/ethnically outside the mainstream"' (p. 19).

Despite the 'sprinkles of everything' and large Anglo-background majority in Easthaven, interviewees overwhelmingly focused their talk on two particular 'groups': the 'Africans' and the 'Aborigines'. At the schools, Seaview High deputy principal William spoke of 'the two main groups . . . Aboriginal . . . and African refugee', while Hillview High deputy Reg referred to 'our three communities . . . the African, the Aboriginal and the "other"', adding: 'The "other" one has more in it [he listed Thai, Chinese, Indian and Burmese], but they [African and Aboriginal] are the two that are more prominent . . . in size at our school.' Missing from both of these characterizations is mention of the huge Anglo-Australian majority: again, 'cultural diversity' here is 'other', non-Anglo people. This echoes the findings of the unpublished 2009 study on Easthaveners' perceptions of their community cited in the previous chapter. Historically, Indigenous Easthaveners have been the largest non-European-background group in the town (as in most regional communities), and 'Black/White' the dominant racial-cultural paradigm. Physically, the new settlers from Africa are easily identifiable and their mutual 'Blackness' allows them to be readily constituted as a group, despite the extraordinary heterogeneity and hybridity of their national, ethnic, cultural, linguistic and religious backgrounds. More than anything else, it was the arrival of the refugees from Africa that was seen as marking Easthaven's transformation into a recognizably 'multicultural' centre. At the same time, the settlers from Africa, through their very Blackness, have disrupted the historical Black/White (Indigenous/Anglo) binary in a way that no other immigrants into Easthaven have done.

Culture, Cultural Diversity and Cultural Identity

Culture as Being, Believing, Doing, Feeling

One question posed to almost all interviewees was: What do you understand by the word 'culture'? Not surprisingly, the responses varied greatly while also showing several common themes. One group of understandings shared a notion of culture as normative – sets of rules, values, beliefs and practices that both produce and maintain distinctive social groups:

> It's the way things are done around here. (Stephanie, deputy principal, Seaview High)

A set of values that are endorsed by the society and passed from one generation to another. (Neil, principal, Hillview High)

It's the dos and don'ts . . . the respect, the hierarchy. (Celine, Year 11 ESL student, Seaview High)

A second group shared notions of culture as difference, as something 'other' people had – such as this comment from Year 7 student Isabelle (Hillview High): 'Like, if there was only just Australian people, no Aboriginals, no Sudanese, I don't reckon culture would be a word because there isn't different people in the world.' Here she appears, in fact, to be talking more about race: if there were no Black people, there would be no difference.

Another view was of culture as varying in intensity and importance between nations and groups: 'It probably means more to people who have a longer chronological culture than, say, White Australians do, but – ours can be a bit jingoistic' (Trudy, parent, Seaview High). Culture was also seen as varying along a continuum from fixed and visceral (as in the first two interview excerpts cited below) to flexible and more intellectual (the latter two examples):

Who you are and where you're from . . . it's the language, the places, sacred sites, the people . . . it's deep within [you], it's in [your] blood. (Kai, AEO, Hillview High)

It's where you belong, and where you feel you belong – where your soul attaches to. (Monica, parent, Seaview High)

For us in Australia, where you can choose who your group is, you don't have to be the same culture as your village. (Caryn, parent, Hillview High)

Some of my best friends classify themselves as Australian . . . They weren't born here, but they've been here since they were twelve. They have a good strong culture but still have an Aussie culture as well. Their culture – what they do is different to their parents, it's a combination. (Sharon, ESL teacher, Hillview High)

Ideas about the relationship between race/ethnicity and culture varied as well, from being essentially the same thing – 'in [your] blood', as Kai said above – to quite separate, as Hillview High parent Erica explained about her son's 'Chineseness'. 'He looks Chinese but we don't do "Chinese" things [at home]', she said. 'So I'd say his cultural background is still not Chinese . . . it [Chineseness] is part of his *racial* background.'

. . . but 'Diversity' as Looks and Seeing

Despite their (general) understanding of 'culture' as embedded in and enacted through beliefs, values and practices, when interviewees were asked about cultural *diversity* they overwhelmingly spoke in terms of people's appearance, not their beliefs and practices. The word 'see', for instance, was frequently connected with 'diversity', as in the following examples:

> [Y]ou can see [the] diversity all around you. (Glenys, NSW DoE regional consultant)

> To see all those different cultures walking around [now], it's just sensational! (Fiona, also a NSW DoE consultant)

> You only have to go out there [the playground] now at recess and see all the multicultural kids ... [and] the Australian kids. (Brody, teacher, Seaview High)

Like the P&C 'culturally diverse' misunderstanding recounted above, here the 'Australian kids' are the *Anglo*-Australian (and possibly Indigenous Australian) students, while the 'multicultural kids' are the brown- and black-skinned immigrants. Such a positioning was even more explicit in a comment by William, deputy principal at Seaview High, when he referred to 'our non-Australians' – although he immediately corrected himself with '... who are now *new* Australians'. While comments such as Brody's and William's are brief, made almost in passing, they reflect and perpetuate discourses that construct White Australians as the *real* Australians – the ones who incontestably can claim the single-word identifier: 'Australian'. Brody alluded to this when he recounted his own experience growing up in a working-class NSW town:

> My best friends when I was a kid, one was Yugoslav and one was Lebanese and I was Welsh, but we were all born in Australia. But I was considered to be the 'Australian' one because I had blond hair. But their parents had been here longer than [mine] had.

Interestingly, there was a moment of insight towards the end of Brody's interview – in which he had spoken at length about his interactions with African-background Easthaveners – when he said:

> Well, I've sat here for forty minutes or something and banged on about Africans. It's only now that I've mentioned [the] South Americans [in the town] – because you get into that visibility trap, the cliché of 'hey, they look different, so therefore there's diversity'.

Occasionally aspects of appearance such as the height or brightly coloured clothes of the African-background Easthaveners (or, in the broader community, the turbans or beards of the Indian-background residents) were mentioned as visible markers of difference. Above all, however, it was skin colour that was the focus of distinctions. This was sometimes directly expressed – words such as 'race' and 'colour' as well as 'black' and 'white'. More often, national or geographic words, such as 'Sudanese' and 'Asian', stood in for 'colour' words (respectively, 'black' and 'brown'). 'African', for example, never meant simply 'from Africa'; in Easthaven, it always denoted 'Black refugees from northern Africa' – not to be confused, say, with skilled migrants of European descent from South Africa.

These data are consistent with the findings of a large-scale US study on race, religion and multiculturalism by Bell and Hartmann (2007). Although interviewees in the study spoke of 'cultural diversity' in the abstract in broad and inclusive terms, when they spoke of their *personal* experience of 'cultural' differences their accounts almost always centred on *ethnic/racial* otherness. In other words, while 'race' may have been largely expunged from the language of diversity in favour of categories based on ethnic, linguistic and religious background, it remains a powerful lens on difference. 'Race refuses to remain silent because it isn't just a word', Goldberg (2006, p. 337) writes. 'It is a set of conditions, shifting over time. Never just one thing, it is a way (or really ways) of thinking, a way(s) of living, a disposition.'

Identities and Identifications

As the discussion above highlights, there was a significant disjunction between most interviewees' conceptualizations of 'culture' as primarily about ways of being, thinking, doing and/or feeling, and their representations of 'diversity' as primarily a visual phenomenon – that is, more akin to notions of race. This understanding of diversity can be seen as a product of entangled national and local, historical and contemporary influences – reflective, for example, of how historical emphases on phenotypical features as key markers of difference are continued in contemporary discourses and images such as corporate communications, media reports and the front cover of multicultural policy documents.

If culture is in effect reduced to race in people's understandings of cultural diversity, this will circumscribe recognition of the multiplicity and intersectionality of identities that constitute our being-and-becoming selves (Hall, 1990a). The NSW DoE's Fiona, quoted above, talked about 'different cultures walking around', as if 'culture' is something people 'have' as a constant over their lifetime (like the colour of their skin). If this is a dominant conceptualization of culture in the context of cultural diversity, 'culture' will also be understood as quantifiable. One Easthaven parent said she was always 'amazed' at 'particularly the older generation, who still say things like "Oh yeah, they're an eighth Aboriginal", like it's this measurement'. A Year 7 student referred to another student (not in the focus group) as 'half-caste'; a Year 9 student described herself as 'three-quarters Italian, one-quarter Irish'; Hillview High principal Neil said he was 'half-Australian, half-Hungarian'; a teacher spoke of her 'mixed-race' children. Hillview High deputy Vince, meanwhile, identified himself as 'an Italian' – even though he was born and had lived all his life in Australia – and said:

> Even with my own children, I tell them, 'You are Italian.' 'No, but I'm Australian', [they say]. I say, 'No. You're Italian because you're a minority group, you come from a minority group.' [. . .] My kids tend to say that they're Italian now, but . . . when they were younger they've been taught [by their Anglo-background mother], 'You're not Italian. You're English. You're born in Australia. You don't want to speak that foreign language. It's – lower-class people speak things we don't understand.'

Here again we see a view of culture as something a person *has* – that is inherited, intact, through genes or genealogy – and thus is intrinsic to who one *is* (cultural identity). In Vince's narrative, however, there is a strong sense of identities being *made* (and remade, in the face of contestation) as well as of a heritage being expressed. Vince does not merely identify himself as Italian but as *an* Italian, also insisting that his third-generation-Australian children see themselves as Italian and 'a minority group'. The identity, then, is not only ethnic/cultural but assumes a position within a social hierarchy – that of being a 'minority' and, according to Vince's (former) wife, 'lower-class'. This is a further effect of diversity-as-strength discourses: if that proposition is 'true', it becomes important to keep 'cultures' and identities discrete.

While such essentializing may not stand up to the test of lived reality in today's hybridized world, it has historically had, and continues to have, enormous *practical* value (or cost) in daily life – to the identifier and the identified, the colonizer and the colonized, individuals and institutions. For one thing, as Baumann (1999) points out, it promotes group-making and conformity within groups. As for dealing with strangers:

> it helps one stereotype them with the greatest of ease and to make commonsense predictions of how these others might think and what they might do next. An American will act like an American, an ethnic like an ethnic, a Muslim like a Muslim. One need not ask who they are if one knows what they are. (Baumann, 1999, p. 84)

The most immediate way to identify 'what' someone is, in everyday encounters, is to look at them: there is little concealing the colour of one's skin, for instance, or the shape of one's eyes. Caryn, a Hillview High parent, said she was 'privileged' (her word) because her work brought her into daily contact with people from diverse backgrounds, and she had to 'get to know them and accept them for who they are'. But most Easthaveners, she said, 'still . . . will see a Chinese-looking person and think they arrived last week, [even though] they've been here longer than your family's been here'. Another Hillview High parent, Erica, whose husband was of Chinese heritage, described how he 'wore two hats', Australian and Chinese, and would sometimes 'put on' the latter:

> If someone comes and knocks at the door, he's quite happy to pretend that he doesn't understand what they're saying: 'No, I don't speak English' sort of stuff. But he's also – sounds Australian too, so – They [Australian-born Chinese] wear two hats easily, so I don't think he feels at all like he doesn't belong in Australia.

From the safety of his cultural belonging, Erica's husband can strategically take advantage of his ethnic foreignness. As discussed shortly, however, this flexibility is not open equally to all non-Anglo Australians.

What's in a Name? What's in a Colour?[2]

Given Australia's history of settler colonialism, the issues of culture, cultural diversity and cultural identity become particularly complex and controversial in relation to

Indigenous identity and skin colour, and are regular topics of public and media debate (Overington, 2012). Vince, for instance, said of Hillview High's students: 'A lot of our Aboriginal kids here don't know about their own identity. It's been lost over – through the Stolen Generation.[3] . . . They're Aboriginal but they're not.' A Year 7 student at Hillview High who identified as 'Aboriginal' echoed this view in her enthusiasm about the school's plans to start teaching the local Indigenous language: "'Cause we're like walking around saying that we're Aboriginal but – Aboriginal people lived on the land and used to talk that way [the local language], so I think we should learn that too.' Again, in these comments there is a view of culture as something that is inherited but, paradoxically, can be taken away or lost, diminishing a person's 'true' identity. This points to 'loss of culture' as a problem for which 'restoration of culture' is the remedy – as if 'Aboriginal culture' is 'out there' and needs only to be 'rediscovered' and revived. It also points to the sort of blurring of ethnicity and culture, heritage and identity, that multicultural policies have tended to promote through their changing and inconsistent terminologies and their focus on 'ethnic groups' maintaining 'their' culture.

'Culture', then, is often assumed to map reasonably accurately onto 'ethnicity'. A person who looks 'Chinese' may be assumed to be culturally Chinese (see Caryn's and Erica's comments above); a person who looks more 'Aboriginal' (i.e. has darker skin) is likely to be assumed to be more 'Aboriginal' culturally. Kai, the AEO at Hillview High, recounted:

> I've even heard some of the staff say, 'Oh, they don't look Aboriginal 'cause they're too white' . . . [or] 'Oh, they're half-caste' or 'They're only 50 per cent; they're only half Aboriginal'. And I go, 'Yeah mate, which half, the top or the bottom half?' You either are or you aren't.

Later in the interview Kai returned to this theme:

> It's hard for the fairer-skinned Aboriginal people, but you just gotta let the world know who you are. You can't go hiding behind – you can't be Black in this circle and then be White in this circle, whenever it suits you. It's got to be Black all the way, Aboriginal all the way, or identify as being non-Aboriginal all the way. You either are or you aren't.

The insistence on a singular identity, in this age of cultural and ethnic hybridity, may appear perverse, but needs to be understood in its historical as well as contemporary and local contexts.

To Be or Not to Be Aboriginal

The majority of Australians who identify as Indigenous have mixed ancestries. Notwithstanding this heterogeneity, asserting a multi-ethnic identity 'is neither common nor straightforward because racial loyalty demands that anomalous individuals choose to be either exclusively Indigenous or exclusively non-Indigenous' (Paradies, 2006, p. 357). As mentioned in Chapter 1, Black/White boundaries were vigorously policed and defended by the residents of regional Bourke, despite the mixed ancestry of most. 'We all carry these categories in our imaginations and inhabitations', Cowlishaw (2004b, p. 60) writes. 'Skin colour, in particular, is the focus of all kinds of struggles and contested significance not only between groups, but also within them.' At a more mundane level, administrative systems, including in schools, also require Australians to choose between Indigenous and non-Indigenous identity; you either tick the 'Aboriginal or Torres Strait Islander' box or you don't. You either are or you aren't. Thus the singular identity of 'Aboriginal' may be imposed (by state or social group) or consciously chosen – but the latter is always in some way a product of the former.

The intricacies of skin colour, identification and identity are vividly captured in Seaview High parent Monica's account of her sons' experiences and enactments of 'Blackness' in Easthaven. Monica describes herself as 'ancestrally' European and 'culturally, I'd say I'm [*pauses*] – I'd say I don't really like to box myself in', while her husband is of South Sea Islander and Aboriginal descent. Asked how her sons identified, she said:

> The way they'd put it is 'I'm part Black and part White, I'm Black and White'. And it's interesting because apart from – all of them [*pauses*], yeah I would say all of them, have had racial slurs, even as littlies. And even though that's always been the Black part [i.e. the racial slurs have always been about their skin colour], they will *always* prefer to be known as Black. They see being Black as very . . . hip or cool . . . particularly with the Afro-American hip-hop artists [. . .] And it's funny to listen to them [her sons] talk amongst themselves . . . they'll rate each other: 'Oh, but I'm the darkest, aren't I?' and 'I look blacker than you.' Or come summer, when they all tan up: 'Oh, you know, we look like *real* Blackfellas now!'

Although Monica's sons are of Aboriginal and European descent and come from a middle-class family, their dark skin precludes them from claiming a plain 'Australian' identity. Locked out of Whiteness, they appropriate the 'cool' of African American blackness to enhance their cultural cachet. At the same time, paradoxically, being blacker appears to be equated with 'authentic' Aboriginality.

Her eldest son's particularly dark skin and strong identification as Black had had significant academic and social impacts, Monica said. Although she felt he had been well supported at Seaview High, she was concerned that some of the teachers at the school had low expectations of Aboriginal students:

> I still think there's a level of or a degree of segregation, and . . . a degree of expectation that the Koori kids will – that there needs to be some sort of, not leniency, but there's more or less this unspoken – I suppose it *is* a degree of leniency: 'Oh well, he's Koori; of course he's gonna excel in sports . . . but we can't expect too much of him academically.' And for him [her son], he's gone from being above average academically to basically the bottom classes right across the board.

Her son had recently participated in a mentoring programme, explaining that he had been enrolled in it because 'I've got anger management issues and I'm Black'. Socially, his friendship circle had narrowed to almost exclusively other Aboriginal students:

He's gone from a primary school where he was mixing with White kids, Asian, he had a really good Asian mate. But now it's just this – there's maybe one or two Anglo-Saxon kids amongst it, but it's all dark-skinned kids, whether they're Kooris or Maoris or – And you'll hear that group of kids talk about 'the Sudis' . . . how many 'Sudi' families are here [now].

While Monica, as someone of European heritage, is able to avoid 'boxing herself in', her dark-skinned sons had been regularly called names such as 'Black cunt' and 'dirty Blackfella' since they were toddlers. Their individual and collective response to being told they were Black (and worse) was to take on strongly Black identities – and, in the case of Monica's eldest son, a 'bad Black' identity. Being competitive, including academically, was seen as 'trying to be White' and hence rejected.

Identities, Hall (1990a) writes, are 'the names we give to the different ways we are positioned by, and position ourselves within, the narratives of the past' (p. 225). The trauma of colonization for Black people lies not only in the ways in which dominant (White) cultural regimes constructed Black people and their knowledges and experiences as 'other' but how, in doing so, the regimes made Black people see *themselves* as 'other' (Hall, 1990a) – even, in the case of Indigenous Australians, within a continent they have occupied for thousands of years. People are not necessarily fixed by the names they are called (Ang, 2001; Hall, 1991): as noted in Chapter 1, the word 'Black', historically a signifier of inferiority and oppression, can be repurposed as a term of pride, solidarity and even 'cool' through its contemporary association with hip-hop and rap. However, as Hall (1991) emphasizes:

> [T]o say something new is first of all to displace all the old things that the words mean – to fight an entire system of meanings . . . . The whole history of Western imperial thought is condensed in the struggle to dislocate what Black used to mean in order to make it mean something new, in order to say 'Black is Beautiful'. (p. 11)

'Black', in short, is not simply a word; it is 'an entire system of meanings', steeped in unequal relations of power – a signifier that can never be free of its pasts.

Long Shadows

The impacts of the 'struggle' highlighted by Hall (1991) reverberate throughout education. The overall academic underperformance of Black students in countries including Australia, Britain and the United States has long been recognized and, despite decades of policy, pedagogic and curriculum reform, remains persistent in many places (Ford, 2013; Ladson-Billings, 2003; Vaught & Castagno, 2008; Wilson, 2016). Writing about the United States thirty years ago, Fordham and Ogbu (1986) proposed that a major reason for many African American students' underperformance at school was their development of what the authors called oppositional social identities and oppositional cultural frames of reference. They argued that centuries of substandard schooling, low teacher expectations and restricted employment options on leaving school had produced a perspective among many Black youth that behaving according to what they saw as White values and practices – such as working hard at school – was 'acting White' and therefore undesirable. The oppositional identity is not simply not-White but 'includes devices for protecting their identity and for maintaining [ethnic and cultural] boundaries' (Fordham & Ogbu, 1986, p. 181). While US and Australian historical, ethnocultural and educational situations are different, evidence of such 'devices' can be found in Monica's account of her son's social and school practices: the narrowing of his friendship circle, the homogenizing of the Koori and Maori boys into 'Blackness' (what Fordham and Ogbu call 'fictive kinship'), and their strong identification with African American cultural expressions. Further, not only do these boys largely separate themselves from their Anglo-Australian peers, they also actively distance themselves, spatially and discursively, from the 'other' local Black people – the recently arrived refugees from Africa, whom they homogenize as the 'Sudis'.

The concept of fictive kinship can be linked to Zerubavel's (1996) ideas about lumping and splitting. It is characterized as a world view and collective identity constructed around (for example) 'Blackness', and reinforced through kinship terms such as 'brother', 'sister', 'blood', 'my people' (Fordham & Ogbu, 1986). Hillview High AEO Kai, for example, described culture as 'in [your] blood' and spoke extensively about his 'mob', aunties, elders, cousins, ancestors, spirits and so on. Such conceptualizations of culture and kinship may be fundamental to ontologies and epistemologies very different from dominant Western ones, but are also inevitably shaped by mainstream beliefs, discourses and other social practices (Nakata, 2007). It may be difficult to reconcile notions of cultural identity as 'deep within' (Kai) with notions of identity as performative; it is less difficult to understand the 'strategic and positional' (Hall, 1997, p. 17) advantages for some Indigenous people of adhering to a singular identity – how 'Black', for instance, can be taken up as 'a political colour to be worn with pride against colour-based racisms' (Brah, 1991, p. 55). However, merely *being* black (in colour) neither means an individual will assume an oppositional identity (Fordham & Ogbu, 1986) nor, as the example of Monica's son and the 'Sudis' illustrates, that he or she will be accepted into a localized collective Black identity.

Even 'Black is beautiful' discourses are a 'potential prison-house' (Ang, 2001, p. 11) for Aboriginal students if the priority in schools becomes simply promoting respect for and appreciation of 'their' culture. 'The culture put into capsules, which has vegetated since the foreign domination, is revalorized', Fanon (1964) writes of this phenomenon. 'It is not reconceived, grasped anew, dynamized from within. It is shouted' (p. 42). Such 'shouting' can be heard not only in Kai's 'you just gotta let the world know who you are', Black or White, but in his approach to Aboriginal education, articulated thus:

> One of the things that Aboriginal students need is a touch of their culture within them. It's *in* them; we just gotta know how to draw it out of them. And the way we're doing it here [at Hillview High] is through dance and [the local Indigenous] language.

Aboriginal students were also taken into the surrounding bushland and to meet with local elders, he explained:

You might read 1000 books, but you're never gonna get that [same] feeling [as] if you're out there in that rainforest or along that ocean . . . And when you're in those significant [Aboriginal] areas and then you hear about those stories – and those stories are tens of thousands of years old. Those pyramids [in Egypt], they're only 4000 years old; these stories go back tens of *thousands* of years, and they're from this area.

Here Kai constructs as 'lesser' both books and the Egyptian pyramids as part of a discourse that privileges the local (connecting with 'country') over more 'distant' (spatially, culturally, affectively) experiences: Aboriginal culture was better, in short, because it was already and forever 'present' ('It's *in* them').

By contrast, Gary, one of Seaview High's Aboriginal support staff, emphasized the need to 'dynamize from within', to use Fanon's expression. For Gary, the challenge was to shift the focus from 'either/or' (Black/White) to 'both/and':

I think we [Indigenous Australians] have to be able to adapt . . . Aboriginal English has its place, yeah, and so does mainstream English [Standard Australian English]. . . . To be successful and to advance the rights and the self-determination and all that thing that Indigenous people are seeking, we need to be able to step into mainstream [*sic*] and understand how it works, and then change it from there.

Gary and Kai clearly have very different perspectives on what their students 'need', along with different spatial and temporal orientations. Kai is oriented to the past and to the local, seeing 'reawakening' of 'culture' as crucial to his students' engagement and empowerment. Gary, in contrast, is focused on equipping his students with the knowledge, skills and motivation to flourish in a technology-driven, globalizing world – allowing for broader imaginings of what it might mean to be 'Aboriginal' in and beyond a regional community in NSW.

Blackness in a Mostly White Town

Since it was established as a town about 150 years ago, Easthaven has been a 'mostly White' settlement – ethnically, but more importantly in its institutions, infrastructure, landholdings and industry. In the post-war period 'White' has expanded to more or less include light-skinned Aboriginal-background people along with immigrants from Italy, India, Vietnam and the former Yugoslavia, among others – people considered to have proven themselves by working hard and contributing to the economic and social life of the community. However, in a space of still predominantly 'blond heads and blue eyes' (Hillview High teacher Winsome), the presence of ethnic and cultural 'others' is not yet 'normal'. 'Anybody that's different to what is the White Anglo-Saxon thingo, they're still getting commented upon', said one parent. Another woman who had lived in the area since emigrating from Spain more than thirty years ago described how, when she went to open a bank account, the teller asked for how long she was visiting Australia. 'That would never happen to me in Sydney', she said. In

Easthaven, in other words, there is some level of assumption that anyone who looks or sounds 'different' must be a visitor or tourist; they do not accord with imaginaries of the 'local'.

Into this space, from the early 2000s, have come the refugees from Africa, Burma and the Middle East. Although when the fieldwork for this study was undertaken, there were almost as many settlers from Burma as from Africa, it was the 'Africans' whom most Easthaveners talked about, at length, in the interviews and also in casual conversations. 'The Africans, at first, *really* stood out as something quite extraordinary here in [Easthaven]', said Debbie, a counsellor. They were 'seen as very exotic – people would touch their skin' (Carla, resident); they were 'gawked at' (Henrietta, retired ESL teacher). A decade on, 'we're all used to going to Woolworths and seeing Africans in the queue with us', Henrietta said. However, she added:

> I think some people in the [Easthaven] community think, 'Oh, it's all very well to have *some* new people, but why have we got so many?' . . . Because they're very *obvious*. And it's interesting, you get that comment about the African – various African communities; you never get it about the Burmese, because nobody notices them. Because they're small and they don't look that different . . . they just blend in.

Henrietta's comments were echoed by Graham, who had a daughter at Hillview High:

> People said, 'They [the families from Africa] seem to be everywhere'. Well, they *weren't* everywhere. They were only in the main area [the town centre], because that's their culture; their culture is to meet in a certain area and chat and socialize. . . . So people just assumed they were everywhere. And they were *conspicuous*. . . . They were a Black person, so you knew they were there and there. And people seemed to imagine that they'd taken over the whole place.

And this from Kerry, who worked in settlement services:

> If you were to ask the average person in the street [about the cultural make-up of Easthaven], they would go 'it's mainly Anglo-Saxon and Sudanese'. They associate every Black person as being Sudanese. Not much talk about the Burmese, which is quite surprising, because we've got quite a lot of Burmese arriving here now, but not many people seem to have the same reaction to Burmese as African. African, there seems to be a lot of fear generated, particularly if there's more than two or three talking together.

These comments capture issues with 'numbers', the amplifying effects of 'obviousness' and anxieties associated with perceived declines in certainty and control. The 'Africans' were seen as 'space invaders' (Puwar, 2004a) by some longtime Easthaveners, but also as having displaced these longtimers from their *own* favoured meeting places. Such discourses reflect Hage's (2000) argument, outlined in Chapter 1, about the meaning of 'too many'. He writes:

> Most humans perceive ants as a different species, and certainly as an inferior species. Yet, just on the basis of this belief, they do not perceive them as 'undesirable' or as 'too many'. They do so only when ants are seen to have invaded spaces where humans find their presence harmful such as in their houses or on their plates. (p. 37)

What Hage (2000) calls 'ant-like discourses' about space and belonging are explored further in the following chapter, with particular attention given to discourses about Africa, 'Africanness' and 'Blackness' and their intersections with discourses about rurality. For now, I note that 'fear' was frequently collocated with 'African' (or 'Sudanese') throughout the interviews and, further, that that fear appeared to be considered quite natural: 'Africans' generated fear because they were black, tall or loud, and so evidently 'foreign'. Two casual encounters I had during my visits to Easthaven add to the picture of the African-background residents' 'conspicuousness'. One time I was on a bus, sitting next to an elderly, well-dressed (White) woman, when a group of teenage (Black) African girls exchanged a few words with the bus driver as they disembarked. 'These Sudanese, they're always *arguing!*' the woman confided to me, shaking her head. I had not heard any argument, only a somewhat more exuberant than 'usual' exchange. The second encounter was a conversation I had with a taxi driver, who told me how he and his family had emigrated from the Netherlands when he was five. He expressed strong feelings about African-background Easthaveners continuing to speak their own language ('It's wrong!'), explaining that his parents had gone to great effort to assimilate and had always spoken only English at home. 'When I see a couple of Sudanese women talking [in the street], I go up to them and say: "Can't you *speak* English?"' he said. I later mentioned this conversation to Seaview High parent Hope, who mused that if the women had been Caucasian and 'were speaking German, would the taxi driver have gone up and said the same thing? Probably not'.

Hillview High parent Caryn, recounting how her father had refused for weeks to visit her house 'because there was a Black man there' (they were hosting an African-background student), said:

> The issue of course is that the Africans that come in *look* different and there's always been that Black/White thing that's gonna be an issue for people [. . .] But it's that – not black and white skin, but Black and White attitude [towards ethnic differences].

By being so 'Black', the refugees from Africa have disrupted Easthaveners' habitual ways of 'seeing' their town. The newcomers are a conspicuous sign of change in a country town that interviewees repeatedly described as conservative and highly stratified. Further, they have detonated the Black/White binary that has dominated social relations in the region for decades. This dynamic was captured by Hillview High deputy principal Reg (Anglo-Australian) when he said:

> The Aboriginals were the main ones we had. I think some people would see almost that there's the Whites and the Aboriginals, the White and the Black. And all of a sudden that was upset because there's another Black, and it was a *darker* Black, and

that causes problems.... And people saw that and all of a sudden it was: 'Hold on, it's not just White and Black, because' – without being – it sounds racist [*inaudible*] but – 'there's *shades*.' Let's say the African black is jet black; there's the Aboriginal black and – A lot of them aren't very dark-skinned, a lot of them you wouldn't even know they're Aboriginal; then there's – let's say the White: 'Well, hold on, in that White you talked about before, there's not just White; there's the Asians, there's the Indians, there's –' ... Before, it was just one or two cultures.

The nature of the 'problems' caused by the Africans' 'darker blackness' is discussed in the following chapters. However, the 'ant-like' nature of Reg's discourse about 'cultures' (races) can be seen in his use of 'we' in the first sentence of this excerpt ('the Aboriginals were the main ones *we* had').

The taken-for-granted dominance of 'we' (Anglo-Australians) in and beyond Easthaven was evident also in Reg's highlighting of contestations over 'ownership of things', which he explained thus: '[I]n our history... the White has owned things, and [now] the Aboriginal has wanted some of them back ... land rights and this sort of thing.' Here, White people are constructed as 'naturally' owning things – such as land – which the 'Aboriginal' has wanted *back* (despite never having ceded it in the first place). That Reg was concerned about threats to Anglo-Australians' power and privilege was underlined later in the interview when he said:

I've done a bit of travelling – the number of people who complain about the fact that the Aboriginals own Ayers Rock[4] and you're not to walk on it and [the local Aborigines] charge you to go and look at it, when it was something we went to for years for nothing. Those decisions, 'it's ours and you've got to pay for it', cause a lot of resentment.

To Reg, no longer being able to go to 'Ayers Rock... for nothing' is a form of Aboriginal discrimination against Whites, and one that White people are quite justified in being annoyed about. At the same time, in order not to risk being seen as racist, he constructs the 'complaints' and 'resentment' as other people's. This strategy makes it 'safe' for him to express his grievances without imperilling his image – possibly in his own eyes as well as others' – as a tolerant, fair-minded Australian.

Unasked Questions, Silences and White Fantasies

As documented, the fact that the African-background residents 'stood out' in Easthaven was mentioned frequently by interviewees. There is a crucial link between this 'standing out' and imaginings of Easthaven, as a regional town, as an essentially White space. The answer to the question 'why do the new Black people stand out?' is perhaps obvious: because the vast majority of people in the area are White. But it is the next question that appears to be rarely even contemplated, let alone asked: Why are most of the people in the area White? Because European settlers took over the land from the Indigenous inhabitants and named, tamed and assigned title to their landholdings, thereby securing their territorial and economic power. In all forty-eight interviews and focus groups, only one Easthavener recognized this logic and the silence surrounding it. Joseph, who had lived in Easthaven for seven years after fleeing his home country of South Sudan, first shared his own experience of being Black in a mostly White town:

> I think of myself as Australian, but my colour doesn't [*laughs*]. Because up to now, many people are still asking 'Where are you coming from?' and 'Are you enjoying Australia?' and 'Do you find it safe here?' and all that. All those questions sometimes make me feel that although I pretend to be Australian, still my skin doesn't show me to be Australian. And unfortunately many, many Australians are expecting that Australia is a country of Europeans. . . . They didn't recognize that Australia is a multicultural place, where if you get Black or you get White or you get Brown person, it's an Australian.

Later in the interview he said:

> If it comes to the truth, Australia is the country of Black people, the Aboriginals. . . . To my surprise, Aboriginal or Torres Strait Islander, I didn't get somebody asking me that question, 'Where do you come from?' and 'How do you find it here?'. Not that, no. Instead, people who are coming, also they are migrants, are asking me and thinking that Australia is their own. No.

According to Joseph, it is only the Anglo Easthaveners, not the Aboriginal ones, who repeatedly ask him where he is from – and this is because the Anglos, 'also . . . migrants', think 'Australia is their own'. The fantasy of Australia as a 'White nation' – one in which 'Aboriginal people and non-White "ethnics" are merely national objects to be moved or removed according to a White national will' (Hage, 2000, p. 18) – remains strong in Easthaven, in Joseph's experience. Belonging, whether national or local, is contingent on where White people draw spatial and sociocultural boundaries. Further, in rural and regional communities, belonging may mean being accepted not only as 'Australian' but as a 'local' – a process that typically takes many years. Council employee Claire (Anglo), for instance, who had moved to Easthaven from Sydney eighteen years before, said she was 'still not classed as a local, but I'm getting there'. Anglo-Australians' claim to belonging is steeped in denial and diminishment, Garbutt (2011) argues: 'Being local is constituted, it has its origins, in forgetting, silence, not seeing – a lack of recognition of Aborigines initially, but with implications for all Australians in multi-racial contemporary Australia' (p. 29).

'Really Really Different Different'

People who 'look different' in Easthaven might attract attention, but they do not necessarily attract genuine curiosity or connection. Sisay and Celine, two Year 11 refugee-background students at Seaview High, both from Africa, spoke of how conspicuous they often felt both within and beyond the school:

> Sisay: Some of them [Easthaveners] don't think they're doing it, like the way they look at you, even – the way they look at you, somehow they just ignore you. They just – it's like you're not there. You're just like –
> Celine: A ghost.
> Sisay: Yeah. And it doesn't feel nice.

Grace, who was born in a Ghanaian refugee camp to Togolese parents, captured similar sentiments in a song she wrote shortly after arriving in Easthaven:

> *Everywhere that I go, Everyone is talking about me*
> *Because I'm so different from them. Really really different different*
> *I don't know what to do because no one cares . . .*

Her 'really really different different' is a powerful expression of how acutely Grace felt 'fixed as a foreigner' (Back, 2012, p. 146) during her early months in Easthaven. Being 'so different from them' – Easthaven's other residents – made her feel she was an object of constant surveillance and commentary. Five years on, Grace said she now felt 'Australian' ('getting citizenship, that make me feel Australian'), had strong friendships and was generally happy in her new country. However, like Joseph, she remained unsure that she was yet accepted more widely as Australian: 'Everywhere that I go, everyone's going to know that I'm African, I'm not Australian.' Hence she sees herself, at the same time, as Australian and not-Australian – her 'footing on the ladder of inclusion . . . neither stable nor clear but contingent and always subject to scrutiny' (Back, 2012, p. 149).

Sisay's, Celine's and Grace's comments resonate with those of two Sudanese-background girls at a rural Australian high school in a study by Edgeworth (2014). The students spoke of how, in the predominantly White rural setting, they felt defined and set apart by their skin colour – Black and therefore irrevocably alien. The dominance of Whiteness, in imaginaries of rurality as well as in demographic reality, 'renders the Black body at once both hyper-visible and invisible' (Edgeworth, 2014, p. 358) – 'gawked at' but also 'a ghost'. In such an environment, even an act as 'innocent' as a slightly longer gaze can amplify the 'unbelonging' of the conspicuous (Edgeworth, 2011): as Matthews (2008) points out, 'racialisation does not require a word to be spoken' (p. 37).

Crowley (1999) has written about the 'extraordinary ordinariness of whiteness' (p. 106), which allows Whiteness and White people to go uninterrogated while also empowering them to interrogate those whom they construct as 'other'. The others' presence in particular spaces requires constant justification. Longtime Easthaven resident Morris, for instance, said there had been some resentment in the community when the refugee families from Africa began arriving:

> And . . . there is still a bit of resentment – they see them grouped around in a particular location [and ask,] 'Why aren't they working?'. You go through the stages of saying, 'Well, where they're grouped together, they're waiting to go into an English class'. 'Oh, *that's* the reason they're there!' . . . It's taken a while to get that – not so much fear, I suppose but – that understanding why they're coming here.

Whiteness in a Mostly White Town

Faced with the impossibility of a return to ethnic and cultural homogeneity, powerful (White) individuals and institutions devise myriad ways of defining and policing boundaries – from official classification systems to everyday naming practices, selective surveillance, the casual questioning of some and not others, particular looks and so on. '[T]he fantasy of white restoration is replaced by a racial reordering . . . a selective process of rearrangement and ranking, featuring in the most intimate aspects of social life', Back (2012, pp. 140, 141) writes. Understanding the ways in which belonging is achieved, granted, withheld and rejected in particular institutional and geographical spaces therefore requires attention to both the continuing relevance of colonial racism and the 'new forces that divide, rank and order' (Back, 2012, p. 140). In Easthaven in the past, when ideas about 'races' and White superiority were pervasive and accepted (among Anglo-Australians) and the town's population was less diverse, social relations were enacted within a hierarchy of White (Anglo) at the top and Black (Aboriginal) at the bottom. This ordering was underpinned and reinforced by spatial constraints: denied access to their traditional lands as the Europeans parcelled out property rights, most Indigenous Easthaveners were forced to live on reserves or in camps on the fringes of town, a pattern repeated across Australia. While race has given way to theoretically non-hierarchical notions of ethnicity and culture, the data presented above reveal that Easthaveners are 'raced' in very different ways. In other words, 'ethnicities' and 'cultures' can still be, and are, ranked – as are languages and accents (Piller, 2016), genders, sexualities, occupations, places of residence and so on.

What follows is the beginnings of a mapping of a racialized hierarchy of belonging in Easthaven – an exercise that continues over the next two chapters. Hierarchies, of course, change over time and depending on the context and space within which social relations are enacted. They also vary from one person to another, depending on their life experiences and beliefs – so it is more accurate to speak of racialized hierarch*ies* of belonging in Easthaven. The comments by Kai, for example, suggest that he ranks local Indigenous knowledge, language, (hi)stories and other cultural practices above Western ones. Further, I am not suggesting that race, ethnicity and/or culture are the only, or necessarily always the most salient, mediators of belonging. However, examining the distinctions and assumptions Easthaveners make about different 'groups' in the town provides a pathway to better understanding their expressed views about whether diversity is a strength, and how they respond to other/Other people – especially within the studied school communities.

New Hierarchies of Belonging

As noted, it was the 'Aborigines' and the 'Africans' who were the subject of most commentary across the interviews and focus groups – and not because of any direct questions about Aboriginal- and African-background Easthaveners. While most of the Anglo-background interviewees (who accounted for most of the sample) had no hesitation in naming these 'groups', they often seemed unsure, and even uncomfortable, about what to call themselves when asked about their cultural background. For example:

> Um [*long pause; laughs*] I don't actually think about that! Cultural background – I grew up in a Catholic family, I went to a Catholic school . . . yeah, sort of [*pauses*] White lower-middle-class, I suppose. (Sally, principal, Seaview High)
>
> Well I'm probably what [*pauses*] is known as a fairly typical Anglo, um, White Australian whose [*pauses*] – has something like six or seven generations going back within Australia, with the odd bit of Irish coming in from time to time, but yeah, yeah [*pauses*] – typical White, basically. (William, deputy principal, Seaview High)
>
> Australian and probably English. My grandfather was from Wales, I think. I'm not one who traces family trees and looks into it. I'm just happy with where I am and what I am sort of thing. So I don't worry about all that. (Reg, deputy principal, Hillview High)
>
> I'm [*laughs*] Australian, and I'm White Australian, but I'm very open and do a lot of work with other cultures. (Roslyn, ESL teacher, Hillview High)
>
> [*pauses*] I – just – oh, Anglo-Saxon-based, yeah, that's it. (Lois, teacher, Seaview High)

There is much work being done in these simple sentences in terms of subject positioning. What I want to draw attention to, however, is that Anglo-Australian Easthaveners are not used to thinking or being asked about their cultural and ethnic background, as indicated by the pauses, self-conscious laughs and qualifiers ('sort of', 'probably', 'just') that punctuate the interviewees' responses. Several interviewees also echoed Seaview High parent Hope's sentiments when she said: 'That's an interesting question; I don't think I've ever been asked that [about her cultural background] before!' These Easthaveners do not have to think or 'worry about all that' (their cultural identity and background) because they are part of the ethnic majority – in contrast to Joseph, Sisay, Celine, Grace, Kai and Monica's sons, whose physical appearance constantly identifies and locates them as outside of 'White' and thus outside of 'typical'. As Dyer (2005) writes:

> As long as race is something only applied to non-white peoples, as long as white people are not racially seen and named, they/we function as a human norm. Other people are raced; we are just people. There is no more powerful position than that of being 'just' human. (p. 10)

The easy power of this position can be heard in Reg's comment: 'I'm not one who traces family trees. . . . I'm just happy with where I am and what I am.' Dyer (2005) further observes:

> We (whites) will speak of, say, the blackness or the Chineseness of friends, neighbours, colleagues, customers or clients, and it may be in the most genuinely friendly and accepting manner, but we don't mention the whiteness of the white people we know. (p. 10)

If White people can construct themselves as without ethnicity, they can also construct themselves as without culture, imbuing their beliefs, values and practices with universality rather than particularity. This gives them unique access to political, economic and social power: 'The claim to power is the claim to speak for the commonality of humanity. Raced people can't do that – they can only speak for their race' (Dyer, 2005, p. 10). Applied to the Australian education system – the product of centuries of Western teaching and learning – schools might therefore be imagined and represented as sites for the neutral passing on of universal truths. Deputy principal Reg seemed to subscribe to such a view when he said of Hillview High's students: '[T]hey can . . . see pathways for them to go through and embrace, whether it's their culture, this culture, that culture or just *no* culture, just educational value' – educational value that in practice accrues more to the non-raced than to those who are raced as goals are set, curricula designed, pedagogies enacted, disciplines imposed and assessments conducted on a daily basis.

Beyond cultural background, how did Anglo-Australian Easthaveners see themselves and their fellow residents, and *in relation to* their fellow residents? In other words, what appears to be in their 'Anglo-Australian' schemas, and what appears to be in their schemas of 'other' categories of Easthavener who were named? A clue to one perspective on 'Anglo-Australian' lies in ESL teacher Roslyn's description of herself (quoted above) as '. . . White Australian, but I'm very open . . .' – the 'but' suggesting she considers openness and cross-cultural engagement *not* to be attributes of most White Australians, in contrast to the data presented in Chapter 2. Overall, characteristics attributed to Anglo-Australians ranged from 'civil', 'friendly' and 'hard-working and fair' through to 'racist', 'jingoistic' and 'superior'. The 'Australian way of life' was highly valued, although interviewees found it difficult to articulate what that was beyond 'we drink, we surf and we party' (Hannah, Year 11, Seaview High). The most common characteristic attributed to Australians in general, however, was 'accepting', as in this exchange among Year 11 Hillview High students:

> Sam: Australia's so multicultural, we've learnt to accept different people, and not just people from different backgrounds but differences in people like disabilities or, what else, sexuality, religious –
> Victoria: I get what you mean. 'Cause we accept different cultures as well, whereas other countries don't necessarily. They just have their culture; they don't accept other ones, whereas we *do* accept other cultures. I think we get on better [than people in other countries].
> Kyla: And 'cause we understand them as well, I think.

The students' comments about Australians' openness towards and understanding of people from backgrounds different from their own (and presumably, as self-identified 'Australians', they are including themselves in their 'we') echo national-level narratives about Australia, Australians and the Australian multicultural success story. However, an exchange earlier in the focus group casts serious doubt on the claim 'we understand them' (Kyla) in relation to the refugee-background students at the school. The exchange followed a question about how well students from different cultural backgrounds mixed in and out of the classroom:

> Thomas: Well, all the Africans hang out with each other; there's no real mix [*giggles*]. That's not funny. That's my comment.
> Neroli: And is that in class and in the playground as well?
> Thomas: Um – pretty much.
> Neroli: Why do you think they hang out with each other?
> Thomas: Because they can speak the same language to each other and not be afraid of what, I don't know, we have to say or think.
> Neroli: *Do* they speak the same language? Or do they speak lots of different languages?
> Thomas: I don't know, I can't understand them [*giggles*].

Asked about the cultural make-up of Hillview High, the students – who had already mentioned 'Aboriginal' and 'Sudanese' – offered the following:

> Thomas: Thai – I don't know, there's a person –
> Victoria: Asian?
> Thomas: Afghanistan, is that a –
> Kyla: Where's [student's name] from? He's from –
> Zoe: Kazakhstan.
> Victoria: No, he's from somewhere –
> Kyla: Where's the exchange student from?
> Zoe: Norway, there's an exchange student from Norway.
> Neroli: What about other African groups – you mentioned Sudanese. Is there anybody else here?
> Thomas: Oooh – [*pauses*] they said it in assembly but we just – I dunno, people just say 'Sudanese'.
> Victoria: There's more than from Sudan, though. They want us to call them 'African', not 'Sudanese'. 'Cause they're from more places than Sudan, but we don't know where [*giggles*].

For these students, 'accepting' appears not to be an active term – showing interest in, engaging with – but rather an absence of ill will: we do not hate them; we do not fight with them; they can share our space as long as they do not trouble us. A similar notion of acceptance was evident in a focus group with students in Years 9 and 10 at Seaview High:

> Sophie: Yeah, they [the LBOTE students] usually stick together. They don't really mix with different people, like White people compared to them. It's – I don't know why, but they just –
> Jonathan: Yeah, there's no grudges or tension between any backgrounds, but it just seems to work that way, that we're separated.

Here Sophie and Jonathan (both Anglo-Australian) present as natural that they and the other-than-Anglo students 'are separated'. Through the use of impersonal sentence constructions for themselves ('*it* just seems to work that way') but active sentence constructions for the LBOTE students ('they . . . stick together'), the pair place all of the responsibility for mixing onto their LBOTE peers. Safe at the top of the social hierarchy and protected by the discourse of Australia as 'open to everybody' and 'really relaxed' (Lucy, Year 9, Seaview High), the Anglo-background students have little need to think about or engage with people different from themselves. This position may be particularly pronounced in historically White country towns: 'Who counts as human in this [rural] space – who is deemed to belong in terms of being seen to be worth knowing – are those who are familiar to the established inhabitants . . . those who are alike, known, recognized – socially, culturally and ethnically' (Edgeworth, 2014, p. 361).

This tendency towards marginalization-through-indifference (as opposed to overt exclusion or rejection) was confirmed by Hillview High ESL teacher Roslyn. If students were specifically asked to do an activity with someone from outside of their usual group, she explained, 'Yes, most of the time they will' – but such interactions were generally not sustained beyond that activity. She cited the example of one refugee-background student, Elaha, who had confided that many of her classmates had never spoken to her, even though she had been in their classes for two years. The extent of her classmates' knowledge, according to Roslyn, was that she was from Afghanistan and 'very bright. End of story. They don't know anything else . . . they don't ask.' Again, Baumann's (1999) words come to mind: 'One need not ask who they are if one knows what they are.'

Comments by parent Catriona point to similar social dynamics at Seaview High. She said the school had tried to encourage the Anglo-Australian students to mix with and include the small number of refugee-background students, but with little success:

> They [the refugee-background students] are really well accepted, like, on the sporting field – it's like, 'great, we've got the refugee kids on the soccer team!', because they're really good at it. But they haven't always been embraced really kindly by other teenagers [at the school] only because I think it's a group – it's sort of a mob mentality with teenagers anyway.

Catriona offered the following story by way of illustration:

> My daughter and her girlfriends, they all went to Sydney on a school excursion last year and two of the refugee African kids went. And when they came back, our girls were really complaining about how much these girls smelled and how they didn't shower properly. And I was saying, 'Well, if you'd grown up in a refugee camp, daily showers and deodorants, they're not – you're just trying to survive' . . . But because it's a teenage age group and the way I think teenage girls are especially, they weren't very accommodating to the other girls.

Catriona's comments suggest a couple of things – first, an instance of interest convergence (Bell, 1979), whereby the non-refugee-background students are prepared to embrace the refugee-background students to the extent that the latter benefit the former (through their sporting prowess, for example); and second, despite her reported efforts to encourage 'our girls' to be more empathetic towards their classmates, an inclination to normalize the (Anglo) girls' behaviour as 'only because' of their teenagerness rather than race-, class- or gender-based ostracism. A potent aspect of Whiteness in Easthaven and its schools is the lack of awareness of many Anglo-Australian Easthaveners of Whiteness as 'ethnic' as any 'ethnic minority' (De Lepervanche, 1980), and of their own part in (re)producing racialized differences and inequities. Discourses of tolerance and benevolence, together with the non-naming of Whiteness, are crucial to maintaining such unawareness.

As for the refugee-background students' experience, this is the account given by Year 11 ESL students at Seaview High:

> Sisay: They [other students] can be friendly but they don't interact with us –
> Celine: . . . you tend to feel like an outsider, because in class they [other students] are talking but then they ignore you. So you have to try and make yourself so they know you're there.
> [. . .]
> Sisay: We try to be friends with them sometimes but sometimes it just seems they don't want it, and we don't want to force it on anyone. 'Cause friendship comes naturally, you know; you don't have to force anyone – like, 'I don't have friends; I need friends'; that's just sad.

Celine said that at church she had 'really good friends', but at school she felt 'really lonely':

> [Y]ou come to school from Monday to Friday, for eight hours, just sitting in the corner of a classroom, trying to pay attention to class, getting stares from everyone for putting your hand up and asking a question. . . . And then your accent, it's like '*What* did you say? I can't hear [understand] you.' And it's really discouraging.

Celine and Sisay also believed they were (still) widely seen as 'refugees' and treated differently as a result, including in class. While staff at Hillview High tended to refer to their refugee-background students as the 'ESL children', certainly staff at Seaview High (the girls' school) did mostly talk about this cohort as the 'refugee children'. Not surprisingly, then, the girls spoke of 'refugee' as a term 'we can never really escape' – one they did not altogether 'mind' (their word), but that they thought sometimes marked them as objects of 'pity'.

Celine had been living in Easthaven for five years, but despite being extremely outgoing, articulate and sporty, she appeared, at school at least, to feel like an 'outsider' most of the time. At church and playing basketball she 'felt Australian', she said, but the classroom and playground were environments in which she was frequently reminded of, and remained acutely conscious of, her 'difference'. Each 'incident' – (still) being referred to as a 'refugee', being the subject of 'stares', having to repeat yourself in class, being shunned on excursions or ignored in the playground, being called 'Sudanese' when you have indicated you would prefer to be called 'African' – may be brief and relatively minor in itself for students such as Celine. But small acts accumulate

(Wilson, 2013); they 'permeate the micro-spaces of social life in which shame, displacement and status anxiety damage the quality of social encounters' (Back, 2012, p. 150). Some of the consequences of such damages have already been touched on – for example, in Monica's account of her son's experiences – and more are explored in the chapters that follow.

Conclusion

This chapter has focused on names and namings, and their intersections with numbers, in Easthaven and its public high schools. To most of the residents interviewed for this study, their regional town was now quite a 'multicultural' place, with 'sprinkles of everything' – immigrants from all over the world. Despite this diversity, interviewees' talk typically centred on just two 'groups': the 'Africans' and the 'Aborigines' – the new and the old Black people. Other, much larger ethnic and cultural 'groups', such as immigrants from Italy and India, not to mention Britain, did not feature in the accounts of the town and its people. In other words, for most of the interviewees, 'diversity' inhered primarily in visible difference from the Anglo-Australian norm.

In mostly White Easthaven, this selective naming of ethnic and cultural 'others' has been integral to the construction of new hierarchies of belonging in the face of demographic change. Paradoxically, belonging (and the power that confers) may be most efficiently claimed and maintained through strategies of silence and invisibility: '[W]hiteness has long reserved the privilege of making everyone but itself visible, lest it be exposed as a position within a constellation of positions . . . . By and large, whites . . . believe they are individuals and not a racial group' (Leonardo, 2002, pp. 41, 45). As the quotation at the beginning of this chapter points out: 'We do race and ethnicity – all of us, every day' – yet White people in particular may rarely be conscious of this.

Other invisibilizing strategies presented and discussed in this chapter include the neutralizing and naturalizing of White perspectives, values and practices, especially in schools; and narratives through to individual sentence constructions that mask or absolve White people's agency in social and educational processes. Although there was a range of views among the interviewees about the extent to which Easthaveners from different ethnic, cultural and linguistic backgrounds mixed, including at school, the consensus was 'not much'. Hillview High deputy principal Vince summed it up thus: 'Like birds, they all share the same sky, but they don't mix' – a sense, by and large, of 'parallel lives' (Valentine, 2008). Few Anglo-background Easthaveners appeared to see such 'living-apart-together' (Ang, 2001) as a problem.

However, Richard, an ESL teacher at Seaview High, did express concern about the ethnicizing in Easthaven, saying: 'When you compartmentalize [people] into groups, you dehumanize, and then you take the individual humanities out of everyone and you look at things as numbers.' He later related a story about a relationship he had seen develop at Seaview High between the (Anglo-Australian) school captain and some of the Burmese-background students:

> They didn't necessarily know everything about each other's culture. They just liked being together and they learned from each other, and now they can speak English to each other ... and she [the school captain] speaks a bit of Burmese.... She's not really just looking for a person that she thinks is there and that she's happy with and 'I'll put you in a box now, I know who you are'. She's actually kind of stuck it out and really looked deep to find out who these people really are.

Such friendships were the exception in Easthaven, Richard said, adding that he saw cross-cultural contact as fundamental to successful multiculturalism:

> Because if they [students] get that cross-cultural experience, it takes them outside their circle, their own little bubble, and then it means that their bubble can expand to incorporate new ideas anywhere in their life, wherever they do [sic], whatever they do.

Richard's understanding of multiculturalism as involving sustained engagement and mutual enrichment informs his evaluation of the potential benefits of diversity – that is, the opportunity to take students outside of their circle, their 'bubble', and develop in them a lifelong openness to new perspectives and practices. In Easthaven, where White dominance has never been challenged and White world views rarely questioned, such opportunities may be unsettling as well as promising. Where this chapter has sought to analyse understandings of diversity and difference in Easthaven and its schools, the next chapter continues the work of relating these understandings to discourses about the *value* of diversity, particularly for young people in this regional community.

5

'Yes, but . . .'

Discourses, Affects and Sentiments

Introduction

A key point in the previous chapter was the disjunction between how Easthaveners spoke about 'culture' and their understandings of 'cultural *diversity*'. Despite the wide range of opinions about the meaning of 'culture', cultural diversity was frequently narrowed to a focus on ethnicity; and notions of ethnicity as singular and fixed – more akin to notions of race – rather than hybrid and performative. Further, race, ethnicity and culture were often seen by Anglo-Australian Easthaveners as invested primarily in 'other' (non-Anglo) people, and above all in those who were 'visibly different' (from the White norm). The aim of this chapter is to link those understandings to discourses about diversity and multiculturalism in the town. In doing so, a particular focus is on interviewees' *evaluations* of cultural diversity, and how these might be influenced by the orientations promoted in multicultural policies. More specifically, do people in Easthaven and its high schools feel positive about *local* demographic changes, and how do they articulate those feelings?

This points to a focus on affect and how affects/emotions are expressed in discourses about diversity, what positioning work those expressions do, and how that in turn impacts on social relations in the school and broader communities. A distinction was made in Chapter 1 between affect and emotion as registered in and on the body (corporeal productions) and sentiment as a *discursive* rendering of affect/emotion. Chapter 2, for instance, documented high levels of agreement among Australians with statements such as 'accepting immigrants from many different countries makes Australia stronger' and 'it is a good thing for society to be made up of different cultures', indicating not only support for but positive feelings about diversity. The drumming teacher's comment 'All of the different skin tones make us even more colourful!' could be said to reflect this orientation. However, people's responses can be influenced by their perception of what is socially desirable, by the wording of the question, by contemporary media commentary and other relational and situational factors (Valentine & Sadgrove, 2014). Further, questions about *specific* aspects of immigration, multiculturalism and diversity (as opposed to general statements) tend to reveal ambivalences and caveats: it is clear, for example, that some immigrants are viewed more favourably than others. In other words, quantitative and qualitative data together suggest that the dominant discourse among Australians about the benefits of diversity could be characterized as 'Yes, but...'.[1] The 'Yes' can be read as shaped, to some extent, by official discourses about diversity. However, it is the 'but...' – and what follows it – that is the focus of this chapter, for it is here that the complexity of people's discourses, affects and attitudes is most evident.

In reality, 'Yes, but...' is not one discourse but a collection of discourses, embodying a range of affects and sentiments. As recorded in the previous chapter, the 'new' diversity in Easthaven had provoked a mix of responses – from excitement and interest through indifference to anxiety, fear and even disgust. Boler and Zembylas's (2003) models of difference provide a useful starting point for examining the discourses about diversity and its impacts at Seaview and Hillview high schools.

The three approaches to difference outlined by Boler and Zembylas (2003) are celebration/tolerance, denial/sameness and natural response/biological. The authors do not see these models as mutually exclusive but rather as often co-existing within a person's belief system, despite any contradictions between them. Such cognitive dissonance is likely to show up in interviews in inconsistencies, ambiguities and lack of specificity or depth. Boler and Zembylas (2003) also propose that different 'emotional stances' are associated with the different models, raising another potential point of tension given the emotional stance towards diversity promoted by multicultural policies. The analysis that follows therefore pays close attention, as van Dijk (1993) recommends, to 'the presence or absence of hedges, hesitations, pauses, laughter, interruptions, doubt or certainty markers, specific lexical items, forms of address and pronoun use' (p. 261).

> Reg, Hillview High deputy principal, for example, deployed various discursive strategies to distance himself from perspectives that might be perceived as racist. At one point he described how, 'All of a sudden ... there [was] another black, and it was a *darker* black. And that causes problems'.

In this text, the refugees from Africa (objectified as 'there' and 'it') are said to have caused 'problems' by being 'a darker black', thereby upsetting the (naturalized) Anglo/Indigenous order in Easthaven. When asked whether he thought diversity was a strength, Anglo-Australian Reg – who had lived in Easthaven for over thirty years – replied:

> [*long pause*] Hmm [*pauses*] I don't know, I haven't thought about it. I can think – I'm trying to – I can think of strengths *and* weaknesses. I don't think it's all – It's not all positive, I've gone through some of the positives there [earlier in the interview]. I suppose – I'm not confronted with it [*sic*] but the one you hear a lot on the news is the women with their burqas and their headgear and this sort of thing. And I can see that's causing problems. So the multicultural there – without saying if it's right or wrong, what they [the burqa-wearing women] are doing, it's causing problems. So anything that causes problems isn't a strength.

Reg's comments encapsulate many of the patterns and themes that emerged in other interviewees' responses to the core question: 'Do you think diversity is a strength?'.

These patterns and themes include hesitancy in stating an opinion, possibly pointing to ambivalence about diversity; citing *other* people's opinions and experiences; the influence of media discourses in defining and shaping ideas about cultural 'others', especially in less-diverse communities; impersonal representations of cultural 'others', which Fairclough (2003) notes 'can dehumanize social actors, take the focus away from them as people' (p.150); and the logics used to rationalize negative comments (the burqa-wearing women, like the 'darker black' Africans, are 'causing problems', and 'anything that causes problems isn't a strength'). Overall, interviewees saw the increased cultural and linguistic diversity in Easthaven and its schools as bringing opportunities *and* challenges, having benefits *and* drawbacks – a perspective captured in the 'Yes, but . . .' title of this chapter, and echoed in research on attitudes to multiculturalism across Australia (Ang et al., 2006). Data presented in the previous chapter indicated concerns on the part of some Easthaveners about segregation and immigrants 'sticking together' – whether by choice (the perspective of many of the Anglo-background interviewees) or because they were not routinely included (the perspective of some of the ESL teachers and the refugee-background students). The paradox with diversity, Ang et al. (2006) conclude, is that it is 'seen as both good and bad, and there are clear limits to what people find acceptable levels of difference' (p. 21).

Diversity Discourses in Easthaven

As these examples highlight, people's beliefs about, and approaches to, diversity are often full of inconsistencies, ambiguities and ambivalences. This messiness – inscribed in but also produced by the varied histories of diversity-related terms, tensions within and between diversity-related policies, the affective dimensions of lived diversity and the performativity inherent in interviews – is as of much interest in the following analysis as the advantages and disadvantages of diversity identified by the participants. It is, after all, essential to making sense of the schools' responses to their changing populations. As Puwar (2004b) writes: 'The arrival of . . . ethnically different bodies does not mean that our institutions have become multicultural. The newcomers' presence generates a sociospatial impact that brings into clear focus what has hitherto been taken for granted' (p. 77). This exposing of the 'taken-for-granted' will have its own sociocognitive and affective impacts, potentially discernible in interviewees' discursive and other social practices.

The analysis of the discourses in Easthaven that follows begins with the 'Yes' discourses – those that are most positive about diversity – and proceeds through to the more openly questioning or negative discourses. As with Boler and Zembylas's models of difference, these discourses are not discrete or mutually exclusive but rather overlap and co-present within the interviews.

New Delights![2]

The aspect of diversity that interviewees in Easthaven were most frequently and unequivocally positive about was food. The variety of cuisines available in rural and regional Australia has traditionally been extremely limited, and many interviewees said they welcomed the new arrivals' additions to the range of eating options in the town. Hillview High teacher Winsome was one of those who appreciated the culinary diversification, saying, 'I *love* cultural diversity because I'm a bit of a foodie'; Seaview High staff member Rita was another to nominate 'the food' as something she liked about diversity. Drumming, dance and other forms of cultural performance were also mentioned by interviewees as things they valued and enjoyed – for instance, Hillview High parent Fleur: 'I've certainly enjoyed some of the aspects of performance that they [the refugee newcomers] have brought to the community.'

However, the full responses of Winsome, Rita and Fleur to the question 'Do you think diversity is a strength?' present a different picture:

> Oh gosh, I don't know. I *love* cultural diversity because I'm a bit of a foodie, I like to eat different foods, and I like – I'm interested and I travel a lot so I like to learn about other people's cultures and – yeah. I don't feel that it is – I come from the dominant culture but it [diversity] doesn't make me feel threatened at all…I worry that people often feel threatened by new groups. (Winsome)

> I guess, you know, the food for one thing. The Australian food years ago was pretty bland and ordinary, so they [non-Anglo immigrants] brought a lot of their recipes to Australia, plus some of their different vegetables and things. When I was growing up – I mean, I love Thai food, and when I was growing up there weren't the vegetables that you can get at the supermarkets as what there are available these days. That's about all I think they've brought to the country, though, is food. Apart from a lot of their gang wars. I can't understand them. I don't know why they want to do what they do, a lot of these people. It's just disruptive. (Rita)

> Um [*pauses*] well I've certainly enjoyed some of the aspects of performance that they have brought to the community. It hasn't really impacted on me in any way so I can't say – apart from enjoying their performances and their presentations of aspects of their culture, I haven't as a person living in [Easthaven] felt any differently, so I can't say that – you know, I haven't had a personal positive relationship with someone from that culture. But I haven't had a negative. (Fleur)

These answers are riddled with hesitancies and ambivalences, with initial responses quickly undercut by qualifications and conditions – from Fleur's 'I can't say' through Rita's 'That's about all' to Winsome's 'worry' about other people's reactions. These interviewees' enthusiasm about diversity is quite 'thin' (Bell & Hartmann, 2007), but there is also a concern with *appearing* to be enthusiastic. Even Rita, who was resoundingly negative about diversity for most of the interview, seems to have felt obliged to come up with something positive ('I guess, you know, the food . . .') when asked whether she considered diversity a strength. The message from official discourses extolling the virtues of diversity is that difference should evoke affects such as interest, excitement and joy (Ahmed, 2008). Against such expectations, owning to misgivings and anxieties about diversity is likely to be uncomfortable – certainly in front of a 'stranger' (such as an interviewer) and in such 'politically correct' spaces as classrooms.

Good for Our Kids, Good for Our Country

It was not always clear in interviewees' comments whether the views they expressed were in relation to diversity at a global, national or local level, or a mix – and the question 'Do you think diversity is a strength?' was intentionally general so that interviewees could respond as personally or abstractly as they wished. With regard to Easthaven, however, another perceived benefit of increased diversity in the town was that it was, or would be, good for young people. For instance, Seaview High teacher Lois said of her previous time at Hillview High:

> We spent time actually developing our multicultural programs because we knew our kids would go to Sydney, for university or for work, and we felt that they wouldn't be able to cope with the plural cultures down there. So we had developed quite a strong multicultural policy because we thought our kids would be disadvantaged [otherwise].

Parents articulated these benefits as well:

> And I'm glad that [son's name] is having that association [with Burmese-background boys], because at university he will no doubt encounter lots of people from different cultures. So it's a really good stepping stone for him to develop the ability to have a relationship with someone outside of what he knows culturally. (Fleur, Hillview High)

> But by the time my kids are through school, the impact of those African kids is gonna be – [the school] would have probably had far more successes in sports, there probably would be an African restaurant [in town], the kids would have all learned to do African drumming or whatever. You can see – and all of our kids are gonna be better off for taking that on board. (Catriona, Hillview High)

The 'our kids' are the children born and/or raised in Easthaven, such as Fleur's son and Catriona's children – all Anglo-Australian, and by length of residence, ethnicity and culture automatically part of the local 'we'.

Teachers said having greater diversity in their schools had more formal teaching and learning benefits as well. Hillview High's Reg, for example, said: 'I think having many cultures is great for teaching. It's not something you read in a book. You can see it. You can experience it' – a view echoed by Gary, one of the Aboriginal support staff at Seaview High:

> We never had the refugee students in the school [before] and we were never aware of other cultures out there, I guess. Only from what we read from books and stuff. But now that we have the internet and these students actually in here, it's great to learn from them and learn about their country, their culture. And they like to learn about ours as well.

As for the students, Declan (Year 9, Seaview High) saw diversity as providing a happy combination of culinary *and* academic benefits:

> I think it is a strength. From things like food, we have a huge variety of food. I like food, personally [*laughter*] but we've got so many different types. . . . But also things like, how I was saying, my friend is very smart at maths. . . . Asians now in universities, there are so many Asian people going now. I think that because they've been pushed, their parents are so – they want their kids to be really good, really smart, and work really hard. I think that will push how smart our country is maybe, and push that up a bit higher.

His classmate Lucy appeared to combine the celebration and sameness models of difference when she said:

> We're all one in the end. We're all human. Diversity, yeah, it *is* a strength. There's so many more different things that are coming into Australia. We've got different food, we've got different types of living, we've got different – a whole range of different things that we can learn from. It's really good.

Difference here is seen as benign (Balint, 2010) – different foods, different musical genres, different lifestyles – which facilitates a celebratory stance vis-à-vis diversity. Overall, however, teachers', students' and parents' enthusiasm for learning from and about 'other cultures' appeared to be quite instrumental: equipping students for assumed futures in more culturally diverse spaces and places, including university; enhancing school sports results; and boosting Australia's international competitiveness through the influence of smart, hard-working 'Asians'. Even so, as in the previous section, there was concern as well as enthusiasm, conveyed by Lois's articulation of diversity as something to be 'coped with' – that is, as inherently challenging.

Perspectives on diversity depend in part on the specific backgrounds and relative proportions of different ethnic and cultural 'groups' in an area. Rita spoke of the 'gang wars' of 'a lot of these people', although it was unclear which particular immigrants she had in mind (or, for that matter, which place/s). Longtime Easthavener Morris, on the other hand, was full of admiration for the well-established Italian community in the town. They were 'a funny lot', he said – cursing each other one minute and laughing together the next – but 'you couldn't get better people'. Their cultural idiosyncrasies notwithstanding, the immigrants from Italy (and their descendants) were woven into Easthaven's social fabric and had 'contributed a lot to this region'. As Seaview High principal Sally explained: 'The European cultures tend to mix – we don't notice them.' Likewise, the 'Indians' in the town were 'considered to be workers' and were well integrated economically, if not always socially. Like the 'Asians', within the schools they were also endorsed as good students.

Media and popular discourses about 'model minorities' have been the subject of much scholarship in Australia and other Western countries over several decades. In educational contexts in particular, the 'model minority' label has been most associated with students of north-east Asian and Indian heritage (Ho, 2020; Watkins & Noble,

2021), who have been identified as the main 'groups' responsible for the overall outperformance of LBOTE students in Australian schools (Lingard et al., 2012).

Similarly, there was little association of equity and social justice with multiculturalism and multicultural education in the interviews. The word 'equity' came up in only five of the forty-eight interviews – much less frequently than 'food'. Only one interviewee spoke about equity at length, and with hesitancy. Glenys, a NSW DoE regional consultant, spoke of 'various different cultural groups living in Australian society, and hopefully all-in-all harmoniously' before adding:

> And equity, I haven't mentioned equity. Equity's a big issue and distribution of wealth or distribution of services, whatever, are unevenly distributed. That's something I haven't really mentioned. I feel like I'm diverting from my [NSW DoE] role and going on to what I feel as a person. Yeah, equity – can I divert here?

It appeared from the broader context of the interview that Glenys saw an interest in equity as more of a 'personal' than a professional concern.

The enormous complexity – and cost – of addressing the legacies of histories of race-based inequality is one reason the less demanding celebratory/tolerance approach to difference tends to predominate in institutional spaces. In a survey of NSW public school staff, Watkins and Noble (2021) found that while teachers endorsed equity and antiracism as two of the chief goals of multicultural education (in line with NSW DoE policy), their strategies for promoting inclusion were more likely to centre on multicultural days similar to Seaview High's. In their US study, Bell and Hartmann (2007) reported that social justice proved to be an awkward topic in interviews:

> [It was] so problematic that some of our interviewers simply stopped asking the question in order to maintain rapport and keep the interview moving. Although most interviewees were asked the question [about the relationship between diversity and inequality], only a handful were willing or able to put together coherent thoughts about inequality after having talked extensively about diversity. (p. 906)

Such findings are products of education discourses and datasets that are engineered to obscure more than expose systemic inequalities – and, in rendering them difficult to 'see', dampening interest in and dialogue about them. Equity, Gillborn (2007, p. 493) notes, 'has constantly to fight for legitimacy as a significant topic' in contemporary neoliberal regimes that promote ability and effort as foundational to success. A simple question to ask is the *cui bono* question raised in Chapter 3: Whose benefit do education policy priorities serve? Yet this can be an unsettling question for policymakers and educators (most of them White), who historically have been 'schooled' *not* to see advantage (McIntosh, 1989). Further, as Castagno (2014) points out, talking about inequity may be seen as not 'nice':

> A nice person is not someone who creates a lot of disturbance, conflict, controversy, or discomfort. Nice people avoid potentially uncomfortable or

upsetting experiences, knowledge, and interactions. We do not point out failures or shortcomings . . . but rather emphasize the good, the promise, and the improvement we see. (p. 9)

Teachers may be particularly invested in seeing themselves as caring and 'nice' (and undoubtedly most are) and are trained to focus on the positive, including helping students to 'feel good' about themselves: education, after all, is a 'nice field' (Ladson-Billings, 1998). But it is not a culturally, politically or affectively *neutral* field. In the absence of unsettling discussions about power and privilege, racialization and racism, progress towards more equitable social and educational outcomes will be compromised. 'The niceness running through diversity-related policy and practice in schools is only good for whiteness,' Castagno (2014, p. 10) argues.

Certainly in the interviews, Easthaveners' talk about the benefits of cultural and linguistic diversity centred almost exclusively on the benefits *for Anglo-Australians* – whether in terms of educational or social advantage or expanded cultural forms for consumption. In terms of the connections between language and power relations, two issues are worth highlighting. The first is the reduction of diversity to 'variety', with 'difference' located in 'other' (non-Anglo) people. As Ahmed (2007a) points out, 'if difference is something "they are", then it is something we [the dominant group] "can have"' (p. 235), for profit or for pleasure. The second issue relates to this expectation of pleasure. As hooks (2006) memorably writes:

> mass culture is the contemporary location that both publicly declares and perpetuates the idea that there is pleasure to be found in the acknowledgment and enjoyment of racial difference. The commodification of Otherness has been so successful because it is offered as a new delight, more intense, more satisfying than normal ways of doing and feeling. Within commodity culture, ethnicity becomes spice, seasoning that can liven up the dull dish that is mainstream white culture. (p. 366)

Again, Fairclough's work on the marketization of discourse is relevant here, to the ways in which ethnicity and difference have been bundled together as 'Otherness' and promoted as delightful 'spice'. The principle of interest convergence can be applied as well: that is, that diversity is embraced to the extent that it benefits primarily the dominant (White) culture – through tastier food choices, better sporting results, more exciting entertainment options and so on. Similarly, diversity is tolerated to the extent it does not alter 'the way things are done around here', to use Seaview High deputy Stephanie's definition of 'culture' in the previous chapter. Seaview High parent Trudy showed an awareness of this as she recounted a shift in perspective she had experienced only the day before, after talking with a local refugee support worker:

> Two things I was made aware of yesterday . . . which I'd never thought about before. One is that our new arrivals to Australia don't want to be called – well, they're *not* refugees, and they don't want to be called refugees because they're no longer refugees once they're here. . . . And I thought, 'I bet most Australians don't

think that'. . . . And the other thing is that they don't always want to just do things that are particular to their culture. . . . They didn't come to Australia to share their culture with Australia; they came to Australia – I mean, yeah, for lots of political and humanitarian and other reasons, but now that they're here they want to be part of Australia. And [support worker's name] said they don't always want to go to African feasts or Burmese film nights or – and I thought, 'well, that's interesting', you know? . . . I mean, it's great if we want – it's great for the school if the 85 per cent [Anglo-Australian students] gain an understanding of African cultures and the Burmese cultures [*she stresses the 's' sound*] – because there's more than one – but more to help those kids understand . . . the Australian culture as well . . . I reckon we tend to think that we should be soaking up all *their* stuff, but it does work both ways.

These ideas – that Easthaven's latest immigrants might not want to be distinguished as 'refugees', and might not always want to do only 'ethnic' things – are genuinely new and 'interesting' to Trudy. Through policy, political and media discourses, she has been encouraged to focus on the benefits of diversity for her as a member of the dominant Anglo-Australian population. Nonetheless, when asked whether diversity was a strength, Trudy was cautious:

Hmm. Well personally I would say that I would think diversity *would* be a strength. However, especially with contact with some of the African people here in [Easthaven], who [*pauses*] um [*pauses*] have issues with other African nationalities who are here, which surprises me – I know as a White Aussie, we think Africans are Africans, but to Africans, you know, if you're from Eritrea or Liberia or Sudan, that can be widely different. And trying to force them to live here harmoniously together after I don't know how long conflict . . . You know, we couldn't hope that if they can't – if they fled their own country because of that conflict, or that conflict was part of the issue, why would we expect that living in Australia would resolve that?

As with the examples given earlier in this chapter, Trudy's response appears to reflect a desire to endorse diversity as a strength, if very conditionally. Immediately, however, she moves on to her concerns about diversity, particularly with regard to the recent arrivals from Africa and her fear that they will not be able to 'live here harmoniously together', threatening Australian harmony.

Not *Too* Multicultural

Uncertainty about how recent demographic changes both nationally and locally would play out was a strong factor in the widespread ambivalence about diversity and multiculturalism in Easthaven. This is captured in Hillview High Year 7 student Ruby's perspective on diversity: 'Like, it's good but it's not good. Because I've heard them saying that in the future, instead of more Australian and Aboriginal and all that, it's gonna be more, like, Asian people.' Her classmate Madeleine added: 'Yeah, because they could become more populated than us. And then it could be *their* culture and we'd be, like, more in their culture than ours.' The girls' conclusion was that they wanted to 'keep it [the nation] Aussie . . . . You still wanna keep it multicultural. . . . But you don't want it *too* multicultural.'

The girls' views bear traces of politically conservative discourses about immigration, asylum seekers and 'Australian values' that have been prevalent both locally and nationally throughout their childhoods. Their exchange conveys concerns about numbers – that having 'too many' (Hage, 2000) immigrants might threaten these young Australians' beliefs, privileges and lifestyle. The pronouns the students use – 'we', 'ours' and the impersonal, universalizing 'you', compared with 'they' and 'theirs' for immigrants – also indicate their confidence in their ability and right to speak for all, reflecting the power of White normativity (Dyer, 2005).

What is equally interesting, however, is what Ruby's and Madeleine's comments highlight about the variable relationship between ethnicity and culture, the historical and situational flexibility of Whiteness, and the influence of other factors such as class on individuals' identities and positionings. At the beginning of the focus group the girls described themselves as 'Aboriginal', but subsequently shifted between 'we' and 'they' when talking about Indigenous people and practices. Ruby, for instance, spoke about Aboriginal 'paintings [which] tell the stories about what they do and that's – when all Aboriginal people get together, that's what they usually act like'. But she said her own 'first goal' was to 'get a job . . . not to just hold back like all the other [Aboriginal] people'. Ethnically, Ruby is of mixed heritage; culturally, it appeared her main access to local Aboriginal knowledges and practices was through activities organized by the school, such as when elders 'take them [Aboriginal students] to their backgrounds and do . . . ceremonies . . . tell us the language and what they used to do'. The girls' comments also suggest they had fairly stereotypical views of 'Aborigines' but tending towards the negative, necessitating a mix of identifying and distancing strategies vis-à-vis their Indigenous ancestry (reflected in the shifting pronouns).

One orientation towards diversity, then, could be summed up as 'diversity is good as long as it is good for us' – although exactly who is included in 'we/us' at any given moment in any given place is often hard to pinpoint. A related orientation, discernible in several of the interviews quoted above, could be distilled as 'we have no issue with diversity provided it does not bother us' – an echo of what Zizek (2010) argues is 'emerging as the central human right in late-capitalist societies . . . the right not to be harassed, which is the right to be kept at a safe distance from others' (para. 8). This was evident in some of the data presented in the previous chapter, in the perspectives on mixing between people from diverse backgrounds within and beyond the schools (Vince's 'birds sharing the same sky'), and the accounts of how difficult it was for the refugee-background students to form friendships outside of their 'group'.

As Long as They Integrate/Assimilate

As several of the interviews presented above reveal, 'others' – people whose forebears were neither Anglo-Celtic nor Aboriginal – were often framed as (potential) threats, whether to Easthaven or Australia more generally. The nature and scope of these threats are explored below, but one consequence of this framing appeared to be a preference for assimilation as a way of 'managing' diversity – in other words, a view that the risks associated with diversity could be mitigated by 'them' learning to do things 'our' way. Certainly the dominant understanding among those interviewed was that the goal of diversity-related policies such as multiculturalism was, or should be, assimilation – a stance consistent with Garland and Chakraborti's (2006) findings in rural communities in England. Seaview High principal Sally, who had taught for many years at a high-LBOTE school in Sydney, said she thought a preference for assimilation remained widespread in Australia, but was pronounced in Easthaven:

> I think we want people to conform. . . . And I will hear that here [in Easthaven], 'they've got to learn our way of doing it'. Which is different to learning how to operate here. So there's a discourse of 'they need to do it our way'. And I mean – that's backed up by politicians. . . . There's constantly this [local political] discourse, 'we're living in the best part of the best state of the best country in the world', and I nearly vomit. . . . There's that pride [in 'Australianness'], and that sense of 'other'.

Here Sally makes a link between local political and everyday discourses about immigrants, Australia and national pride. While her perspective on Easthaveners' orientation towards diversity is quite succinct, she also distances herself from this perspective through her very visceral 'I nearly vomit'. As noted earlier, such strategies were common throughout the interviews, another indication not only of many interviewees' concerns about diversity but their concern with how their expressed views might reflect on them as individuals – as if, given the orthodoxy that diversity is something all Australians should prize, they felt a national and moral obligation to do so.

Significantly, Sally's views on 'good diversity' appeared to lean more towards assimilation than integration, even though 'integration' was the word she consistently used. Commenting on the 'quite strong' presence of immigrants from South Africa in Easthaven, she said they tended to 'mix in', noting that one of the school's vice-captains that year was South African: 'Quite dark-skinned . . . Afrikaans-speaking, and he was elected vice-captain within twelve months of being here. So, perfectly – beautifully integrated and popular.' What Sally seems to be saying here is that ethnic and linguistic differences (from Seaview High's Anglo norm) are not necessarily a bar to power and popularity, provided the person adapts to prevailing (Eurocentric) social and educational norms. There is little suggestion of a two-way process other than at the level of cultural art forms (sport, music, food and fashion). As with the turn to ethnicity/culture from race, the turn to multiculturalism/integration from assimilation does not necessarily change underlying schemas, supporting structures or everyday practices. '[T]he use of these terms . . . must not be taken at their face value, but critically inspected', Modood (2013, p. 3) warns.[3] In the interviews, both 'assimilation' and 'integration' were used, often interchangeably. On balance, it appeared from the interviews that while some Easthaveners had learnt to use the 'newer' word of integration, the predominant belief was that assimilation was the best strategy for ensuring social cohesion and safeguarding the 'Australian way of life'.

A preference for assimilation may also, of course, reflect a desire among longtime Easthaveners not to have to do things differently – an idea explored in the next chapter. Assimilation puts the responsibility for 'adjusting' on the newcomer, thereby minimizing the disruption to oldtimers' lives. Several interviewees recounted that some service providers had resisted using interpreters when dealing with NESB immigrants, even after they had been shown how to do so. Kerry, who worked in settlement services, related the following experience:

> I'm saying, 'My client needs an interpreter'. [They say] 'Oh, what? We've never had to use one before. We don't see a need for using an interpreter. Why should we have to get an interpreter for them?' . . . Unfortunately there are people who go 'We've got our way of doing it, if they come here they should talk like us, they should dress like us, they should do as we do', as if we're superior in some way.

Generational Differences?

Reflecting pre-1970s orientations towards diversity in Australia, assimilationist views, along with overt racism and racial stereotyping, might be more expected among older Easthaveners. Seaview High parent Catriona, for example, said that 'especially in the older vanilla world, you have these preconceived notions [about people from non-Anglo backgrounds] and they do take a while just to knock out of the community'. Hillview High parent Erica was more cautious about assuming generational changes in attitude, commenting that a lot of Easthaven's retirees were 'racist [and] they're quite happy to say it out loud . . . [whereas] people my generation are more aware that – if they're racist, they're racist quietly'. Multicultural discourses of celebration and tolerance have rendered naked racism socially unacceptable, or at least risky.

The Anglo-Australian students interviewed mostly characterized themselves as more accepting and less racist than their parents and grandparents. Hannah (Year 11, Seaview High) said her grandmother had a 'total dislike' of anyone and anything 'Asian', because family members had been killed in the Second World War – but 'I'm fine, I don't really mind what happened'. Her classmate Jeremy said his father 'tends to not like the ethnic countries with the Sudanese and that sort of stuff'. Like Hannah, Jeremy said he did not share his father's prejudices. However, his singling out of the 'Sudanese' (who are not only from Sudan) as 'ethnic' and his reference to 'that sort of stuff' (presumably other 'ethnics') raise questions about his own orientation towards 'difference' and diversity.

Other comments during the focus group suggest that these young people's views were less progressive than they appeared to imagine. Asked her opinion about cultural maintenance – a fundamental principle of Australian multiculturalism – Hannah offered the following:

> I would like to encourage the people that come here to maintain their culture and keep Australia nice and cultural – like, diversity. But . . . you see a lot of, I guess, foreigners come to Australia and they get in trouble because they don't really know Australian law or they don't really want to abide by it 'cause they did it differently in their home country. So, personally, I wanna see – like, I wanna see their culture,

I wanna see their food, their dancing and their language. But I want them to also realise that they're now in Australia, we speak English as our first language, and we abide by the Australian law.

Her classmate Riley agreed, saying he was 'happy' to have 'more different nationalities and more different types . . . as long as they do follow our rules, our laws, and they don't keep causing problems like some of them are at the moment'.

Similar views were expressed by Year 11 students at Hillview High. Thomas recounted a class discussion about immigration in which most of his peers said 'they [immigrants] should pick up our customs and they should lose theirs'. His classmate Victoria added:

It kinda depends on what it is. . . . They [immigrants] should still be allowed to speak in their own languages and eat their own food and things but . . . like, they wanted to come here, so they should – well, they *have* to go by our rules.

In fact, Victoria said her (Anglo-Australian) mother was 'more accepting' of 'other' cultures than she was: 'I think it's 'cause she *didn't* go to school with them [people from backgrounds different from her own] as much and she didn't see how they act . . . how they treat other people.' In contrast to findings that young people are more comfortable with and positive about diversity than older generations, Victoria at least is prepared to declare that she is *less* accepting – a position she presents as justified by her experiences of how 'they' act and 'treat other people' at school.

Overall, these students showed a preoccupation with immigrants' legal compliance and repeatedly constructed them as actual or potential law-breakers – and hence risks to social stability and moral order. This threat was most strongly associated with one particular group, the 'Sudanese' (typically used to refer to all refugees from Africa). This may have been partly due to negative stories in the local media about 'Africans' and crime (mentioned by several interviewees) but also the students' experiences at school. At Seaview High, for instance, Principal Sally recounted how two African-background students had been expelled for repeated stealing:

The difficult part was that it created tensions, in that they were two students who were persistently, over a long period of time, doing the wrong thing. But if they'd been two Anglo-background students . . . doing the wrong thing, it wouldn't have created 'the Whites are doing this', but it did create for a while there 'the Africans', that sentiment of 'the Africans', because they came to be representative of the whole group [of refugee-background students].

Because Black people are highly visible in mostly White Easthaven, their actions – especially their transgressions – are more visible. Further, as Sally observes, their actions are more likely to be causally linked to their ethnicity (the most obvious way in which they are 'different') than sociocultural factors such as financial situation, family history or mental health. This was commented on by Seaview High parent Catriona as well: 'Every time an African person in our community . . . one of them might get done once for drunk-driving, and ten whities would have got done for drunk-driving as well, but somehow the papers [report on] the African or the Indigenous person.'

While such incidents seem minor, they are integral to the construction of 'visibly different' Easthaveners as disruptive and potentially dangerous. As Swanton (2005) points out, the power of stories, stereotypes and other forms of classification lies in their repetition, so that they become mundane and 'commonsense'. Seaview High student Hannah was able to confidently articulate a 'truth' about the UK's largest city (which she had never visited) saying:

> You can't find an Englishman in London any more. . . . I know they have a lot of issues over there . . . but in Australia I just don't think there's that many ['foreign'] people, they're still a minority. . . . I don't think it [diversity] is a problem here because we just don't have the numbers that other countries do, where they have the conflicts.

Notwithstanding the inaccuracy of her representations – Australia's largest city, Sydney, actually has a higher proportion of overseas-born people than London (ABS, 2016a) – and her lack of experience in a highly diverse community, Hannah associates 'foreigners' with 'issues' and 'conflicts', and greater diversity with more problems. If 'difference' is routinely linked with 'conflict' – if non-Anglo-Australians, for example, are constructed as threats – a preference for assimilation, as a policy of minimizing 'otherness' and the assumed level of threat, is logical (Salter & Maxwell, 2016).

Influence of the Media

Despite a common construction of immigrants as potential problems, different non-Anglo Easthaveners were seen as problematic to different degrees and in different ways. Concerns accrued to three particular 'groups': the 'Africans', the 'Aborigines' and the 'Muslims' (although there were scarcely any Muslims in the town). Indeed, the black-skinned newcomers were the object of myriad fears – not only crimes such as 'stealing, break-and-enter and that sort of stuff' (Jeremy, student) but promiscuity and rape ('I had this woman say to me "you gotta watch out for all those African Blacks, they're gonna try and get as many White women pregnant so they can start really spreading their blood around town"' – Catriona, parent), 'gang wars' and tribal conflicts ('we never had that sort of thing before all these people started coming to live in our country' – Rita, staff), and contamination and filth. Former Hillview High student Grace, of Togolese background, recalled her experiences when she arrived in Easthaven: 'You'll be walking past . . . and they [her Anglo-background classmates] will be like, "Oh, Africans", they'll be like "oh, look at her skin, they don't have shower, that's why they're Black"'. Refugee support worker Kerry reported fielding regular phone calls from real-estate agents worried that their properties were being 'abused' by refugee families from Africa: 'There's this – just this underlying – that they don't know how to care for themselves.' Clearly, the refugee families *do* know how to care for themselves, having survived civil conflict in many cases and years of living in refugee camps. The discourse, then, carries an unspoken specificity: they don't know how to care for themselves *according to our standards*. Some of the fears about the people from

Africa might relate to their histories as refugees, or they might be more grounded in colonial narratives about 'Africanness' (Edgeworth, 2014). Certainly there was some evidence for the latter – Hillview High's Reg, for instance, spoke about the 'bad temper' (his words) and anger of some of the African-background students, explaining: 'That volatility comes from the culture.'

I want to suggest here that 'African' may have a particular potency in rural spaces. Conceptually, there is the contrast between European narratives about Africa as the 'Dark Continent' (Hall, 1990a) and imaginaries of the rural as 'White', civilized, ordered and safe. Historical European discourses about Africa's inhabitants being more primate than human – deployed to justify the taking of slaves, annexing of lands and exploitation of resources – continue to erupt in public name-calling: Hillview High teacher Winsome, for example, recounted attending local soccer matches where the coach would 'say things like "Get back in your cage, you black monkey!"' to the African-background goalie. Contemporary notions of Africa's 'darkness' are sustained through news stories about seemingly never-ending wars, corruption, diseases (Ebola, AIDS), droughts and famines (Colic-Peisker & Tilbury, 2008). Africa, then, may be 'seen as the antibook of, and thus a *particular threat to*, the rural idyll' (Colvin, 2017, p. 231) – and immigrants from Africa as potential vectors of conflict and chaos. Seidman (2013) writes that 'figures of difference' become 'other' if they are symbolically associated with excess and ungovernability. Such 'others' are constructed not merely as 'strange' or deficient but as defiled:

> [T]his defiled state trades on more than the anxiety of disorder; it is linked to disgust. . . . As a figure threatening chaos and ruin, the Other may be subject to forms of governance that suspend routine customary and juridical conventions. . . . Moreover, the defiled threatens an ever-widening circle of contamination, moral ruin and civic disorder. (pp. 6–7)

The more of 'them', the bigger the threat – reflected in comments quoted previously about fears the immigrants from Africa were 'taking over', and of Black people gathered together.

Although all the refugee settlers in Easthaven had come to Australia through UNHCR programmes, support worker Kerry believed political and media discourses about 'asylum seekers', 'boat people' and 'illegals' had magnified some residents' fears about the newcomers. Some evidence of that was provided by Seaview High's Rita. Asked how the school population had changed over the eight years she had been on staff, she said 'the Sudanese and Burmese . . . have been coming in in boatloads'. In reality, none of the new arrivals had come to Australia by boat and together they accounted for only about 1 per cent of Easthaven's population. As suggested in Chapter 4, however, the 'Sudanese' and the 'Burmese', notwithstanding their common 'refugee-ness', were positioned differently by longtime Easthaveners. In addition to differences in 'visibility' and cultural practices between the African- and Burmese-background newcomers, another reason the latter were perceived as 'blending in' could be that they did not come to the town so 'already known' (Cowlishaw, 2004b) as the people from Africa. Burma does not carry the same weight of colonial narratives as Africa, while contemporary mainstream media coverage is largely limited to political developments and elections. It also is not associated with Muslims and Islamic terrorism as some northern African countries are.

Political and media discourses about increasing immigration from Middle Eastern countries, Islamic fundamentalism and global terrorism had considerable resonance in Easthaven. Several residents expressed concerns about Muslims, their growing numbers ('We'll all be Muslims in fifty years' time; they're outbreeding us' – the taxi driver quoted in Chapter 4) and especially the burqa – a visible marker of 'otherness'. Here the international and national entwined to produce localized discourses of fear and suspicion, even though there would not have been more than a couple of dozen Muslims in Easthaven. Hillview High parent Erica, for instance, said Muslims were 'more of a challenge than the African [sic] and the refugees'. Fellow Hillview High parent Fleur said:

> Certainly there are some aspects, for example the burqa, which have created quite a bit of negativity and distress within – you know, how does that fit with our society and with our laws, even? And you've only got to look at the media to see that that has been an issue.

The media, of course, both reflect and create 'issues'. In rural and regional communities, where interaction between people from different backgrounds tends not to be the norm, the media are likely to have heightened importance as a source of information about cultural 'others' (Swanton, 2010). In the absence of personal contact – and cultural mixing in Easthaven was not routine – there may be little to challenge media images and narratives that construct particular ethnic, cultural and religious 'others' in a mostly negative light. This is not to suggest that contact necessarily breaks down stereotypes and prejudices (Amin, 2002; Santoro, 2014): retired ESL teacher Henrietta, for instance, said increased contact had in some cases hardened existing prejudices, while in other cases it had been beneficial for individual and community relations.

Refugee-Background Students' Perspectives

Despite many longtime Easthaveners' apparent support for assimilation as an approach to managing diversity, the refugee-background students had rather different ideas about their relationship with Easthaven and Australia. This exchange comes from a focus group with Year 11 ESL students at Seaview High.

> Celine: I think being – I think learning Australian is fun, but also to keep hold of who you really are, which is African – well, for me it is . . . I think it's finding the balance between still being true to yourself without changing yourself to fit a new society, still staying yourself but also making other friends and also learning their language to socialize with other people as well.
> Sisay: It's good to know you're different, because my culture and my background is a really big part of me and I wouldn't like to lose it 'cause if I didn't have it I would just be – I don't know [. . .] Sometimes – people from Ethiopia, friends

of mum, come to my house and they wear those traditional clothes and then they make coffee, like coffee in the Ethiopian cultural way ... And they sit together and they make popcorn and it's – when I look at them I just feel happy, 'cause I'm like 'oh yeah, that's me'.

For these students, being 'Australian' clearly does *not* mean giving up their languages, traditions and transnational connections but rather finding a 'balance' between their former and current lives as they fashion new cultural identities. After five years and eighteen months, respectively, in Easthaven, Celine's and Sisay's emotional attachments to their childhoods in Africa remain strong, and they see their 'African' selves as their 'true' selves. As Sisay explained: 'I had a *life* back in Africa. It was good. Well, I would go back there if there's no problems.' For Hillview High teacher Winsome, the continuing 'home' orientation of some of the refugee-background students was problematic. Some of the boys from Africa were acquiring cows to buy brides with, she said, adding: 'Their life is still in Africa, their minds are still in Africa, their traditions are still there, and they have no wish to be other than that.' In other words, she saw them as making little effort to integrate.

For Elaha, who had come to Easthaven from Afghanistan five years before, 'when you belong somewhere, there is like – you are in love with that thing and you always want to go back there even though you have a great life in Australia'. Despite her sense of displacement, the Hillview High student saw her resettlement journey as immensely enriching:

> It makes you mature ... it will teach you a lot quicker than someone who lived in a country with no trouble. .... The way you think is a lot different to the others, you know how to live by the time you are fourteen, fifteen ... because you are handling problems every day. ... You say, okay, I have all of these problems, but one day I will be a doctor, I will be an engineer ... all of these problems will be gone.[4]

These students' views of their past, present and future lives are markedly different from most Anglo Easthaveners' perceptions and expectations of them – as Seaview High parent Trudy, quoted earlier, came to realize. They see themselves as resilient, capable and having much to share.

As a whole, the interviews suggest that in mostly White Easthaven, many Anglo-background residents saw assimilation as the basis of 'endorsable' diversity – although some harboured doubts about whether the refugee newcomers (and in particular those from Africa) *could* assimilate. For their part, the newcomers seemed to feel, at least at this stage of their resettlement, that they would never become truly 'Australian' and in some respects did not want to, as that might mean giving up cherished practices or aspects of their identity or risking family relationships.

The *Real* Problem

Other Easthaveners were willing to give the newcomers the benefit of the doubt on integration/assimilation and saw the *real* problem as the 'Aborigines'. Local police officer Phil, for example, said the refugee-resettlement process in Easthaven was 'going all right' and that, contrary to the Seaview High students' perspectives, there were no 'dramas with the multicultural people here':

> It's not going pear-shaped like it is in some places in Sydney. We don't have people getting bashed because of the colour they are. . . . I often hear comments about 'Oh, don't the ladies look lovely' and stuff like that. So people are starting to come around.

Here, 'going all right' seems to be associated with an absence of physical violence (unsurprising, given Phil's profession) coupled with compliments from longtime Easthaveners about the African women's appearance (they dressed 'beautifully', as several interviewees mentioned). He explained that the local police had a much better relationship, and fewer problems, with the 'CALD community' than with Aboriginal locals:

> The Indigenous community – I shouldn't say, and this is stereotyping, but *some* people within the Indigenous community hate the cops. . . . They see us as being the people that have taken the country, the whole lot [of us]. This is something that personally really annoys me, is the fact that they're [Indigenous parents and elders] still passing that on to the kids . . . they're going to grow up to hate the cops, and they're going to end up in the same merry-go-round that some of the older kids are on. [But] I've noticed with the CALD community that that doesn't seem to happen. Once they realize that we're different to the cops back home, then they encourage their kids to come and talk to us, they're comfortable.

The sedimented history of Indigenous/non-Indigenous relations in Australia is articulated here as the pre-eminent social problem in Easthaven, and it was also seen as a leading problem, educationally and socially, in the schools. Jeremy (Year 11, Seaview High) commented that the African-background students were 'willing to learn' and did 'pretty well' at school, whereas 'Aboriginal kids tend to not listen and not pay attention' and did not do well. Most staff at the schools spoke of the refugee-background families as having a positive attitude towards schools and education and wanting their children to succeed academically. Aboriginal families, on the other hand, were sometimes characterized as not caring (because of their 'culture' – 'they don't seem to have the same ethic to rise forward', Seaview High teacher Lana said) or having an inviolable antipathy towards schools because of past negative experiences. As Gary, one of the Aboriginal support staff at Seaview High, explained: 'Because [Aboriginal] parents have had – how shall I put it? Schooling hasn't always been good for parents. . . . They've struggled with it. So their children seem to say, 'Why – it's not working for us, either''.

Similarly, while the antisocial behaviour of refugee-background students might be understood as linked to the traumas they had endured growing up in war-torn countries and refugee camps, the traumas of dispossession and discrimination suffered by many Aboriginal people have largely receded, or been pushed, into history. As Seaview High principal Sally noted:

> On the one hand, [people] can accept intellectually the place of Indigenous people, [but then] they're confronted with the reality of poverty or drunkenness or violence, or all those other things that go hand in hand with the history of the Aboriginal people and displacement.

This disconnect between knowledge of Australia's colonial history and the everyday realities of its legacy was evident in the observations of (Anglo-Australian) Fleur, mother of two boys at Hillview High. Fleur was positive about the African-background families ('they have attempted to integrate') but reported that she, her parents and her sons had had repeated 'negative interactions' with local Indigenous families. 'I don't fully understand the reasons behind that', she said. 'But I've just felt that there were negative feelings towards me, when I have done nothing to warrant that.' Her younger son had recently completed a unit of study on Indigenous history and culture, she said, and had expressed 'some sympathy for the types of atrocities that were enforced on the Indigenous population by European settlement – and he certainly didn't approve of that'. However, he also felt 'that was 200 years ago and that he can't be held accountable for that and we should move forward'. She added: 'Unfortunately I think he has a perception that – as do a lot of us, that – and I don't want to sound nasty, but basically they [Aboriginal youth] are allowed to get away with things that he's not.' Here Fleur constructs her son's negativity towards Aboriginal people as 'unfortunate', but well founded and shared by other Anglo-Australians ('a lot of us'). She expressed her 'sadness' at the level of 'presumed prejudice' towards Indigenous Australians, and clearly did not want to be 'nasty' (or perceived as nasty). Throughout the interview, Fleur deployed a range of discursive strategies – recounting personal experiences, invoking other people's views and experiences as corroboration, emphasizing emotions ('sympathy', 'sadness') and expressing incomprehension ('I don't fully understand the reasons behind that') – to validate her perspective and make it socially acceptable.

This is not to suggest that Fleur and her family had *not* had unpleasant experiences with local Aboriginal people but rather to highlight the complex interconnections between discourses, affects and attitudes. Public and media discourses linking Aboriginality and antisocial behaviour may make this the default lens through which Fleur 'sees' most Aboriginal-looking Easthaveners, whereas antisocial behaviour on the part of White people may be more likely to be attributed to class/personality factors, or experienced as less upsetting. Cowlishaw (2004b) observes that Indigenous Australians are 'often overwhelmed or enraged by the fact that they are already known to others, not as they experience themselves but in the plethora of images, stereotypes and discourses which have made them known in the public domain' (p. 64). This 'knowledge', created and sustained through discourse, mediates expectations and actual encounters on both sides. There may also be a country-town dimension here, consistent with Cowlishaw's (2006) comments quoted in Chapter 1 about the tensions between white rural residents' 'pragmatic, empirical knowledge of Aborigines', developed through years of contact, and city dwellers' 'romantic views' (p. 433), often based on little contact. Like Fleur, the 'Whitefellas' in Cowlishaw's Bourke study felt hurt not only by Blackfella incivilities and misdemeanours but by (potentially) being branded racist when they recounted those experiences – in other words, doubly victimized.

What about Us?

A related but broader discourse concerned Anglo-Australians having to be accepting of and empathetic towards people from minority groups even as they were denied the cultural, social and financial benefits available to these 'others'. The exchange below, with an Anglo Hillview High student, followed a question about whether events such as Harmony Day, NAIDOC Week and Sorry Day helped the Year 11 interviewees to understand or interact with people outside of their usual social/cultural group.

> Sam: We had to put our hand into the ground to say sorry. I was really – I was kind of confused about that.
> Neroli: So you don't really understand the context?
> Sam: I do but – like, it wasn't us that did it. I don't – I've forgotten what it was all about, but I think it was just a bit weird that they made the whole entire school put our hand into the ground to say sorry.
> Neroli: So nobody explained the point of it?
> Sam: I think they did but I didn't like it [. . .] And they're [Aboriginal-background students] not discriminated against at school. And we are, sort of.
> Neroli: How are you discriminated against?
> Sam: Well it's not discriminated but – we get left out a lot. Like I'll use Aboriginal people as an example: they get taken out of classes, they get tutoring for free, and I know at the canteen sometimes they get free food and stuff.

Sam's comments point to two related complaints – first, being forced to participate in an act of acknowledgement and reconciliation for injustices that he constructed as temporally irrelevant; and second, that it was no longer Aboriginal people who were discriminated against (or 'left out') but him and his Anglo peers.

Seaview High staff member Rita – who described herself as 'a White Australian, I don't have Aboriginal blood in me' – echoed this complaint:

> The Aboriginal Australians get a hell of a lot more than what the White Australians get, and they're the ones always up in arms about – you know, they want to have equal rights. So yes, that [equal rights] is something *I've* always wanted. When my eldest son was in sixth class . . . [he] was going on a Canberra excursion. And two of the little Aboriginal girls in his class went up to [him] and went [*mocking tone*]: 'Ha-ha-ha, we get to go to Canberra for nothing and you have to pay!' And I thought [*sarcastic tone*], 'Yeah, that's really fair, isn't it? That's really fair.' Same here with the refugee kids. . . . They get everything given to them, whereas the Aussies have to battle and get the second-hand clothes, and they have to pay off this and pay off that, and yeah, it's a bit unfair. But that's the way it is.

Together, dehistoricization, Black/White binaries and the potency of the 'r' word ('racism') (Nelson, 2015) leave little space for recognizing and discussing the grievances on both sides, Indigenous and Anglo – the latter explicit in the comments of Fleur, Rita and some of the students quoted above. Hillview High's Sam said he understood what

Sorry Day was about but 'it wasn't us that did it', and he 'didn't like' being 'made' to participate in the activity. In this discourse White people become the victims of equity measures and the equity measures themselves are cast as 'unfair', divisive and racist (Gillborn, 2010), *contra* the 'Australian values' of inclusion and egalitarianism. Against the weight of White hegemony, such measures are rendered fragile and vulnerable to challenge.

Denial and Worrying

Affects and sentiments can also imperil social justice initiatives. Fleur, Rita and Sam, quoted above, had different socio-economic backgrounds, pointing to different levels of 'class' privilege, but a common obliviousness to White privilege (they were all of Anglo-Celtic descent). They also shared a resignation, even fatigue, about Indigenous/non-Indigenous relations. Acknowledging White privilege, according to McIntosh (2010), is 'not about blame, shame, guilt, or whether one is a "nice person"'. Yet these not-so-nice affects/emotions (Probyn, 2005) can be a barrier even to small acts of recognition and restitution. As McIntosh (1989) argues: 'The silences and denials surrounding privilege are the key political tool. . . . They keep the thinking about equality or equity incomplete, protecting unearned advantage and conferred dominance by making these taboo subjects' (p. 12). Thus 'Harmony Day' promotes discourses, affects and activities very different from those suggested by 'the United Nations International Day for the Elimination of Racial Discrimination' – including its foregrounding and valorizing of 'otherness' and lack of attention to White normativity.

Another aspect of White privilege evident in Easthaven was the perceived threat posed by non-Anglo Australians to the privileges historically enjoyed by most Anglo-Australians. Rita, for example, sees both Aboriginal and refugee-background students as receiving unearned privileges at her expense. This sense of injustice ('it's a bit unfair') is accompanied by a sense of lost power: 'That's the way it is. I can't change the rules. I'm not allowed to.' Rita is an example of the 'white-and-very-worried-about-the-nation-subject' who Hage (2000) argues is central to imaginaries of Australia as the rightful domain of the White, working-class male. Worrying, whether privately felt or publicly declared, may help alleviate a sense of loss of control (Hage, 2000, p. 10). Insecurity feeds fear and fear feeds insecurity (Back, 2012), entrenching the White worriers' efforts to 'protect' the nation, their own position within it and the 'Australian way of life'. This tendency may be particularly pronounced in rural and regional areas – the last bastion of the 'old' Australia, the focus and repository of colonial ambitions (Colvin, 2017). Relatedly, White privilege is likely to be less visible in mostly White country towns; it is simply 'normal'.

Another interviewee whose comments suggest he was a 'White worrier' was Hillview High deputy Reg. As reported in the previous chapter, he expressed (albeit indirectly) concern about the fact that Aboriginal people had gained land rights over Uluru/Ayers Rock and made decisions limiting the access of people such as himself to the site. During a later discussion about decisions and who had the power to make them, Reg said:

If we talk in races and colours again ... I think the story of the Stolen Generation, the kids who were taken from their families – everyone's trying to do all this and redress that and change it ... Not buying into right or wrong, now, looking at it, but I think at the time the people who made the decisions thought they were doing the right thing. They didn't do it to be nasty. And some of the people who have spoken against it have admitted, 'without being taken out of that Aboriginal family which was poor, I've been put in a White family and given an education ... '. So I think the people who made the decisions meant well. Right or wrong? I'm not going to go into that one. It's not for us to say.

In the face of contemporary moves to recognize native title, circulate the stories of the Stolen Generations and apologize for past mistreatment of Indigenous Australians, Reg reasserts more colonial-era narratives about White benevolence, reinforced by reported Aboriginal gratitude. Implicit in these narratives is a construction of other-than-Anglo people (often Indigenous peoples in particular) as 'less than' – deficient and needy. In this discourse what matters is 'doing the right thing', meaning well, not being 'nasty'; White people cannot be held responsible for actions or outcomes, only for intentions. Even so, given countervailing discourses that do emphasize 'redress' and 'change', Reg at the same time seeks to distance himself both from those long-ago decision makers and from judging them: 'Right or wrong? It's not for us to say.' I am not suggesting that Reg's view was typical among the staff at Hillview High; he, his fellow deputy Vince and principal Neil appeared to have very different experiences of and perspectives on diversity and education. However, it is worth considering that Reg's views may have had particular influence within the school not only because of his executive position but because he had been a teacher there for thirty years.

Loss and Longing

Another aspect of the 'What about us?' discourse is hinted at in Rita's 'But that's the way it is'. As noted, Rita expressed some of the most negative views about diversity among the interviewees At the same time, Rita recognizes that multiculturalism and Australia's 'multicultural future' is a lost battle. Even country towns no longer offer a haven from the sorts of demographic flux and social change usually associated with cities. In an exchange about cultural identity and what it took, in her opinion, to become 'Australian', Rita said people should be 'one or the other ... then there's no confusion. Black and White [*laughs*]. It's easier that way, but it never will be like that. It never will be. Not any more.' Her sense of loss and disorientation was perhaps most palpable at the end of the interview when she reflected:

I'm lucky, I think, that I grew up when I did. I think it was a safer world back then . . . .
There's too much I enjoy from years ago. It'd be nice for things to slow down a bit.

Nostalgia is intimately connected with privilege: looking back in time – 50 years, 100 years, more – is 'a pleasure trip for some and a horror story for others' (Smith,

2016, para. 6), depending on class, race, gender, sexuality and so on. The 1950s and early 1960s, when Rita was growing up, may have been a 'safer world' for most White people, but it was not for most Indigenous Australians (who did not yet have national voting rights) or immigrants. Although Rita may not have been privileged in terms of socio-economic status, she at least had the certainty of her position at the top of the ethnic hierarchy. Now she appears to feel she has lost even that. Discourses about embracing diversity make recognizing and addressing the real sense of loss that may attach to demographic changes particularly challenging (Nelson, 2015).

'Natural' to Be Afraid

Perhaps the most common discourse of all among interviewees was that if (some) Easthaveners felt worried about or threatened by diversity, that was only to be expected. According to this discourse, people are 'naturally' afraid of, or at least resistant to, change, and 'naturally' wary of 'strangers' – Boler and Zembylas's (2003) biological/natural response model of difference.

Certainly 'fear of the unknown' and 'fear of change' were repeatedly cited as reasons for people's reservations about diversity. Seaview High teacher Brody offered this perspective:

> Well, people who think that diversity can lead to cultural animosity, they're exactly right. . . . We fear the people on the other side of the hill because they might steal our women and our food. So, you know, you've *got* to worry about the other people from the other tribe. They look funny, jeez, and they talk weird. That's part of the human make-up.

Here Brody constructs fear of 'people on the other side of the hill' as a survival mechanism, an evolutionary imperative. Other interviewees linked fear of the 'other' to experiential factors – or rather, lack of experience. NSW DoE consultant Fiona, recounted going to the weekly growers' market and seeing 'women walking across the street with an *abaya* on':

> I mean, that's just – that was unheard of in this area ten years ago. . . . It's still incredibly confronting for many people. . . . It's probably mixed with a bit of fear of the unknown. . . . Having all these different cultures come in, it's making people confront issues and fears, and they have to think about the world beyond [Easthaven], which I don't think a lot of people necessarily have done.

Fiona's comments point not only to the shock of a 'strange' new sight for longtime Easthaveners but also to the discomfort – whether actual or anticipated – of having to think and act differently because of the new presences. She saw this discomfort as being magnified in rural areas – areas marked by low ethnic and cultural diversity, social and political conservatism, and hyperlocalism.

Similar perspectives are evident in the following excerpts:

> I think [lack of cross-cultural mixing] is actually not even judgment. I think it's fear, I think it's a fear of the unknown because they don't know anybody that's living in Australia who's African, or who's – probably they don't even know any Kooris. (Caryn, parent, Hillview High)

> I think generally, once Australians develop a relationship, then there's a kind of acceptance. I think the unknown is – that fear of not knowing a person. But I think once there's a bit of a connection there – that's where school is so important, to get that connection happening early on. So then they're not afraid of approaching the African person in the street. (Stephanie, deputy principal, Seaview High)

Again, in these examples, it is striking that 'fear' is linked specifically to the 'Africans' (and perhaps the 'Kooris'). As highlighted throughout this and the previous chapter, the immigrants from Africa elicited attentions, affects and sentiments in Easthaven that no other ethnic 'group' appeared to. This is true beyond Easthaven: in the 2015 *Australians Today* study (Markus, 2016), which included 500 African-background respondents among its 10,500 total, more than three-quarters of respondents from South Sudan (n =166) reported having experienced discrimination in the past twelve months. Markus (2016, p. 72) writes: 'It seems that differences of skin colour are a significant issue for many Australians, for whom there has been little interaction with very dark skinned people.' The report cites an anecdote from a focus group about a tall, dark-skinned, tribally scarred South Sudanese man who went to work at an aged-care facility:

> As soon as [the man goes there], all the older people start standing up, running to their rooms. And some of them start falling down . . . 'get away from him, get away from him, he'll kill you too, he'll kill you too'. . . . They [the facility operators] couldn't take that guy on, they had to send him back. (Markus, 2016, p. 73)

. . . Especially of Black People

I cite the excerpt above because of its similarity to a situation recounted by Seaview High parent Catriona. Asked whether she thought attitudes towards diversity had changed over the past decade as Easthaven's population had changed, Catriona said they had, 'but not enough':

> And a prime example is that we own a computer business and we were advertising for a new technician. And one of the African refugees came to us and he'd had a lot of IT experience. And this is awful, but we felt we couldn't give him the job, because we send our technicians into people's houses, and we knew that if a Black African guy rocked up at someone's house to try and fix their computer, they would not always be welcomed in all – would not always be – look, it would not be something that [Easthaven] was ready for yet. And that's awful. It sounds awful when you say that, but that's – the reality is that . . . I would've loved to have been able to give him a job, because I really believe in that. But I had to sort of think about it from my business point of view. . . . [T]hat's the really sad thing about this

town, is there's still that degree of redneckery. And then also there's – the question you have to ask yourself is 'Well, how could we effect change by having someone – well, we should employ that guy anyway.' But could we afford to do that for our business, you know? It's all a bit awkward.

Asked why she thought her customers might not be 'ready' to have a Black technician enter their homes, Catriona replied:

> I think it's probably just fear of the unknown . . . there's been no indicators whatsoever to say these people are bad or they're gonna rob you or they're gonna kill you . . . in the general perception there's been no indicators that I can think of that would say, 'You are at risk by having this person come to your house or to your business'. . . . [But] it would be really great to see some African-type restaurants or some African bands doing more stuff or whatever, just to hammer home how good it [diversity] is and how it's not – how it doesn't bring a threat.

There is much to analyse in these excerpts – Catriona's account complementing Hillview High parent Caryn's account (in the previous chapter) of how her father had refused to come into her house when she had an African-background student staying there. First, there is the intimate relationship between the social and the spatial, with sociocultural hierarchies maintained by spatial as well as discursive practices. While Anglo-Australian Easthaveners may have come to accept the presence of their African-background neighbours in public spaces, they are presented as not (yet) 'ready' to accept them in that most private of spaces, one's home. As 'spatial managers' (Hage, 2000), they have the self-bestowed right – and responsibility, Catriona's comments imply (she does not want to upset her customers) – to determine who can go where, and when – and who is who in the first place. It is in this sense that Leonardo (2002) likens Whiteness itself to (private) property, writing: '[L]ike a house, whiteness can be demarcated and fenced off as a territory of white people which keeps Others out' (p. 38).

A second point concerns Catriona's use of sentiments in her account of her decision not to risk sending a Black technician into White people's houses. These sentiments – 'awful', 'sad', 'awkward' – may indicate that Catriona is not altogether comfortable with her decision. However, it is also possible to read her account as a performance of niceness, informed by multicultural discourses and even, ironically, notions of equity and a 'fair go': she, after all, 'really believes' in diversity and 'would've loved to have been able to give [the technician] the job'. In reality, she was perfectly 'able' to employ him, as she owned and managed the business – but the fears and prejudices of 'others' are cited as reasons she ultimately could not act in accordance with her 'values'. She concedes that there is no evidentiary basis for Anglo Easthaveners' (presumed) fear of the dark-skinned newcomers ('there's been no indicators whatsoever to say these people are bad') – but the automatic assumption is that Black people *are* a threat (more likely to 'rob' or 'kill'); and, further, that it is natural to be afraid of the 'unknown'. As Noble and Poynting (2010) write, victims of racial vilification are not discriminated against primarily for their actions, but for who they are – 'or rather, being who they are where they are (where they don't belong). They transgress by being there' (p. 496). In mostly White Easthaven, the qualified computer technician transgresses by being Black – but Blackness can at least be contained by keeping it out of White people's homes.

Third, Catriona showed no recognition that her decision might not just be regarded as regrettable, but was in fact illegal. Acts of racial discrimination such as the one she relates are by no means unique to Easthaven and other mostly White settlements. Both national and international research on employment decisions – to take one important life opportunity – indicate that discrimination on the basis of race/ethnicity, as well as religion, language background/accent, class, gender, sexual orientation, age and other sociocultural dimensions, remains pervasive despite anti-discrimination laws (Abdelkerim & Grace, 2012; Audit Office of NSW, 2012). A three-year study of refugee settlers' job-seeking and employment experiences in Western Australia (Colic-Peisker & Tilbury, 2007; Tilbury & Colic-Peisker, 2006) provides a valuable broader context for Catriona's comments. While many employer participants in the Western Australian study expressed goodwill towards migrants and refugees, the researchers reported that almost all denied that racial discrimination was a problem in Australian workplaces (Colic-Peisker & Tilbury, 2007). However, detailed analysis of the interview transcripts illuminated a range of strategies deployed by participants to deflect responsibility for potentially discriminatory practices. These included discourses about egalitarianism/meritocracy; inadequate cultural knowledge on the part of the migrants; 'the market'; and, as with Catriona's account, the alleged prejudices of their clients or customers. By constructing the 'redneckery' in Easthaven as the problem, Catriona is able to absolve herself not only from legal culpability but also from guilt over her actions.

Finally, it is worth drawing attention to Catriona's reiteration of 'how good [diversity] is' and how 'it would be really great to see some African-type restaurants or some African bands doing more stuff or whatever'. The latter statement, together with other data presented in this and the previous chapter, illustrates how discourses of Whiteness can be used to develop topographies of belonging. In these topographies 'Africans', for instance, are discursively positioned as 'fit' for sporting fields (soccer, running), performance stages ('bands', dancing) and restaurants; somewhat 'controversial' in the mall; and 'absent' from White people's property and from positions of social, intellectual and economic leadership – also 'White property' in CRT scholarship. As a result, contemporary rhetoric about acceptance and inclusion can, in given spaces (such as rural spaces), be

> simply incorporation in another guise, a process of fitting 'the excluded' into positions in the mainstream economy where they can be more efficiently exploited at the same time as some of these excluded groups are featured in seemingly positive and progressive representations of multicultural societies. (Sibley, 2006, p. 401)

Of course, topographies of belonging are established and maintained through non-discursive means as well, as already argued: stares, smiles, interactions in the playground and so on. Such practices and their consequences are examined further in the next chapter.

Things Get Better with Time

A related but slightly different perspective on the fear of 'others' was that change is always difficult at first, but that acceptance 'naturally' develops over time. Hillview High principal Neil, for instance, said:

> You look back to when I was a kid and 'wogs' and 'dagos'[5] – I look back on that and then I look at now that we actually celebrate Greek culture, and people love to go to Vietnamese restaurants and things like that . . . I think we're an awful lot better society than we would have been had it [mass immigration] not happened. But I do think racism, it's still there . . . it takes generations to get rid of that. Maybe fifty years from now we'll have an even stronger society.

And more from Seaview High's Brody:

> I think that when you say that multiculturalism will cause conflict, of course it will, but that's part of human nature is to change, and conflict is part of that. . . . And people who say that cultural diversity is a bad thing, I bet they've eaten pizza, and I bet they have a doner kebab occasionally. . . . So to say that multicultural leads to – it's a double-edged sword. . . . Having people from different cultures will always cause conflict, because they don't trust each other; but then they learn from each other, so then that means it *doesn't* cause conflict.

Brody and Neil construct as 'natural' the tendency to distrust or ostracize immigrants, but suggest that new consumables (pizza, doner kebabs, Vietnamese food) can help foster familiarity and eventually acceptance. I do not question that immigration and multiculturalism have been broadly positive in strengthening intercultural understanding and engagement in Australia, as well as modifying prejudices and segregations. However, it should not be assumed that occasional community celebrations along with regular interactions in spaces of association such as restaurants and schools translate into full inclusion (Wise, 2011). Nor should it be assumed that 'social progress' is linear. Discourses in relation to Muslims in Australia and elsewhere in the wake of the 2001 terrorist attacks on the United States are one example of the capacity for sudden shifts in affects, attitudes and actions (Noble & Poynting, 2010).

Critiquing the trope of incremental improvements in social inclusion and cohesion has been, and is, a central mission of race-critical scholarship. Dixson and Rousseau (2005) tie this to broader critiques of liberalism and liberalism's 'faith in the system as an instrument of justice' (p. 16). Similarly, Gillborn (2007) questions a view among policymakers (including in education) that policy evolves in a rational and linear fashion towards more equitable outcomes. The reality, he argues, is that inequity and racism are not 'aberrant or accidental phenomena that will be ironed out in time' (Gillborn, 2007, p. 498) but rather are built into policy settings (notwithstanding good intentions), institutional structures and everyday discursive and material practices. The trope of improvement over time can thus be another way of avoiding macro-level or individual responsibility for effecting here-and-now change, as in Catriona's case.

'I Look at All Kids and Think They're All the Same'

This chapter opened with a review of Boler and Zembylas's (2003) three models of difference: celebration/tolerance, natural response/biological and denial/sameness. The data can be seen as overwhelmingly aligning with the first two models, or a mix of them (diversity as good *and* bad). The White victimology discourse ('What about us?') discussed above can be seen as a variation on the denial/sameness model – not 'we are all the same' but 'we should all be *treated* the same', or rather 'they' should not receive special treatment.

Among the school staff interviewed, however, only one person articulated an orientation aligned with the denial/sameness model as presented by Boler and Zembylas (2003). This was Hillview High deputy Reg, who said: 'I look at all kids and think they're all the same. Some people would say you shouldn't look at them like that, I guess. But I think, yeah, they're all the same. . . . I see them all as average kids.' Later he said:

> I'm getting to the stage now where I just accept them all. I don't think I didn't before, but I don't notice now if a culture is or [is] not performing something. . . . [Y]ou have them in front of an assembly or in front of parents here, doing their drumming, and you don't sit there and count 'oh, there's three Africans and one of these.' I couldn't tell you now – you might've noticed, but I couldn't tell you what cultures were in that [drumming performance earlier in the day]. I just saw a group of our kids putting on a show.

Here Reg constructs himself as (now) 'postracial'. He claims not to notice colour or culture and to 'accept them all' as 'the same . . . [just] average kids'. Yet his talk about diversity was riddled with anxieties and resentments, as documented, and deeply racialized throughout. It was also replete with cultural stereotypes, from 'the African boys love their soccer, the Aboriginal boys love their touch football' to 'the Irish are always a bit different!' and the 'Asian' students being more 'sensitive . . . a lot of them in their culture are very quiet'. Again, Reg's comments illuminate the hierarchies and topographies of belonging in Easthaven and its schools: the 'Africans' and the 'Aborigines' on the playing fields, excelling at sport; the 'Asians' in the classroom, embodying a 'model minority'; the Anglo-background children (and adults) everywhere but unraced, unplaced and often absent as social actors. This pattern of discourse is typical of what Bonilla-Silva (2006) calls 'colour-blind racism' – a contemporary form of racism that 'otherizes softly . . . .aid[ing] the maintenance of white privilege without fanfare, without naming those who it subjects and those who it rewards [*sic*]' (pp. 3–4).

Conclusion

The comments of these Easthaveners revealed a range of orientations towards diversity in the town and its schools, particularly with regard to policy framings of diversity as a strength. Even within interviews, orientations were often inconsistent and conflicted – reflecting an evaluation of diversity, overall, as a 'double-edged sword' (Seaview High's Brody). While seeing some benefits (food and the arts), many interviewees expressed significant and wide-ranging concerns about the demographic changes in their town, and what the changes might mean for them personally and for their regional community. Discourses were also often deeply racialized, notwithstanding a general awareness among interviewees of the 'political incorrectness' of racial stereotyping and the 'unacceptability' of racism.

Race remains socially salient because it is not simply a word but rather a way of seeing and thinking (Goldberg, 2006) – habits that have 'become ingrained in vernacular and institutional practice due to the force of stacked legacies of reading human difference and worth in racial terms' (Amin, 2010, p. 13). Such habits may be especially entrenched in rural and regional areas where Whiteness has enjoyed a long and rarely troubled reign. Multicultural policies' focus on the 'nice, pretty cultural parts' of diversity helps to deflect attention from continuing racialization and racisms while keeping Whiteness unethnicized and therefore 'normal'. Further, as shown, both celebratory and fear discourses about 'difference' (Boler & Zembylas, 2003) can and do animate practices that stratify and spatialize belonging, while sameness discourses can help maintain those arrangements. As Ang (2001) writes: '[R]acially and ethnically marked people are no longer othered today through simple mechanisms of rejection and exclusion, but through an ambivalent and apparently contradictory process of *inclusion by virtue of othering*' (p. 139). They are allowed into the country, into workplaces, schools and public spaces, but they can still be contained by categories, imaginaries, the force of discourse. 'Sprinkles of everything' may be embraced or at least accepted – the 'Yes' part of 'Yes, but . . .', but even 'sprinkles' may provoke concerns among some Australians about challenges to familiar ways of seeing, thinking, talking, feeling and acting (the 'but' part). In view of these tensions, the next chapter, 'Old Ways Die Hard', examines how understandings of and discourses about diversity and difference have translated into material practices in Easthaven's public high schools.

6

'Old Ways Die Hard'

Practices and Consequences

Introduction

This chapter investigates how the understandings of and discourses about diversity detailed in the previous chapters shape material social and educational practices at Hillview High and Seaview High. As argued in the Introduction, different understandings of the world – reflected in and produced through language – are linked to different possibilities for action, and thus to different consequences. A celebratory model of difference is likely to lead to curriculum and pedagogical practices that diverge from those informed by a denial/sameness model (Boler & Zembylas, 2003). Discourses that construct LBOTE students as 'problems' or 'deficient' (whether because of their ethnicity, cultural practices or lack of proficiency in English) will promote practices divergent from those suggested by discourses that construct them as resilient, resourceful and rich in their own knowledges and life experiences. As documented in the previous chapter, many of the Anglo-Australian interviewees in this study appeared to conceive of immigration and settlement as a one-way process: 'they' come to 'us', therefore 'they should pick up our customs and . . . lose theirs' (Hillview High student). Yet that, as noted, is not the ethos of multiculturalism, and has not been an official policy approach to diversity for 50 years (Koleth, 2010).

This chapter explores a range of practices in Easthaven's two public high schools – both those observed during visits to the schools, but more frequently *accounts* of practices. The chapter acknowledges, first, that accounts of practices may not be full representations of actual practices; and second, that factors such as funding, staff backgrounds, administrative systems and access to educational and more general resources, as well as understandings of and orientations towards diversity, affect how multicultural policies are enacted in particular sites – that is, that multiculturalism in practice is a product of both material and conceptual affordances and constraints. Policies are usually concerned with *what* is to be done, leaving the detail of *how* it is done to practitioners; this allows schools to devise responses that they believe are appropriate to their circumstances and priorities. As 'textual interventions', policies can produce significant changes (Ball, 1993). However, educational theorists and practitioners should remain alert to 'the way that things stay the same [and] the ways in which changes are different in different settings and different from the intentions of policy authors' (Ball, 1993, p. 13).

This chapter takes up Ball's advice to ask: How have practices changed, and *not* changed, at Seaview and Hillview high schools over a decade of diversification, and why? According to a number of staff members, the changes in curriculum and pedagogical practices at each school had been limited overall and uneven across learning areas. To Seaview High's ESL teacher Richard, this was reflective of nation-wide imaginative and structural failures to adapt to the realities of contemporary Australian diversity – failures he linked to continuing media and corporate images of the 'average Australian' as 'blond and blue-eyed', though this is changing, evident in the increasing representation of diversity in, for example, advertising. To Hillview High's deputy principal, Vince, teachers' persistence with 'old ways' of doing things was due more to local factors.

Not all interviewees shared Richard's and Vince's perspective on the schools' efforts. However, the argument of this chapter is that, notwithstanding the requirement that all NSW schools implement multicultural education, Aboriginal education and antiracism policies (among many others), 'old ways' of perceiving, thinking and talking about culture and difference, and within schools of teaching, assessing and prioritizing, continue to mediate enactments of policies. These old ways are often racialized, as shown in the previous chapters – but, having been practised for years, they have become 'normal' and thus invisible to many practitioners. Further, old ways may be particular barriers in non-metropolitan schools where cultural and ethnic diversity has not been part of most people's experience; where teachers are typically older and have often been at schools for a long time, so that practices are more entrenched ('the old folk will never change'); and where access to specialist support, resources and professional development opportunities tends to be more limited than in metropolitan schools. As documented, there have been substantial demographic changes in Easthaven – changes that were acknowledged by research participants as having brought unprecedented challenges to the town's public schools. This is against the backdrop of significant changes in education more generally (Salter & Maxwell, 2016) – reflected in Hillview High principal Neil's comment that 'schools' jobs are getting tougher and tougher'.

Major educational reform has been a focus of state and federal governments for over a decade (Connell, 2009; Creagh, 2016a) – yet educational disadvantage in Australia continues to worsen, particularly for students from Indigenous, non-metropolitan and/ or low socio-economic backgrounds. Furthermore, Australia compares poorly with other OECD countries on equality of educational opportunities, equality of outcomes and school segregation (Perry, 2017). This conundrum is central to the analysis that follows.

The chapter begins by examining perspectives on multicultural education, Aboriginal education and the national curriculum capability of intercultural understanding. How these dimensions of education are understood by school leaders and teachers will have a strong bearing on curriculum, pedagogy, pastoral care and other practices in schools. Also important is how school leaders and teachers understand the *relationships* between the varied objectives and dimensions of education – particularly, given the regional context of the study and the schools' populations, the relationship between multicultural education and Aboriginal education. The focus then shifts to the classroom and accounts of teachers' practices, bringing in student perspectives in an effort to shed light on the consequences of those practices. The final section moves outside the classroom to explore a range of broader educational and school practices (multicultural events, school assemblies and cultural performances) and their effects on social relations in Easthaven.

Multicultural Education, Aboriginal Education and Intercultural Understanding

State-based multicultural education and Aboriginal education policies have been in force for decades and apply to all students in NSW schools. The national curriculum, on the other hand, is far more recent (ACARA, 2014). The capability of intercultural understanding was something that school leaders and teachers would or should have been aware of, but that they were not yet officially charged with developing (in accordance with the national curriculum) in students. The same applied to the cross-curriculum priority of Aboriginal and Torres Strait Islander histories and cultures. The relationships between intercultural understanding (national curriculum) and multicultural education (state policy), and between Aboriginal and Torres Strait Islander histories and cultures (national curriculum) and Aboriginal education (state policy), along with the relationships of these with other policies (such as antiracism), general capabilities and curriculum priorities, have up to this point, remained untested.

While the NSW DoE's multicultural and Aboriginal education policies apply to all schools, no specific curriculum is associated with them (Walton et al., 2016). Rather, guidelines are provided, and schools are left to develop priorities and implement programmes according to the particularities of their communities (Watkins and Noble, 2021). While this provides flexibility, it also means that teachers 'have to design curriculum units without a structured curriculum to support critical discussions about multiculturalism' (Walton et al., 2016) – and therefore that enactments depend more heavily on the capacities of individual schools and the capabilities of their teachers, and on the resources available to them, than is the case for other aspects of the curriculum (Mansouri & Percival Wood, 2007). Given schools' obligations of recognizing and catering for the specific needs of particular students, promoting openness towards diversity and working to ensure equitable social and educational outcomes for all students (ACARA, n.d.; NSW DoE, 2016a, 2016c), one area of interest was how staff at the high schools conceptualized and prioritized these responsibilities.

In any school, the executive has a critical role in establishing the nature and scope of diversity-related programmes and practices – making decisions about staff recruitment, professional development, curriculum, pedagogy, assessment, modes of communication, allocation of resources and so on. The executive sets and reports on diversity-related objectives, and determines who will have responsibility for meeting them and how outcomes are evaluated. Understanding school leaders' perspectives on diversity-related policies and capabilities is important for several reasons. First, executive members' responses to questions on these topics help to contextualize formal and informal practices within the schools. Second, the interview data provide insights into the degree of similarity – and points of difference – in the executive members' perspectives, within and between the schools; this was of interest given the different demographic profiles and histories of the schools. The third point relates to research highlighting the importance of a whole-school approach (beginning with strong leadership) in implementing effective multicultural and antiracism programmes (Aveling, 2007; Mansouri & Jenkins, 2010; Walton et al., 2015). For these reasons, data from the interviews with executive members at each school are discussed separately.

Hillview High School Leaders' Perspectives and Accounts of Practice

The interviews with the executive at Hillview High revealed divergent perspectives on multicultural education and Aboriginal education, undergirded by divergent understandings of, orientations towards and lived and professional experiences of diversity and difference. Unlike many of his staff and his immediate predecessor, principal Neil had been at the school for only a few years. Asked what he understood 'multicultural education' to be, Neil's first response – emphatically made – was that it was 'not assimilation'.

He went on to define it as 'cultures valuing the best out [*sic*] from each other and learning from each other so that each different culture grows by learning from the others'. Neil saw the school's Aboriginal and ESL (mostly refugee-background) students as similar in that 'both . . . are coming from very low bases in terms of the opportunities that they've had'. But 'multicultural education is so diverse . . . whereas Aboriginal education is very narrow and catering for a small group. I see Aboriginal education [as] probably under a big umbrella of multicultural'.

Questions about the relationship between multicultural education and Aboriginal education – both as the relationship is at present and as it perhaps could or should be in the future – are complex and contested (Hickling-Hudson, 2003). While Neil saw commonalities between Aboriginal and ESL students (and, he later said, 'the poorest of the poor' Anglo-Australian students) in terms of socio-economic background, his comments also suggest that he saw Aboriginal education as being only for students who identified as Aboriginal – contrary to the NSW DoE *Aboriginal Education and Training Policy* (NSW DoE, 2016a). Conceptually, however, Neil located 'Aboriginal' as 'probably' – or maybe ideally – 'under a big umbrella of multicultural'.

Neil's deputy, Reg, expressed a similar view, saying he thought the separation between Aboriginal education and multicultural education was 'not really right' because 'the word says it, "multi" – many cultures' (including Indigenous). However, he also saw multicultural education very much in terms of the ethnicity of children at a particular school, and the *numbers* of each 'ethnicity'. Thus multicultural education at Hillview High 'tended to be the influx of the African students', he said, adding:

'Now there are some of these other ones . . . the Burmese, Thailand, that sort of thing, Chinese, [but] there's not many of them.' The school tried to 'cater for what we have', Reg explained, offering the following example of how he believed that was done:

> I'm sure our teachers make a lot of allowances in their classes in what they're talking and the way they're teaching for an Aboriginal perspective on things. They're then trying now to make a consciously African perspective. . . . I bet if a Chinese student is sitting in the class, they [the teachers] are not making a Chinese perspective as forcefully as the other two because, 'oh, I didn't realize I had that one', you know?

Some doubt must be cast on Reg's account of Hillview High teachers routinely incorporating multiple perspectives into their lessons: the weight of interview data suggested this was not standard practice at the school. By prefacing his comments with 'I'm sure' and 'I bet', however, Reg avoids any claims to truth. Instead, there is a conflation of perceptions of how things should be (or perceptions of how, as the interviewer and researcher, I might think they should be) with how they presently are, pointing to a desire to be seen as responding 'correctly' to diversity. At the same time, Reg's tendency to see difference through an ethnic/racial lens leads him to homogenize the people he assigns to discrete ethnoracial groups into singular cultural entities – hence '*an* Aboriginal perspective', '*a* Chinese perspective'. Such singular perspectives clearly make no sense given the ethnic, cultural, linguistic and religious heterogeneity within groups named as 'Aboriginal', 'African', 'Chinese' and so on. More importantly in terms of social and educational consequences, such homogenizing of cultural 'others' denies their individuality and even agency: the non-Anglo students are constructed as objects to be 'accommodated' within existing White intellectual, communicative and physical spaces (Hage, 2000), making them more likely to be seen as 'problems' than as potentially enriching teaching and learning resources. The objectification of the non-Anglo students is also reflected in and produced by phrases such as 'some of *these other ones*', 'that sort of *thing*' and 'I didn't realize I had *that one*', further stripping them of individuality, identity and agency and therefore of legitimacy – at least in a mostly White town like Easthaven. Thus a practice that Reg presents as inclusive – incorporating non-European perspectives into the curriculum – may in effect be more marginalizing for the small numbers of 'other' students because of the way they are positioned within the community.

Strikingly, both Neil's and Reg's responses appear to reflect a view of multicultural education and Aboriginal education as about 'the other' (Walton et al., 2016). This is consistent with multicultural education's beginnings as education for migrants (Inglis, 2009), and also with the understandings and usages of terms such as 'multicultural' and 'culturally diverse' documented in earlier chapters. Reg confirmed this conceptualization of multicultural education when he spoke of it as, until recently, 'not relevant to us in our school . . . not relevant to where we live'. But 'need promotes it [multicultural education]', he said, and 'since we've got a lot more of them [LBOTE students] in, it's made people have to understand it more. [. . .] And as we get more multicultural, it'll be easier.' Again, this conceptualization of multicultural education as relevant only to schools with large numbers of non-Anglo students is contrary to NSW

DoE directives that its diversity-related policies apply to all students in all schools, regardless of schools' demographic composition. Reg's perspective was no doubt influenced by the fact he had taught in mostly White regional schools and had done his teacher training when multicultural education *was* essentially migrant education. The name remains the same as it was then – that is, 'multicultural education' – and this perhaps makes it easier to overlook that the objectives, audience and applicability, context, responsibilities and delegations, and monitoring, evaluation and reporting requirements (NSW DoE, 2016c) associated with this field have altered markedly.

Two other segments of the comments merit attention. The first is the comment that the increased cultural diversity at Hillview High had '*made* people *have to* understand it more', suggesting a sense of being imposed upon and concerns about loss of (White) power. At the same time, Reg appeared always conscious that to express such concerns, or to be seen as not embracing multiculturalism, might not be socially or professionally acceptable. A few sentences later he said, in a rather confused qualification: 'When I say "have to", you don't have to because someone's forcing you; you should have to, or want to have to, because you want to make people tolerant of each other and understand each other.' Reg knows the 'right' words to use, including 'tolerant' and 'understand'. There is still a sense of force here, however, in 'because you want *to make* people tolerant', belying a fundamental unease – 'white worrying' (Hage, 2000) – about the impacts of diversity on social relations. As McLeod and Yates (2003) note, knowing 'the right way to speak . . . is not necessarily evidence of a transformation in 'commonsense' and habitual political thinking and orientation' (p. 34). 'Have to' was a phrase that was used frequently in this interview, suggesting broader anxieties about a changing world reminiscent of Seaview High staff member Rita's comment that 'I'm afraid . . . I don't live in the [present] . . . It'd be nice for things to slow down'. Such fears may be understandable among older Australians who have lived in rural and regional areas for most of their lives (which is not to assume that all older rural residents feel this way). The important point is that while negative affects are not 'racist', they can nonetheless prompt and permit practices that *are* racializing and discriminatory, with potentially significant impacts in schools.

The second text segment is the comment that 'as we get more multicultural, it'll be easier'. Despite the challenges of the changes at Hillview High, Reg was proud of how the school had responded. Multiculturalism was promoted 'all the time' at assemblies, he said, explaining that 'we get them doing dance – Africans, Aboriginals, they get up and do different dances. And everyone sits there and appreciates it'. In fact, he said, 'I'd like to see us celebrate *more* cultures'. Here again, creating space at assemblies for African-background and Aboriginal students to perform for the school is presented as 'promoting multiculturalism' and being inclusive. So it may be – but the language used reveals the sort of power imbalance that is inherent in prevailing discourses of tolerance: 'we', the tolerators, 'get them', the tolerated, 'doing dance . . . And everyone sits there and appreciates it'. As with the opening account of Multicultural Day at Seaview High, there is a sense of the 'spectacle' and the spectators – who know that they are expected to value such displays. From other interviews and observations at the assemblies I attended, it seemed there *was* widespread appreciation of the ESL students' performances. However, there was no evidence in this deputy's comments of an understanding of multicultural education as extending beyond recognition and appreciation of 'other cultures' – no concept, for instance, of the equity and antiracism objectives of multicultural and Aboriginal education (NSW DoE, 2016c), but an assumption that things will get 'easier' (for whom?) as diversity becomes more 'normal' in Easthaven and its schools.

By contrast, Hillview High's other deputy, Vince, was emphatic about the need for a stronger focus on equity and for reform of institutional practices. As someone who saw himself as an outsider – ethnically as 'an Italian', culturally as a maverick, and also as a relative newcomer to the school – Vince was sceptical not only about his colleagues' level of understanding of diversity policies but whether they even knew they existed. He related how he 'couldn't even find the Aboriginal education policy in the school ... I can't find the document [*laughs*]. So who do you reckon has looked at it and read it? Hasn't happened! [*laughs*]'. His laughter had a ridiculing tone, consistent with comments he made elsewhere in the interview about schools (and institutions in general) only paying 'lip service' to policies, and policies simply being 'things on paper to make politicians and educational bureaucrats look good'. He believed these bureaucrats had little grasp of the day-to-day realities of schools, particularly in country areas where attitudes, expectations, experiences, resources, priorities and practices were very different from those in city schools and departmental head offices. He added:

> It's like the old boss who used to be here ... said: 'If the department [NSW DoE] has done it, guaranteed it'll stuff up.' Because when you've been in the system that long, you pick out the fads and this [multiculturalism] is a fad, to me it's a fad.

Vince's use of the word 'fad' to describe a forty-year-old policy – one that has long had state as well as federal bipartisan support and been promoted as central to national identity – is noteworthy. From other comments made by Vince, it seems his Italian background and identity had shaped his view of 'Australian multiculturalism' as something mostly play-acted by a still-culturally very Anglo nation, in contrast to the more organic and 'lived' reality of centuries-old diversity in places like Europe.

While I did not ask school leaders and teachers if they had read the NSW DoE's diversity-related policies, research indicates that lack of policy familiarity is not unusual. Watkins et al. (2013) found that almost 40 per cent of executive non-teaching staff in NSW schools reported having either not implemented the NSW DoE's *Multicultural Education Policy* or not knowing whether they had done so. However, there may also be a particular 'rural' dimension to the lack of policy knowledge of staff in Easthaven's schools, reflecting a view of multiculturalism as something imposed by city types/progressives/bureaucrats/idealists on country types/ conservatives/practitioners/realists. Certainly there were suggestions in other interviews – echoing broader media and popular discourses – about a disconnect between 'Macquarie Street' (the NSW parliament) and 'the bush' in terms of decision-making, policy-making, funding and resourcing. Cowlishaw (2004b), for example, reports a 'startling' (her word) finding from her study in the NSW country town of Bourke: that many Murri (the self-description used by local people who identified as Aboriginal) expressed support or even a liking for Pauline Hanson, a federal politician widely criticized in the national capital and other cities for her racist comments about 'Aboriginals' (Hanson's preferred term) and immigrants from Asia. But '[r]ural Aborigines found her language familiar, and appreciated her attacks on urban elites and misdirected or misused spending by governments' (Cowlishaw, 2004b, p. 65). In other words, at this particular time and in this particular place, the Murris' rural or anti-urban subjectivity appears to be dominant over their Indigenous/vilified minority subjectivity. The potential strength of rural identities is noted also by Holloway (2007, p.15) in a study in rural England, where some villagers decried the actions of '[outsider] busybodies with no understanding of [local] traditions' after a particular incident. In the same way, rural identities constructed in opposition to perceived urban identities may be a stronger influence on some long-term regional teachers' everyday practices than their professional identity, engendering a generalized pro-local/anti-Bridge Street (the DoE's head office) orientation.

Seaview High School Leaders' Perspectives and Accounts of Practice

Whereas Neil, Reg and Vince appeared to have divergent perspectives on multicultural and Aboriginal education, the executive at Seaview High seemed more closely aligned in their perspectives. Deputy principal Stephanie described the goals of multicultural education as 'those old-fashioned words of harmony and peace and respect and tolerance' – words that are foregrounded in official diversity discourses. Overall, the approach to diversity was quite assimilationist (although that word was never used) – for example, William, the other deputy, said one aspect of multicultural education was 'integrating . . . kids from another culture into the Australian culture'. Another aspect, he said, was 'awareness raising for the students and their families of different cultures and the importance of working together' – 'awareness raising' being one of the reported rationales for the school's Multicultural Day. Principal Sally saw common ground between the school's LBOTE and Aboriginal students in that 'you've got two groups who . . . have historically not been achieving potential'; the priority, therefore, was 'trying to make sure that they've got equality of opportunity'. Her focus on 'equality of opportunity' differs from the NSW DoE *Multicultural Education Policy*'s objective of 'providing *opportunities* that enable all students to achieve equitable education and social *outcomes*' (NSW DoE, 2016c, overarching objective; emphasis added) – that is, equality of outcomes rather than opportunities. I return to this point shortly.

In contrast to Neil's and Reg's perspective at Hillview High, Lois, another member of the executive at Seaview, was adamant that Aboriginal education and multicultural education needed to be separate. This view, she said, had been shaped by 'a very simple story' related to her by an Indigenous friend:

> She said to me one day: 'It was all right for you buggers to come in, take over our country, dispossess us. But then you open the doors and say, "Hey, everyone else

can come in!"'. And she told me that's the heart of the issue for them [Indigenous Australians], that no one ever consulted with them.

Brody, also a member of the executive, saw land and power as central issues as well:

> Aboriginal culture, as far as I know, has its specific needs, which is acknowledging ownership of the land, whereas multiculturalism is acknowledging an acceptance to *be* in that land, of which we're part of [*sic*]. Anglo – the dominant culture ... tends to dictate, I think, a sense of marginalization for other cultures ... that marginalization comes from a [Anglo-constructed] hierarchy which says, '*We're* marginalizing *you*'.

In both of these perspectives there is recognition that multiculturalism may not be of equal benefit to all Australians and that there is, within the nation's diversity, an ethnic and cultural group that still 'dictates' the terms and conditions of others' 'acceptance'; moreover, that this was not commonly acknowledged, and needed to be if reconciliation and equity objectives were to be met.

The capability of intercultural understanding, meanwhile, appeared to have received very little consideration at either school – not surprising, given the convoluted development of the national curriculum (Adoniou et al., 2015) and its phased implementation across learning areas and jurisdictions (ACARA, 2014). At Seaview High, deputy principal Stephanie said developing intercultural understanding in the school's students was 'going to be a big challenge because we're up against traditional family values and experiences and we've got a very, very crowded curriculum'. Teacher Lois deemed the capability 'just ... a new name for something we've been doing forever', while principal Sally said it was something 'I haven't even begun to think about!'. At Hillview High, Deputy Reg said he thought the best way to develop intercultural understanding in students was 'having many cultures in the school', while sometime Deputy Winsome said it was about 'being able to say, "Did you celebrate ... such-and-such?" or talk about the food they're eating'. Overall, there appeared to be a level of assumption about what the capability encompassed ('something we've been doing forever') despite a lack of familiarity with the ACARA documentation, and a dominant view of intercultural understanding as essentially about Anglo-background students becoming more knowledgeable about and appreciative of non-Anglo students. Absent here is an emphasis on what ACARA in fact foregrounds, which is students 'learning to value and view critically their own cultural perspectives and practices and those of others through their interactions with people, texts and contexts across the curriculum' (ACARA, n.d.). In addition to a continuing preoccupation with 'others' and a simultaneous lack of focus on Whiteness (as the ethnic and cultural majority in Australia and Easthaven), the school leaders' comments do not point to whole-school efforts to promote critical thinking about culture and difference ('... view critically ... ') or, indeed, actively promote cross-cultural 'interactions'.

Teachers' Perspectives and Accounts of Practice

While school leaders' perspectives on diversity-related policies are important in setting priorities and establishing programmes, it is teachers who translate policies and priorities into practice, within classrooms and in their extracurricular involvements. At Hillview High, for example, teacher Sharon not only taught ESL but co-supervised an after-school homework club set up to provide extra assistance for refugee-background students. She was also a lead organizer of multicultural events such as Harmony Day and of community outreach initiatives. Sharon characterized multicultural education as 'trying to be an inclusive school for everyone – and that means not just doing things for ESL kids but getting other kids to understand and appreciate each other's differences, similarities, that kind of thing' – a perspective much closer to the NSW DoE policy than some of the views presented above. However, funding, administrative and social factors often made it difficult to foster that inclusiveness, Sharon said, citing the homework club:

> [It's] funded for ESL students, but it seems very separatist then. . . . I've had other people saying, 'Well, can other kids come? And what about Aboriginal kids, can we run at the same time?' And I say, 'Well, that would be wonderful, but when they did a homework club for Aboriginal kids, not many kids came anyway. And they're *less* likely to come if there's twenty ESL kids because it's gonna be *more* intimidating for them'. . . . Ideally it would be lovely to have an inclusive homework club for everyone . . . if the funding [could be] more across the board, [for] disadvantaged kids, as opposed to ESL, Aboriginal.

For Sharon, the separation between multicultural education and Aboriginal education was not just theoretically problematic but had adverse practical consequences in schools. Rather than educational need, access to homework help was based on funding tied to ethnic and cultural categorizations. Decisions made at a state level may 'hit the ground' in awkward ways: policy-linked structures that are outside the control of individual teachers and schools can have unintended corollary effects, such as creating or reinforcing localized ethnic and social divisions, and fostering resentments among some students about the 'special treatment' afforded to minority cohorts.

ESL Tuition

Both principals reported resentments among some teachers, in this case about the impact of ESL students on their classes. The teachers' irritation related primarily to the way in which English was taught to the schools' refugee-background students, the principals said. In metropolitan centres, refugee-background teenagers typically attend Intensive English Centres (IECs) for up to four terms before entering mainstream high school (Watkins et al., 2019). While IECs may take students a long way towards oral proficiency, research indicates that developing proficiency in academic English takes far longer – up to seven years (Watkins et al., 2019), and often considerably more in the case of adolescents with little or no formal schooling prior to their resettlement (Miller et al., 2005; NSW DoE, 2014). These students often face other significant barriers to learning, including affective and cognitive impairments associated with trauma, family stresses and financial hardships (NSW DoE, 2014).

In regional Easthaven the numbers of refugee-background students were too low for an IEC; children instead went straight into normal classes and were taken out for periods of ESL tuition. At Hillview High, Neil said 'a very small number' of teachers had resisted ESL students being withdrawn from their classes to attend ESL classes – even though becoming proficient in English was vital for these students' educational and social participation ('Unless they get their English and literacy scores up to speed, they are not going to be learning anything anyway' – Neil). These teachers – many of whom had taught at the school for decades, well before students from Africa, Southeast Asia and the Middle East began arriving – may not have been unsympathetic to the newcomers' needs, but rather unused to such disruptions and neither prepared or equipped to deal with them (Dobinson & Buchori, 2016; Miller et al., 2005). The practice of withdrawing ESL students from class had become an issue at Seaview High as well, principal Sally said, although in a different way. Her argument for leaving the ESL students in mainstream classes rather than withdrawing them was that 'that gives teachers ownership of the teaching ... [I]f the ESL teachers are taking on too much ... the [other] teachers can tend to say "not my problem, not my student".'

How ESL instruction is best delivered is clearly a complex issue (Morrison, 2014; Premier & Miller, 2010). While withdrawing ESL students from mainstream classes may be more necessary in regional contexts given the lack of IECs, this practice may help to mark these students as more 'different' and reinforce their social isolation. On the other hand, an 'integration' approach would have left Seaview High and Hillview High classroom teachers having to deal with refugee-background students who had virtually no English and little formal schooling before coming to Australia. The majority of these teachers had minimal or no training in teaching ESL, let alone teaching English to students with other complex learning and wellbeing needs. Practices such as collaboration and team teaching between ESL and mainstream teachers, reported to be both popular and effective in facilitating English language learning (Premier & Miller, 2010), were only just 'starting to happen' at Seaview High, principal Sally said, noting that these practices had been routine at the metropolitan schools where she had taught).

Certainly there was agreement at the schools that anything to do with 'cultural diversity' was the ESL teachers' domain. Even whole-school events such as Harmony Day and NAIDOC Week were mostly regarded as, respectively, the responsibility of the ESL and Aboriginal support staff. This stance reflects one of the factors that Neal (2002) argues distinguish diversity-related practices in rural areas from those in urban areas – that is, that 'raising issues and developing appropriate racial equality strategies' (p. 457), among other multicultural initiatives, tend to be driven by a few individuals rather than occurring at a whole-organization level.

Reflecting this tendency, take-up of diversity-related professional development opportunities was generally low, according to the ESL staff at Hillview High. One of the ESL teachers, Roslyn, perceived that there was in some cases an active racist and resistant aspect to this non-participation:

> Some of them [the mainstream teachers] are really open to [recognizing] that there is these cultural differences and they want to learn more. [But] some of them

couldn't care less. . . . The first lot of students that came in were from Sudan. And now you will *still* hear [a decade later] teachers that just say, 'Oh, those Sudanese students, in that class.' And I say, 'Well, there's actually *no* Sudanese; there's Congolese and there's Togolese' . . . . So therefore they're not interested in the best way to help [those] students, either.

Roslyn's comment about the frequent homogenizing of African-background Easthaveners into 'Sudanese', within and beyond the school, highlights points made about lumping (Zerubavel, 1996), misrecognition, objectification and indifference as subtle practices of unbelonging (Edgeworth, 2014). The exclusionary power of such practices depends in part on their subtlety – their mundaneness and ubiquity. By declining (according to Roslyn) to find out about students' backgrounds, participate in professional development and adapt their pedagogy, these 'resistant' teachers are denying their refugee-background students recognition as individuals and legitimate 'Hillview High students', and obstructing their access to full academic and social participation. I do not suggest that such consequences are inevitable (teachers are only one influence on inclusion and belonging), nor do I suggest that teachers *intend* their practices to have inequitable consequences; rather, that racist attitudes towards (some) other-than-Anglo Australians combined with beliefs in White superiority allow the continuation of practices that potentially *end up* being discriminatory.

A final point relates to how and where the ESL students were typically placed upon enrolment. Like withdrawal/integration, this is a complex area, particularly in the case of refugee-background adolescents. Three interconnected issues are of interest here. One, raised by Hillview High ESL teacher Sharon, was the difficulty of sourcing beginner-level English language texts that were age-appropriate for teenagers, and also texts that were culturally appropriate for people from non-European backgrounds. A second issue mentioned by several staff was administrative and social imperatives for placing students in a year group appropriate for their age, even though educationally many of the refugee-background students were far from ready to join these classes. Because of this, the refugee-background students – at Hillview High at least – were routinely placed in the bottom classes, where the lesson content, structure and pace were in theory easier for them. However, this led to a third issue related to intersections of ethnicity, culture, class and gender: these classes tended to be dominated by students from highly dysfunctional families – many of them products of intergenerational poverty, many Aboriginal and most of them boys. These students had significant social and learning problems and were 'not necessarily accepting of other cultures. So therefore there is name calling and bullying in those classes', ESL teacher Roslyn said. She added: 'If a teacher says "OK, get yourselves into groups of three", the ESL kids will usually get left out. So there's that subtle form of bullying [as well] . . . just that subtle, underlying "well, we're not working with them" sort of thing.'

Georgie, a young history and English teacher, reported pronounced differences in attitude and ability between the top and bottom classes at Hillview High. 'I'll have a discussion with my top Year 8 . . . history class and then I'll have the same discussion with the bottom: polar opposites in their regards [attitudes] to different cultures and races . . . what they think and perceive is very different.' She said cultural perspectives and practices 'comes up a lot in history... [I] ask them questions and challenge their ideas and their perceptions and put them into roles.... Some of them [in the lower classes are] very, very, very, *very* stubborn and will refuse to even look at another person's perspective'.

Again, Roslyn's and Georgie's comments highlight the exclusionary consequences of an array of practices – some of which were no doubt intended to marginalize (such as 'name calling and bullying'), but most of which would not have been, such as placing the refugee-background students in lower-level classes and allowing classmates to arrange themselves into groups for activities. The non-refugee-background students in these classes probably had friendships and habits of interaction developed through years of schooling together; equally, lack of 'practice' at cross-cultural engagement and perspective-taking is likely to have been a factor in the dynamics outlined. There is a logic to the decision to place the ESL students in the lower streams, but localized sociocultural factors mean that this may not have been in the best academic and social interests of these students. An alternative approach would be to place ESL students in the upper classes, where their peers might be more accepting, the newcomers would be exposed more to Standard Australian English and teachers might have time to give them more attention than in the already highly demanding bottom classes. Indeed, Roslyn said that in her experience the results *were* much better when the ESL students were placed in the top classes – 'but unfortunately we can't get them in there'.

Aboriginal Education

Hillview High and Seaview High had had Aboriginal children for decades – far longer than they had had recognized ESL students – but the size of these cohorts had historically been small and 'Aboriginal education', as a concept and an endeavour, had received little attention. In recent years, however, the number of students identifying as Aboriginal had roughly doubled at both schools, and Aboriginal education had become a priority area in terms of curriculum, staffing, attendance, retention rates and academic achievement. The relationship between these two developments – the stronger focus on Aboriginal education and the surge in Aboriginal enrolments – was unclear: according to Hillview High deputy Vince, the 'Aboriginal population hasn't all of a sudden blossomed' but rather students were 'starting to... feel that there are people in the school... who support them and want to help them achieve', and so were more willing to publicly identify as Aboriginal. Small changes, such as having Aboriginal students do acknowledgement of country at school assemblies (rather than the school captain), had also promoted a stronger sense of inclusion and engagement, Vince said. A similar perspective was voiced by Gary, one of the Aboriginal support staff at Seaview High.

Notwithstanding these changes, Hillview High AEO Kai said the attitudes and practices of many of the teachers were 'still the same' as when he had been educated there twenty years earlier. Many staff knew little about Indigenous histories and cultures (including those of the local Aboriginal people), he said, but also had little interest in knowing more; they did not 'have an open mind'. Providing some corroboration for this was a 2010 external review of Aboriginal education at the school, in which the executive, Aboriginal parents and students and staff themselves identified low staff awareness of the local Aboriginal culture and community as a barrier to improving outcomes for Hillview High's Aboriginal students. Teachers were generally caring, the report found – but the school's Aboriginal students continued to stand out for their overrepresentation in the bottom bands in NAPLAN tests, significantly lower attendance rates, and HSC completion rates less than half those for non-Aboriginal students. Aboriginal parents and students also identified low teacher expectations of Aboriginal students as an issue and expressed a strong desire for incorporation of Aboriginal perspectives across the curriculum. Consistent with the points raised above, staff identified a need for better teamwork among the executive and greater knowledge of Aboriginal education and antiracism policies.

As touched on in Chapter 4, Kai and his counterpart at Seaview High, Gary, had very different ideas about the objectives of Aboriginal education – and, for that matter, about 'culture'. Culture, for Gary, was 'family, background, identifying, being part of the community'. Considerable effort had been put into training Seaview High staff in cultural awareness and increasing engagement with Aboriginal parents and elders, he said. One important aspect was persuading parents that things had changed at schools and that there was more flexibility and 'respect' (his word) for students who identified as Aboriginal than when they (the parents) had gone to school. 'And if we change their [parents'] attitude and change the students' . . . the students will develop and succeed.' Success to him was Aboriginal students holding leadership positions within the school, and being able to 'step out of that Indigenous side and . . . into the mainstream'. That capacity, he argued, was crucial to both individual prosperity and wellbeing and the collective advancement of Indigenous Australians. One had to be within the system to change it.

Kai, on the other hand, spoke of culture as 'deep within [a person] . . . in their blood . . . in their stomach . . . in their heart'. To him, Aboriginal education was about making Aboriginal students 'proud' (a word he used repeatedly) by 'reawakening them' – teaching them the local Aboriginal language, taking them on 'bush tucker[1] walks', showing them the local sacred sites and so on. 'Fair enough, we do the normal curriculum stuff', he said. 'But if you wanna engage the students, you gotta get back to culture.' In contrast to Gary, who barely mentioned his background and cultural identity, Kai spoke at length about the history and geography of the area and his spiritual connection with it: 'I'm a saltwater person . . . shown all those old ways of how to get food and to live off the ocean . . . from my father. And I know the bush, the trees, the earth, the animals, everything.' This was what he saw as 'missing' in his students' lives. Here, then, the educational emphasis is on emotion and the revitalization of some assumed 'authentic' self; as argued in Chapter 4, if 'loss of culture' (through dispossession, forced assimilation, language extinction and so on) is seen as the problem, then 'restoration of culture' is likely to be seen as the solution.

While acknowledging local cultural narratives and practices is clearly important for Aboriginal Easthaveners from both a knowledge and affective perspective, a focus on this at the expense of 'normal curriculum stuff' will do little to tackle the 'locked-in inequality' (Gillborn, 2008) that is the legacy of the history of Anglo-Indigenous relations in Australia (Ford, 2013). According to Vince, a sizeable proportion of

Aboriginal parents at Hillview High had left school before they were fifteen, were semi-literate at best and had never had a job. In some cases they had grown up speaking local Aboriginal languages or creoles at home but had never been recognized in the education system as ESL students, and so had not received the language learning support they needed for academic success (Lingard et al., 2012; Nakata, 2000). Their capacity to help their children with schoolwork was therefore often extremely limited – making the school's role in breaking the cycle of disadvantage even more important. Hillview High's awareness of this was reflected in new practices such as creating personalized learning plans (PLPs) to increase Aboriginal parents' and carers' engagement in their children's education, and thus (it was hoped) lift the attendance rates, retention rates and academic results of Aboriginal students.

However, such efforts were countered by lack of change in other areas. Communications with parents and carers at both schools, for instance, were via typed letters (in English) sent home with students. This is a fairly standard practice in Australian schools and in keeping with the cultural norms of White, middle-class families, but potentially exclusionary of families from non-Anglo backgrounds. As Vince commented:

We don't branch out and try and reach them [non-Anglo families] by a phone call or talking [directly] to the parent. [The attitude is] just, 'yeah, I've let the kid know, letter's gone home' ... So it's almost like a negligent duty of care that we [the staff] treat our kids [students] ... like they're the same as us.

Parent Eddie, a refugee from Burundi, recounted his experience of this practice at Seaview High: 'Yes, they send some letter sometimes to explain. ... [But] you can't send me a big letter, one or two pages, in English, and thinking that I'll read it ... I understand maybe 10 words out of 200.' He said of the school 'they don't try hard', adding: 'It is then [when he cannot read the letter] we feel a bit discouraged.' A tendency to treat students and families 'like they're the same as us' is likely to be exaggerated in regional schools where almost all of the staff and a large majority of the students are from Anglo backgrounds; historically, with Aboriginal students expected to assimilate and with very few non-English-speaking immigrants, there would have been little (perceived) reason not to treat them so.

As noted, there are multiple theoretical and practical tensions between the objectives of diversity-related and education policies. This is one factor in the challenges of balancing Aboriginal education objectives including 'improving the educational outcomes and wellbeing of Aboriginal and Torres Strait Islander students' (NSW DoE, 2016a), 'increasing knowledge and understanding of the histories, cultures and experiences' of Indigenous Australians (NSW DoE, 2016a) and 'incorporat[ing] the cultural contexts, values and practices of local Aboriginal communities into the mainstream delivery of education' (NSW DoE, 2016a) against each other and myriad other educational objectives. However, a necessary starting point is recognizing these challenges' basis in conceptualizations of Indigenous knowledges as inferior or at least antithetical to Western knowledges. Just like Black/White ethnic and identity divisions, such conceptualizations militate against an approach that neither devalues nor valorizes Indigenous knowledges and practices (Cowlishaw, 2004b) but rather looks to 'entanglements, synergies', and the conditions under which knowledges and practices developed and remain useful: knowledge not as a 'contest' but as a 'site for extending inquiry, thinking, and problem-solving' (Nakata, 2010, pp. 55–56).

Equality, Equity

Ideas about equality, equity, merit and fairness were explicit or implicit in many of the interviews conducted for this study. Some school leaders and teachers spoke of schools as having a crucial role in tackling social and economic disadvantage, while others put greater emphasis on schools producing 'nice young adolescents' who 'feel that they've achieved something' – not that these are mutually exclusive. Interviewees' comments also indicated that there were significant differences in their conceptualizations of equality. The fact that Aboriginal and refugee-background students received extra assistance and participated in 'special' programmes and activities, for example, was seen as unjust by some students, parents and staff (see Chapter 5). Year 11 Hillview High student Kyla was one interviewee to voice suspicions about government largesse to refugees, saying: 'I know that they haven't got any money and stuff, but don't they get, like, a huge, huge payout as soon as they get here? That's what I've heard, anyway.'

Comments about 'huge payouts', getting 'things for free' and so on echo political and media discourses about the unearned privileges that Indigenous and refugee-background Australians enjoy under Aboriginal and multicultural policies (Buckmaster, 2012; Clarke, 2016). Such discourses have long been, and continue to be, deployed to deny White racism, to deny unearned *White* privilege, and to claim 'reverse racism' (i.e. that White people have become victims of equality measures). All of these discourses involve a double strategy of positive self-presentation (Whites knowing the right way to do things, Whites' benevolence) and negative other-presentation (others not valuing what they are given, others choosing not to learn) (van Dijk, 1992) – a strategy that can be used (not necessarily consciously) to justify White people's resentments and criticisms of ethnic and cultural others, thereby forestalling efforts to tackle racialized disadvantage and preserving White advantage. At a macro level, such discourses may be used to validate cutbacks in social justice programmes. At a local or interpersonal level, they may facilitate a continuation of practices that are in effect (if not intention) exclusionary, such as schools communicating only in written English or ethnic separations in classroom and playground activities. Thus Year 11 Hillview High student Zoe (Anglo-Australian), while she said it was 'good having diversity in Australia', thought it would be better 'if it was more equal', such as 'not giving free scholarships to Aboriginal people – like, making them actually *work* for it instead of just giving them out'. Zoe's comments suggest she does not, in fact, believe that diversity is altogether good because of the 'inequalities' diversity-related policies and programmes allow – hardly 'a strength and an asset'.

According to Hillview High deputy Vince, many teachers had misconceptions about equality/equity as well:

People see equal opportunity as being equal value for money, whereas equal opportunity to a kid who is struggling might mean you've got to give them $10 whereas to another kid who's not struggling can do with $2. So equal opportunity . . . isn't about being equal. It's about [bringing them] up to the same level. And a lot of staff don't understand that.

Seaview High teacher Brody expressed a similar view, saying it was part of the school's welfare and discipline policy that 'everyone's treated equally as best as we can'. But, he added, 'I always say to . . . the students: "I won't treat you equally, I will treat you individually." Because we're not the same.'

Understandings of equality as 'equal treatment' in part reflect the influence of dominant neoliberal discourses that attribute 'success' to hard work and talent, and 'failure' to a lack of these, particularly of effort. Certainly the importance of individual effort was a message heard repeatedly at Hillview High – including, at an awards ceremony, phrases such as 'Success is inside ourselves', 'No matter who you are, if you just get in there, you'll be rewarded' and 'Effort is everything!'; and, during a reading activity, from the librarian: 'People who can read well do well in exams. People who do well in exams have lifestyle choices – they're the ones who get better jobs and get to go on good holidays.' Through this discourse, poor outcomes and disadvantages are not only individualized but dehistoricized and depoliticized, making *structural* factors easier to ignore. Following Crenshaw's (1988) distinction between equality as a result and equality as a process, 'treating students the same' is an enactment of the latter understanding and does not direct attention to differential outcomes; whereas bringing students 'up to the same level' – which may require spending $10 on one child and only $2 on another – is an enactment of the former, outcomes-focused perspective.

This distinction is illustrated by an account of a conversation deputy principal Vince said he had recently had with a senior teacher transferred to Hillview High from another school. '[The teacher] said: "There's something wrong with the kids [here] because I've always taught this way and I've always got good results . . . [T]his is the best way of teaching. It's just that [these] kids are dumber."' Here the students are constructed as the problem if they do not achieve the expected results – because they are 'dumber', or do not have the right attitude or work ethic. Thus broader discourses about equality and meritocracy may amplify the construction of people from non-Anglo backgrounds as deficient (intellectually, socially, culturally, morally), disruptive (of schools' and teachers' normal practices) and the cause of division and disaffection. In localized practice, then, policies and programmes designed to promote 'equality' can wind up entrenching rather than reducing differences and disadvantage.

Inside the Classroom

Accounts of Teacher Practices

The executive at both schools said some staff were less 'tolerant' (Hillview High principal Neil) towards non-Anglo students than they might have been, as noted.

Further, the relatively low numbers of non-Anglo students made it easier for teachers to 'get away with', or think they could get away with, teaching only to an assumed White, middle-class norm (i.e. similar to their own background). Teachers in high-LBOTE metropolitan schools had to adapt their teaching style to cater for the diversity of students, Neil said, 'or you're not going to survive'. In mostly White Easthaven, however, 'a lot of the teachers can get by, by not changing their teaching styles and just catering for that White Australian, White Anglo-Saxon background'.

A case in point might be Neil's deputy Reg, who insisted he saw all Hillview High students as 'just average kids . . . they're all the same'. A former maths teacher, Reg explained his approach:

> When . . . I'm teaching them something in maths – it's a corny line, but in my head I think quite often it doesn't matter what colour you are, what sex you are, where you come from, I'm teaching you about a triangle; we're doing that. The other stuff's left behind; we're just doing this [learning about triangles].

Such an approach ties in with a view of education as socially and culturally neutral – a passing on by teacher to student of objective and useful 'facts' about the world. A triangle is seen as just such a 'fact' (even though it is a construct), and learning about triangles as completely separate from 'other stuff' such as a student's educational, cultural or linguistic background.

A different perspective came from Roslyn, also a former maths teacher but now one of the ESL teachers at Hillview High. Talking about working with the refugee-background students, she said:

> In mathematics, when you're learning the different shapes – square, rectangle, whatever – you always then get up to octagon. And for Australian children that's easy. They've grown up – even though most children have never seen an octopus, they know what an octopus is, they would've seen children's pictures of them, and that's easy: eight legs. But with these refugee children, they've got no idea what an octopus is. . . . So you can't link that in. So you've got to find something [else] to link [the concept] into.

The need for flexible thinking and methods on the part of teachers applied equally to assessment practices, deputy Vince pointed out:

> [W]ith Aboriginal kids . . . if you test them a different way than the Anglo way with pen and paper, the kids will do well. But to put them on a pen and paper NAPLAN[2] [test], they know they're not going to do well and they *don't* do well. And some of them will even purposely not do well because it's easier not to answer; you can't get it wrong if you don't answer it. It's a stigma that you have, that you're dumber, and it's really hard to break that. . . . You don't believe in yourself, that you're capable.

Here Vince recognizes that there are differences in attitudes towards school learning and performance, and that these need to be taken into account if equitable outcomes are to be achieved. However, his comments also suggest a danger of essentializing – of assuming that 'Aboriginal' students (all of them) prefer and perform better under a 'different way than the Anglo way', and that all Aboriginal students see themselves as less 'capable' and lack confidence.

Together, these examples illustrate the need to question assumptions about the effectiveness and equity of education systems – to pay close attention instead to the intersections between categories of difference (including ethnicity and culture), hegemonic knowledges and practices, and social and educational outcomes. It is important also to consider how teachers see themselves, their role and the role of schools in the lives of children and society more generally. Not surprisingly, Reg described himself as 'very practical, I'm not into theory', whereas Vince presented himself as 'an innovator. I want to bring improvement. And every time you try to bring improvement you get resistance'. That 'resistance' was partly a product of many teachers' age and long tenure at the school, according to Vince, but also reflective of what he identified as a broader problem in education – namely, the lack of mandatory professional development for teachers:[3]

> If you're a doctor or an accountant, you've got to keep up with the times, but in teaching it's not required. You got your degree thirty, forty years ago, and for a lot of people, other than a bit of in-service [training], that's it.

The sorts of in-service training mentioned by staff at Hillview High and Seaview High included Aboriginal cultural awareness, working with refugee families, a STARTTS[4] training session and PBL (Positive Behaviour for Learning) – all relevant to the school's student population, but representing more of a piecemeal selection than a coherent professional development programme. The schools' regional location, access to resources and timetabling factors were said to make it difficult to do anything substantial (longer than half a day, for example). Further, Vince said, training was typically scheduled for school development days at the end of the term: 'And it's useless. Everybody is exhausted.' Teaching is demanding and often stressful work, and teacher burnout is a recognized phenomenon (Matthews, 2008). Nonetheless, the comments above highlight a range of issues relating to teaching practices that warrant discussion. The first links to discourses outlined in the previous chapter about its being 'natural' for people to fear change. What these discourses do is make it 'natural' to *resist* change (Reg said he thought that that was 'human nature') – for teachers, for instance, not to reflect on or modify their teaching practices, not to think beyond the classroom, not to take up professional development opportunities. Such discourses may also make it 'natural' to *resent having to change*, adding an affective element to resistances to alternative perceptions, interpretations and possibilities for action. Hillview High deputy Vince thought there was a particular Easthaven 'cultural thing' – what he called a 'syndrome', characterized as 'very holiday-like, very Aussie, "she'll be fine"' – that might account for a lack of effort on the part of some teachers, rather than active resistance to change. Comparing the region's schools with metropolitan schools he had taught at, he said:

> We don't have that hunger [for excellence] here. . . . [And] a lot of teachers don't have that sight of where the benchmark really is, and they think they're teaching

> really well and that they're great teachers. But when you put the kids' results in comparison to the state, we're pretty bad [. . .] We've got some dinosaurs here, a lot of [regional] schools have got dinosaurs in them. They don't care about kids, they don't set homework, they don't mark homework, they don't follow assessment policies. They run their own show.

It is impossible to judge the overall accuracy of this assessment, or how many teachers it might have been true of. Certainly there were some comments about minority-group students increasing teachers' workload, such as Hillview High principal Neil's description of the African-background students as 'another group [on top of the Aboriginal cohort] that are hard work sometimes'. This is not to suggest that the refugee-background students do not present significant challenges for educators but rather to consider how 'holiday-like' Easthaven's demographic changes might influence some teachers' attitudes towards the students.

Questions about 'benchmarks' lead to a second issue, that of perspectives on what makes a 'great teacher'. As touched on earlier, there was some evidence at the schools of conceptualizations of teaching as fundamentally an instrumental process – a transmission of 'neutral' skills and knowledge – rather than as intellectual, affective and inevitably having significant social impacts (Connell, 2009). For educators who subscribe to the former view, being 'very practical' and 'not into theory' may in fact be a point of professional pride (Watkins & Noble, 2021). Seaview High principal Sally also highlighted the problem of teachers thinking of themselves as subject-matter experts and of their classroom as an autonomous domain (where they 'run their own show' – Vince). Moving teachers 'away from thinking they're just delivering content' had been a challenge at the school, Sally said. The persistence of such practices may be due to a combination of lack of professional development (with fewer opportunities in regional areas), changing ideas about what constitutes a 'good teacher' (Connell, 2009), and changing ideas about the role and responsibilities of schools generally.

Teachers are practitioners *and* intellectual workers, and need not only to 'adopt a capacity for critique but to then apply these understandings in productive ways with their students . . . and with their broader school communities' (Watkins & Noble, 2016, p. 43). Further, teaching and learning have affective dimensions (Matias & Zembylas, 2014) that mediate discursive and material practices (Boler & Zembylas, 2003). Schools need to pay attention to these processes and dynamics and to recognize good teaching as a *collective* enterprise (Connell, 2009). Teacher autonomy, while understandably valued by many teachers, can nonetheless undermine the coherence of initiatives 'when it [autonomy] comes to mean "freedom from scrutiny and the largely unexamined right to exercise personal preference"' (Timperley & Robinson, 2000, p. 48).

The third issue raised by the data presented above relates to hegemony and notions of deficit. Among some teachers at the schools, as noted, there was a reported tendency to cast poorly performing students (disproportionately Aboriginal) as 'dumber' (Vince) or 'hard work' (Neil). According to the Year 11 refugee-background students interviewed at Seaview High, some of the teachers there 'put you down' when the students did not understand or know something. Celine, for example, said:

It's really discouraging when they say it and they say it in front of the class as well, and it's like 'Oh you shouldn't do this subject because you haven't [done] this this this this' – 'You don't have the ability to do this.' It's like they're on purpose to tell you, 'You don't have what it takes – just give up and do something else'.

It is true that refugee-background students' interrupted schooling before coming to Australia is often a barrier to their immediately pursuing the subjects and educational pathways they might want (Watkins et al., 2019). However, Celine's concerns appeared to relate more to teacher practices of highlighting her 'difference' and deficits in front of her peers – something she saw as linked to prevailing beliefs about 'Africans'. Certainly racialized deficit discourses are another way in which teachers may justify not reflecting on or altering their practice (Vass, 2014). In a case study of change processes at a US elementary school, where the student population was highly diverse but the staff were not, McKenzie and Scheurich (2008) found that despite the staff's agreement on and collaborative implementation of a reform programme, discourses of resistance to change remained prevalent throughout the process. From Celine's perspective, such resistances also stemmed from teachers' ideas about their own (White) superiority: 'They shouldn't be "I'm the teacher – this is what you do and I want it done like this." They should be a little bit more flexible and understanding of what's going on . . . for different persons in the class.'

The above accounts of teacher attitudes and practices lead to a fourth issue of teacher training and education. As noted, there was reliance on the ESL teachers at the schools to deal with the complex needs of the refugee-background students. Of the Hillview High ESL teachers interviewed for this study, Sharon was primary-school-trained and had recently completed a TESOL[5] certificate, while Roslyn was a maths/science teacher who was not ESL trained but had 'done a few courses'. Neither spoke a language other than English. At Seaview High, the main ESL teacher, Richard, had taught French before moving into ESL teaching and spoke several languages himself. In fact, his transition into ESL had come about because some of the early African-background students spoke French and he had been asked to provide initial bilingual tuition. He did not, however, have formal training in teaching ESL. The staff did have access to regional consultants including Henrietta and Fiona, both of whom had completed ESL training, although these positions were axed shortly after the fieldwork for this study was conducted as the NSW DoE shifted to a decentralized funding model (Michell, 2014).

The Easthaven ESL teachers were not alone in having little formal training in teaching English to speakers of other languages. As recorded in Chapter 2, a survey of NSW public school staff found that only 28 per cent of total respondents had had pre-service training in teaching ESL, with the figure for ESL teachers below half (49 per cent) (Watkins et al., 2013). Only 48 per cent of the total sample reported having had pre-service training in other aspects of multicultural education such as inclusive curricula, antiracism and community engagement. This as a significant issue given policy and curriculum requirements to equip *all* students with the knowledges and skills to live and work in increasingly mobile and culturally complex societies.

A further and even more significant issue concerns the *quality* of training teachers receive, both pre-service and in-service. Here I offer another example from Hillview

High, where the arrival of the refugee-background students had been 'eye-opening', to use deputy principal Reg's word. At first, Reg explained, there were 'a lot of stories that I don't think we could understand – the hardships they [the refugees] had gone through to come here. Staff were happy to sit down and watch videos about the camps.... So that opened their eyes to the background they [the refugees] had come from.' While such information is clearly important, there is a big gap between watching a one-off, mass-produced video and developing new social and pedagogical practices to meet the needs of particular students in a particular geographical and institutional setting. Among the interviewees for this study, finding out about 'other cultures' was commonly articulated as a key aspect of multiculturalism and multicultural education – a perspective consistent with the sorts of understandings of 'culture' and 'difference' documented in Chapter 4, and those promoted by official multicultural discourses. This can also, however, be linked to teacher training, with courses often implicitly presenting 'difference' as either problematic or exotic, and always located in ethnic and cultural 'others', while sidestepping issues of racialization, patterned inequality and power (Santoro, 2009).

Many researchers have raised concerns about the extent to which Australian training programmes develop teachers' critical capacities, including their understanding of culture and identity as multifaceted, dynamic and relational (Santoro, 2009). Integral to this development is helping teachers to see *themselves* as not only classed and gendered but ethnicized human beings, given the 'normalness' and hence invisibility of Whiteness in a majority-White nation like Australia and an even stronger majority-White profession such as teaching. As Santoro (2009) argues:

> [L]earning to teach for diversity requires sophisticated levels of reflective skill, opportunities for practice as well as theoretical understandings of critical race theory, multicultural education and so on. Such knowledge cannot be developed in schools, nor can it be developed in short periods of time. (p. 43)

Acquiring not only the skill but the *habit* of critical reflection takes time; it is not something that can be gained from a video or even a one- or two-day professional development course (which is not to say such offerings do not have a place in multicultural education). Further, if equity is to be a priority in education, teachers need to understand themselves as not only ethnicized but always-ethnicizing – always categorizing (mostly unconsciously) people and making schematized assumptions about them that promote differential (inter)actions and thus outcomes.

An example of this was provided by Richard, the main ESL teacher at Seaview High. According to Richard, his colleagues often assumed that if the refugee-background students did not complete assignments or participate much in class, it was due to language problems and/or 'cultural traits' such as the 'passivity' of the 'Burmese'. It was only through working intensively with these students over past years, he said, that he had come to understand that the barriers might lie more in fundamental differences in life experiences, perceptions and ways of thinking. In Richard's opinion, two things had to change in teaching – not just at Seaview High but in Australian schools across the board. The first was that there needed to be a greater recognition and acceptance of non-mainstream world views:

I know that each country has to have rules, that's fair enough. But maybe just beyond the rules there needs to be an overall acceptance... of the way that different people perceive what they do and accept that people *do* perceive it differently, and that that's OK.

The second change – and one he said could come only after the first – was structural reform. As diversification spread, teachers (and Australians generally) needed to recognize that it was not so much a matter of non-Anglo Australians not fitting the model as the model 'not fitting *them* that well'. Of the refugee-background students, he said:

As long as they feel as if they have some sort of input into something that's different than them, that they feel included in some way – because they're all new members of the community and the community is made up of all of us together. So therefore we have to kind of adjust the structure a little bit to incorporate everybody into that.

Of all the people interviewed, Richard was the only one to talk explicitly about 'structural norms' and a need for structural change. He was also one of the few who appeared to see the ESL students as a resource for teaching and learning (beyond enlivening assemblies with their singing, dancing and drumming). 'If we adjusted things', he said, 'they [the ESL students] would have a lot to offer that we could learn from . . . *we're* missing out on things too, because *they've* got things to offer that *we're* not getting'. He saw integration, as a genuine two-way process, as a cornerstone of multicultural education and essential to broader societal benefits. In addition to openness and flexibility, he emphasized the need for sustained interaction: 'I think you have to go through a lot of experiences to get to that [integration], because there's all these little things we have in us which need to be broken down' – or if not necessarily broken down, brought to light so that they are available for critical reflection and review.

Parent interviewees were generally not asked directly what they thought about teaching practices at the schools; indeed, most said they knew little about the curriculum or staff. Observations did come up, however: Hillview High parent Graham said, 'The teachers, from what I've seen, are just fabulous – inclusive . . . dedicated . . . they're there for the kids 100 per cent.' Two parents spontaneously brought up issues related to some of these points. Burundi-born Eddie, the father of Seaview High ESL student Celine, said he thought teachers could do more to include non-Anglo-background parents and recognize them as resources. He also stressed a need for better teacher education around cultural diversity, saying all teachers 'should be able to demonstrate and understand that every person is an individual, [instead of giving] . . . a stereotype . . . to someone because he comes from Africa or she comes from Asia'. Anglo-Australian Monica, another Seaview High parent, was also critical of what she saw as the continuing Eurocentrism of the curriculum.

Notwithstanding the introduction of practices such as acknowledgement of country, perspectives on Australian history, geography and racial relations remained overwhelmingly 'White', in her view. Before she had children, Monica had lived and worked for a time among Indigenous communities in north-western Australia. That experience had led to 'a real shift in my life philosophy', she said, beginning with an awareness of how she had been 'totally indoctrinated [at school] into this accepted history of Australia . . . I was just given . . . so much wrong information. . . . It was never even questioned that this is what's happened'. That situation had changed to a degree, she said, but making space for non-mainstream perspectives and programmes remained a constant battle: 'It's like we need to [continually] justify why the truth should be there, whether it be . . . the First Fleet or whether it be NAIDOC Week or the Stolen Generation or any of those sorts of issues.' Seaview High excursions were typically to the snowfields or capital cities, never to Indigenous sites or communities, Monica said, adding: 'I mean . . . why isn't that an option?'

Curriculum, Ladson-Billings and Tate (1995, p. 54) point out, is a 'form of intellectual property', guiding students' access (largely through discourse) not only to different kinds of knowledge but also their understanding of the social and economic *value* of different knowledges. As Fairclough (2003, p. 124) writes, 'discourses differ in their degree of repetition, commonality, stability over time, and in what we might call their "scale"' – and thus, ultimately, in the degree to which they become 'truth'. Dominant narratives about Australia's past have historically paid little attention to Indigenous histories, resistances and achievements. These omissions were not accidental but structural, the anthropologist Stanner argued in 1968:

> a view from a window . . . carefully placed to exclude a whole quadrant of the landscape. What may well have begun as a simple forgetting of other possible views turned under habit and over time into something like a cult of forgetfulness practised on a national scale. (quoted in Daley, 2016)

Schools, once pivotal to this national 'forgetfulness', are now tasked with inculcating new habits of remembering (Leonardo, 2004). Resentment and resistance – evident in some of the students' comments presented above, including Sam's 'it wasn't us that did it' response to Sorry Day – may be deployed against acts of recognition. Vaught and Castagno (2008), in a US study of teacher responses to anti-bias training programmes, found that creating 'cultural awareness' did 'not lead to empathy amongst teachers, but resulted instead in a reinvention of meaning that reified existing, culturally constructed, racist frameworks' (p. 110). As the authors point out, it is unrealistic to think that racialization, discrimination and inequality – problems that are long-standing and systemic – can be addressed by 'reforming' individual teachers; Stanner's metaphor above draws attention to the need to reposition the window, not (merely) the viewer. The above critique, then, is intended not as censure of individualized teaching practices but as a dissection of institutional structures and practices (including teacher training), and specific local factors, that sustain systems of racialized privilege and disadvantage. This warrants a further investigation of practices beyond the classroom.

Beyond the Classroom

Celebrations!

As emphasized throughout this book, official multicultural policies and discourses in Australia promote a celebratory orientation towards difference and diversity. This and the changes in the local population had prompted Easthaven's schools to do much more to recognize and include 'other cultures' in their educational and social activities – something which, historically, had been of low priority. Cultural performances and celebrations, as noted, had become regular events on school and community calendars, with Harmony Day in particular a 'big thing' (Hillview High principal Neil). While most interviewees said it was important to celebrate diversity through such events, they often struggled to articulate why. Seaview High teacher Brody, for instance, said it was 'certainly the role of schools' to celebrate cultural diversity 'because it's a multicultural country . . . I don't know. You have to'. He added: 'This school does its best to do that [celebrate diversity], and Multicultural Day the other day did that. But it's difficult in *this* town because it tends to be a fairly conservative sort of place.' Here Brody is quite firm in his view that celebrating diversity is 'very important' and one of schools' (many) roles, but can only offer 'because it's a multicultural country' as a reason. Further, as with interviewee comments reported earlier, there is a sense of multiculturalism as an imposition ('You have to') – and particularly so in the case of schools in '*this* town', regional Easthaven, due to its social, cultural and political conservatism.

Hillview High ESL teacher Sharon was more reflective about the capacity of events such as NAIDOC Week, Harmony Day and Refugee Week to facilitate cross-cultural connection and understanding. She said the school used Refugee Week, for example, as an opportunity for refugee-background students and families to share their stories by 'presenting at an assembly or something'. But '[the refugee-background] kids are just seen; they're not really interacting [with other students]'. The main problem was that such events were 'one-offs', Sharon said, and there was not 'a continuing message [around multiculturalism] throughout the school'. She commented:

> You have to have a plan that's on a deeper level, on a whole-school level, over a period of time, not just a quick 'we've got to organize something' [approach], and have a bit more thought. And supported from top down, not pushed from bottom up.

Here she highlights the need for a whole-school approach to multicultural and Aboriginal education, and for strong leadership and planning in order to ensure that programmes and practices are not one-offs or 'ad hoc' but at 'a deeper level'. This contrasts with common assumptions that 'doing something' multicultural is what matters, when the research evidence suggests that superficial celebrations of diversity can in fact entrench stereotypes, prejudices and divisions, and various forms of disadvantage (Watkins and Noble, 2021).

Importantly, the refugee-background students themselves also expressed mixed sentiments about diversity celebrations – even though a rationale for such events was to make this cohort feel recognized and valued. Burundi-born Seaview High student Celine thought they were 'good things . . . really fun'. But for her Kenya-born, Ethiopian-heritage classmate Sisay, who had lived in Easthaven for only eighteen months, such events seemed above all to reinforce her 'differentness' and isolation. The 'only reason' she liked celebrations and cultural performances, Sisay said, was because they 'bring us [the refugee-background students] together and I like seeing my friends . . . You feel good when you have your friends with you, especially like – you know you're the same'. In reality, her friends, far from being 'the same', were to most Easthaveners the definition of the town's diversity – from multiple countries across Africa, South-east Asia and the Middle East. What appeared to make them 'the same' in Sisay's perception was not only their common status as former refugees but their positionings as outside the norm in Easthaven (Colvin, 2017). Equally, it is likely that Sisay's feelings of 'otherness' and isolation were especially acute at this juncture because of her relative newness in the school and the town.

Both Sisay and Celine were in the popular African drumming group which comprised students from a range of ethnic and cultural backgrounds, including Aboriginal and Anglo, across local schools. However, the girls said the activity had not helped them form friendships outside of their small former-refugee circle. 'We don't really talk, we just sit there', Sisay said. 'You can be like "hey, how's it going?" [to other people in the drumming group]', Celine added. 'But not really friends.' To Sisay's and Celine's well-established classmates, the distinction between 'friend' and 'friendly' might not seem significant. For the former refugees, it appeared to be by far their biggest concern about their new lives in Australia. I wondered, too, whether these students had ever been asked whether they wanted to 'perform' and how they felt about, or what *they* would like to get out of, events such as Harmony Day. Settlement services worker Kerry said lack of consultation was a problem more generally in service provision in the town, with assumptions routinely made about 'what would help them . . . rather than . . . [asking] "Well, *would* you like [to]?" . . . People just think that they know best. . . . Sometimes it can be even trying to be oversensitive, trying to do too much.'

As for the Anglo-Australian students, they said events such as Harmony Day were 'fun' ('I get excited when they have them [performances] at assembly' – Sam) but agreed they did not encourage cross-cultural mixing. Hillview High Year 11 student Victoria explained:

> We don't really get to interact on those days because they [the ESL students] get taken away and they do their special activities, whereas the rest of the school just has normal classes. . . . They take them away as if they're special.

The ESL students being 'taken away' and treated 'as if they're special' appeared to annoy Victoria's classmate Thomas, who said he would 'love to be a part of the drumming group, but I don't think it's offered to me'. Fellow Year 11 student Zoe corrected him: 'Yeah, it's offered to everyone. . . . they [the ESL students] do it with their people, all the Sudanese people.' As noted, the drumming group was very mixed (I attended several performances) and was indeed an activity that was 'offered to everyone'.

Notwithstanding these 'realities', the Anglo-Australian students' dialogue constructs the drumming as something '*they* do with *their* people' (Black people), while ordinary White Easthaveners are 'left out'. This in turn provides moral and affective justification for the Anglo students making little effort to mix with newcomers.

Black v Black[6]

While the increased ethnic and cultural diversity in Easthaven was widely associated with more cultural celebrations, it was also associated with more interethnic conflict – specifically, tensions between some of the town's African- and Aboriginal-background residents (mostly among adolescent males). This came to light in the first interview I conducted, with Hillview High deputy Vince. Describing some of the African-background students as 'very, very aggressive', he said there was 'sometimes . . . conflict between the Aboriginal kids and the African kids . . . It's like a racial thing, you know? Like, "you're not Black; *I'm* Black."' Later in the interview, he said the conflict was 'both verbal and physical', adding:

> A lot of it happens outside the school because, see, both cultures, simply because they're coloured, [the] fact is that they're going to find it harder to get work. The community is largely White around here, and if you come from a coloured background, there's less opportunities for you. There's less employment opportunities as it is [because of Easthaven's regional status], and so the chance of a coloured kid getting work is greatly reduced.

Here Vince adds a socio-economic dimension to the conflicts, with both the attributed 'racial' and employment/financial reasons linked to local demographic and economic factors. It is worth noting, too, his description of 'cultures' as 'coloured', reflecting the enduring racialized nature of much talk about difference and diversity.

The 'Black v Black' phenomenon came up again, unprompted, in the second interview, this one with Hillview High's other deputy, Reg, who said: 'Early on, there was a little bit of talk . . . of the Aboriginals and the Africans not getting on . . . it was almost like [*chuckles*] "You're not Black, *we* are" . . . That just blew me away.' Reg did not offer an explanation for why contestations over 'Blackness' should cause 'the Aboriginals and the Africans' to 'not get on'. From his Anglo-Australian perspective, the idea that skin colour might have any social or affective significance appeared to be astonishing.

Former ESL teacher Henrietta, by contrast, did have an opinion on why 'you're not Black, *we* are' had become a trope in the schools:

> I've overheard Africans saying, 'Why do you call yourselves Black? You're not Black. We're Black' . . . And a Sudanese kid will put their arm beside an Aboriginal kid . . . it's just an inquiring thing that they're doing. But for an Aboriginal to have that said to them – 'You're not Black', when that's their culture and their identity – has been a bit of a slap in the face, really, even if it's not intended to be.

Furthermore, Henrietta said the nature and extent of the reported conflicts between Easthaven's Aboriginal and African-background youth had often been exaggerated: 'It's really a *few* doing it, and they're the same kids who would have picked on somebody else when they weren't picking on those ones.' In other words, she saw the tensions as not especially racial but rather the result of aggressive behaviour on the part of some adolescents who happened to be of African and Aboriginal heritage. As with the stealing and drunk-driving incidents related in Chapter 5, it may be that these skirmishes attracted more attention because those involved were more 'visible', and also seen as generally more likely to transgress. Nonetheless, Henrietta believed there had been a real degree of identity disruption for some local Aboriginal youth – perhaps reflecting the affective dimensions of the fight to reclaim 'Black' as an identity of resilience and pride (Chapter 4).

Henrietta's comments were supported by an anecdote related by Seaview High parent Trudy. A few days after our interview, Trudy emailed me the following about a local friend of hers who had emigrated to Australia from South Sudan about a decade earlier:

> She was telling me that her nephews and nieces were bullied by the Indigenous kids at school. She went to the school with her sister to have a meeting with the principal, teachers and Aboriginal parents. [And] one of the [Aboriginal] men said to her: 'There's only room for one lot of Blacks in this town and that's us.'

In two respects the refugees from Africa had had unprecedented social impacts on Easthaven. First, for Anglo Easthaveners, they were so 'visibly different', provoking a range of affects and discourses about 'Africa' and its people. For Easthaveners who identified as Indigenous, however, the newcomers were 'another Black', unsettling *their* 'Black' in a way that immigrants with other-coloured skin had not. In other words, the new settlers had disrupted not only the 'Whiteness' of Easthaven but the historical Black/White (Aboriginal/Anglo) binary also typical of many regional towns.

According to local police officer Phil, the tensions between Aboriginal- and African-background youth had largely subsided in recent years. Still, the *idea* of them remained vivid in the local imaginary: they were mentioned, usually spontaneously, in almost every interview – including by Year 11 Hillview High student Zoe (Anglo-Australian), who recalled 'a huge riot at school, all these Sudanese people against the Aboriginal people'. Asked for details, she conceded the 'riot' had not actually eventuated: 'I think it was going to, but ... the teachers came along and stopped it. But they were – I remember seeing them [the African-background and Aboriginal students] standing, there was two big lines against each other.' As with the 'huge payouts' to refugees, handouts to Aboriginal students and 'Africans-only' drumming group, the exaggeration or misunderstanding here seems to serve a distancing purpose, reinforcing the boundary between White and 'other'.

Overall, the reported 'Black v Black' phenomenon appeared to be more a source of bemusement than anxiety in the schools and the town, given the antagonism did not involve the Anglo majority. What was fascinating to me, as an outsider, was to hear accounts of some of the (Anglo) practices that contributed to the frictions. One centred on the enthusiasm of most Easthaveners about the addition of African drumming and dancing to school and community events. The popularity of these performances had even sparked demand for Aboriginal cultural performances, which historically had been of little interest to the local Anglo community. Hillview High, for instance, was trying to establish its first-ever Aboriginal dance troupe, whereas it had had African drumming and dance groups for at least four years. Rachel, one of the support staff for the school's Aboriginal students, explained:

> So many times you'll say to the [Aboriginal] kids, 'Let's go out and do some traditional – .' 'No, that's shame', [they say]. 'Why is it shame?' 'Oh, it's just shame. People don't want to see it.' 'They *do* want to see it.' You know?

As Harkins (1990) notes, the word 'shame' has very different meanings and syntactic forms in Aboriginal English to Standard Australian English usage. Often paired with 'be', 'get' or 'make', 'shame' can denote shyness, embarrassment, a desire not to draw attention to oneself – among many other place- and situation-specific meanings. In the situation detailed above, 'shame' appears to reflect both a fear of exposure and historically grounded feelings of not being culturally valued. ESL teacher Sharon agreed that 'the African kids perform a lot more than the Aboriginal kids have ever [done]'. In other words, the 'African kids' had quickly garnered a level of recognition that their Aboriginal peers had never enjoyed.

Another differentiating practice involved the forms of assistance offered to the refugee-background students. Notwithstanding some Easthaveners' overt racisms, many residents had gone out of their way to help the newcomers – giving them lifts, driving them to appointments and so on. Community member Carla said the local Catholic schools had offered scholarships to some of the refugee-background children – but that the schools had never offered scholarships to Aboriginal children. At the schools, there was some perception among students and teachers alike that the ESL students had better staffing and material resources than the Aboriginal students did. At Hillview High, Deputy Vince said:

> The ESL people at the school here do a fantastic job. . . . They are really committed. . . . [T]hey even take kids out for outings and after school and visit the home. And that's what's lacking with Aboriginal education, is that we don't have the resource to do that. In fact, I think African kids get more support than Aboriginal kids in this school.

The allegedly greater support given to the ESL students was particularly unfair, in Vince's view, because the school's LBOTE population was only 13 per cent, whereas its Aboriginal population was about 18 per cent.

The issue of extracurricular teacher engagement with the refugee-background students came up several times in interviews. Kerry, who worked in settlement services, said the relatively small size of Easthaven and the low numbers of refugee-background families meant that those working with the families often developed 'extremely close relationships' with them. As a result, 'personal and professional roles [can] get very mixed ... the client doesn't really know whether they [the service provider, including teachers] are a friend or a worker'. This could lead to unrealistic expectations of the relationship on both sides, she explained. Another example came from Hillview High ESL teacher Sharon, who reflected that some of her colleagues' eagerness to help the refugee families had 'probably created a situation' where the families had become overly dependent on their assistance.

The phenomenon of ESL teachers going the 'extra mile' and extending their involvements with refugee families beyond the school gate was noted by Wilkinson and Langat (2012) in their study of a regional NSW high school. The researchers acknowledge the caring and inclusive approach of teachers towards these new students but critique overall school practices in two main respects: first, the overreliance on ESL teachers to address refugee-background students' needs, reflecting (among other things) limited professional development and the lack of a whole-school, collaborative teaching and learning plan; and second, insufficient critical attention to the discourses that informed material educational practices at the school, potentially compromising those practices' (and broader policy) equity objectives. I do not cite the examples above as criticism of the intentions or even actions of the teachers at Hillview and Seaview high schools. The aim, rather, is to illuminate how local phenomena – including country towns' smaller size and potentially stronger sociality, regional schools' tendency to overrely on ESL staff vis-à-vis refugee-background students, and the demographic mix and community relations history of an area – can help produce effects that are different to those intended. Benevolent 'White' practices, unintentionally, may create or inflame tensions between Easthaven's original 'Black' inhabitants and its much more recent 'Black' settlers.

This temporal dimension – old and new – is crucial to interpreting the 'Black v Black' story at a deeper level. Despite the (perceived) common 'Blackness' of Indigenous Easthaveners and African-background Easthaveners, the relationship between the former and the Anglo majority is very different from that between the latter and the Anglo majority. Thus it is not only ethnic, cultural and linguistic differences per se that affect educational outcomes but the effect of this relationship-to-the-majority on students' identities, expectations and aspirations (Ogbu, 1992). Understanding the importance of this, in turn, is critical to the success of school programmes and practices. Easthaven students whose looks and identity are strongly 'Aboriginal' (such as Seaview High parent Monica's son) may have very different experiences of racism and perceptions of the opportunities and pathways open to them than African-background students, for whom resettlement in Australia, for all its challenges, nonetheless represents a host of *new* experiences and opportunities. A teenager from an Aboriginal family where no one has ever had a paid job may see the obstacles to gaining employment as systemic and permanent, for instance, whereas a refugee-background student may see any barriers as more individually located and temporary. There was some evidence of this at Seaview High and Hillview High: the refugee-background students were typically focused on professional careers, according to the ESL teachers, while many Aboriginal students saw limited futures for themselves, several interviewees said. The 'new Blacks', therefore, may have been perceived by the 'old Blacks' as not only unsettling their ethnic identity (as NSW DoE consultant Henrietta suggested) but as almost immediately overtaking them in social and cultural status in Easthaven. This is another sense in which 'old ways' – intergenerational positionalities – may 'die hard' in regional towns where one ethnocultural group has a particularly pungent history of discrimination and disadvantage.

In Easthaven, interviewees mostly characterized the Aboriginal-African tensions as racial or grounded in competition for resources. Rachel, one of Hillview High's Aboriginal support staff, expressed bewilderment at the conflict, saying: 'Their cultures are so similar, I don't understand why there's such a big thing between them.' Here the students' common 'Blackness' is used not only to homogenize 'Aboriginal' and 'African' people into singular 'cultures' but to construct their 'cultures' as 'similar' –a difficult position to sustain. However, Rachel's subsequent comments suggested that despite her use of the word 'cultures', what she meant was closer to 'histories' – that both populations had been subject to interethnic violence and oppression, and consequent separation (to varying degrees) from community, language and lands. Hillview High parent Caryn echoed this argument, attributing the intergroup tensions to 'lateral violence', which she defined as 'people who are oppressed, or feel oppressed, start to lash out at each other laterally instead of upward at the oppressor'. Caryn worked in Aboriginal health and said lateral violence was a common topic at conferences she attended: 'Every bloody conference . . . "lateral violence". So you just get used to seeing it happening.'

What is noteworthy in all of the explanations above is an absence: a lack of explicit recognition of the role of *Whiteness* in creating the conditions for tensions – from classification systems that spawn programmes and practices that differentiate and divide to the way in which Whiteness systematically makes itself invisible. I am not suggesting that different people do not have diverse capabilities, aspirations and needs, but rather that more attention must be paid to the way in which Whiteness listens to and caters for these, and the histories that have shaped them. With Whiteness unseen and unnamed, 'Black v Black' is inevitably about 'them'; it is outside of Whiteness and, being thus, feeds back into White narratives about Black unruliness, aggression and criminality. The explanation for the 'way they are', in short, is located not in history but in ethnicity. The dominance of discourses of 'bad Blackness' means that 'you just get used to seeing it happening' – and even more so in a mostly White town like Easthaven.

Conclusion

This chapter has analysed some of the ways in which diversity-related education policies are enacted in regional Easthaven's public high schools. It has shown how personal and localized understandings of and discourses about diversity have combined with other affordances and constraints to shape the schools' responses to changes in their student populations. By creating space for interviewees, particularly students, to 'name their own reality' (Ladson-Billings & Tate, 1995), the chapter has also sought to shed light on some *consequences* of practices within and beyond the schools.

Some of the practice issues identified are grounded in challenges common across rural and regional areas, while others are specific to Easthaven, reflecting the microcultures of place (Amin, 2002). Some have their origins in macro-level structures, such as the conceptual and material cleavage between 'multicultural' and 'Indigenous', and the general absence of Anglo-ness, in diversity discourses and initiatives. Yet other issues reflect a combination of macro and micro, such as gaps in teacher training and education and anomalies in funding and resources.

Above all, the objective has been to bring attention to how 'old ways' – of thinking, talking, planning, administering, engaging within and beyond the classroom – can affect the situated outcomes of multicultural policies and programmes. The association between diversity and celebrations – promoted by official policies and discourses – can lead schools to focus on helping students 'feel good' about cultural differences while ignoring or glossing over the structural bases of those differences. The danger with such 'positive' approaches to diversity lies not only in the simplistic and essentializing notions of culture and difference they tend to uphold but in their failure to recognize and address the relationships between education, knowledge and power. In a mostly White town such as Easthaven, where Whiteness remains pervasive, largely invisible and hence 'natural', such an undertaking is especially critical. 'The hidden curriculum of whiteness saturates everyday school life', Leonardo (2004) writes, 'and one of the first steps to articulating its features is coming to terms with its specific modes' (p. 144). This chapter has sought to take those 'first steps': to reveal the work of Whiteness in the processes of change and stasis (Ball, 1993; Fairclough, 2003) – what Whiteness willingly allows in Easthaven and its high schools, what it less willingly allows and what it does not. The Conclusion to this book considers what some of the next steps might be, particularly with regard to regional schools and enduring tensions within and between multicultural and Aboriginal education.

Conclusion

Towards a Multiculturalism for All

Introduction

This book opened with an account of Multicultural Day at Seaview High, one of two public high schools studied in the regional NSW town of Easthaven. Multicultural Day featured a range of activities designed to increase students' awareness and appreciation of cultural practices different from their own, while also giving the school's LBOTE students an opportunity to 'celebrate their heritage' (as the school reported). The account was used to begin to explore the central themes of this book: the sorts of understandings of diversity that multiculturalism has helped to promote; the impact of multicultural policies' positive framing of diversity on everyday discourses about culture and difference; schools' changing roles and responsibilities; and the ways in which all of these, as well as local histories and pervasive imaginaries of the rural, might inflect responses to cultural diversity in regional communities and schools.

Multiculturalism, of course, has never been simply about food and festivals. As a policy, it has always had, to a greater or lesser degree, formally stated equitable intentions (Koleth, 2010). Yet it remains a long way from being 'about all Australians and for all Australians' (as *The People of Australia* proclaims) in practice. As Ball (1993, pp. 12–13) explains:

> [W]e cannot predict or assume how they [policies] will be acted on, what their immediate effect will be, what room for manoeuvre actors will find for themselves.... the enactment of [policy] texts relies on things like commitment, understanding, capability, resources, practical limitations, cooperation and (importantly) intertextual compatibility.

The preceding chapters have documented instances of all of these in Easthaven and its public high schools, and discussed the ways in which regional and/or specific local factors may have been involved.

However, the dimension emphasized by Ball, that of 'intertextual compatibility', is one I want to consider further in this conclusion. Multiculturalism, in both theory and practice, has challengers – and challenges – at all levels. At a global level, there are forceful discourses about meritocracy – that systems reward those who have talent and work hard, regardless of ethnicity, class, gender and other dimensions of difference. At a national level, there are potent narratives about Australian egalitarianism and tolerance, and regular political speeches and media reports about Australia's multicultural success (as well as speeches and reports about multiculturalism's perils). And at a micro level – a town, a school, a classroom – there are all of these, along with local stories, experiences, understandings, concerns, priorities, structures, practices and so on. In such multiscalar social and physical spaces, it is indeed impossible, as Ball (1993) contends, to anticipate how policies will 'hit the ground'; to fully understand how they *are* interpreted and enacted; and to link social and educational outcomes directly to particular programmes and practices. As Rachel, one of Hillview High's Aboriginal support staff, reflected: 'In reality, how *do* you deal with different cultures? There's no set, guaranteed answer that's going to work. And what might work at this school might not work two schools over.'

Looking Back: The Study in Review

Multicultural success, as Amin (2002) reminds us, is a product of 'local context and local energies' (p. 976) – and recognizing this is of course crucial to considering the relevance and value of this study to other regional and school communities. The study has shed light on how multiculturalism was understood, valued and lived in specific regional institutional spaces at a specific point in time. That time has already passed: the town's demographics have changed and the schools have changed (including new leadership and staff), as other regional areas have changed.

Notwithstanding its spatial and temporal particularities, this study has illuminated more general respects in which Australian multiculturalism needs critical attention. These are summarized into four interrelated areas: conceptual/discursive, affective, spatial and structural. The first of these, conceptual/discursive, relates to the way in which multiculturalism, through its foregrounding of culture and difference, masks power and privilege. Three policy elements have been shown to be central to this outcome. The first is terminology: while the epithets of 'multicultural' and 'culturally diverse' have become commonplace and are ostensibly non-hierarchical, in both official and everyday use, they continue to denote 'other' – that is, other-than-Anglo. Thus in Easthaven and the studied schools, interviewees often spoke about 'the Australians', 'the multicultural community' and 'the Aborigines', constructing the town's large Anglo majority as the norm against which 'difference' was marked and measured. Indeed, it is by *seeming* neutral that the language of diversity can naturalize ethnic and cultural categories, thereby obscuring how they are constructed, by whom and ultimately with what effects – such as leaving other-than-Anglo Australians discursively positioned outside of 'Australian'.

The second element is policies' positive framing of diversity. The strong emphasis on multiculturalism's benefits appears commendable but can also deflect attention from its many challenges, damping discussions about the knowledge, skills and structural changes needed to broaden and sustain multicultural success. Such discussions may be particularly pressing in regional areas as diversity spreads and intensifies. The third element is the way in which this positive orientation helps to dehistoricize and depoliticize prevailing conceptualizations of and discourses about culture and difference. Multiculturalism sounds modern and progressive (in contrast to the White Australia policy, for example), but in practice it remains hostage to national and local historical factors, institutional structures, and the adaptability and inventiveness of race and racism. Racialization processes, and impacts, can thus be highly localized.

The second area relates to the affective dimension of perceptions and experiences of cultural differences, and how this mediates responses to individuals and groups from backgrounds different from our own. As well as documenting the ways in which official positivity regarding diversity was echoed, challenged and resisted by interviewees in their talk about diversity, I have highlighted signs of affect (i.e. affects that were not verbally or directly expressed) in the research data. In mostly White Easthaven, where cultural diversity had not been part of most residents' lived experience, the study found there were significant anxieties about the recent demographic changes in the town and its schools. These anxieties typically emerged in what I have characterized as a 'yes, but . . .' discourse, where initial declarations of support for diversity (in line with official discourses) were quickly undercut by hedges, qualifications and even contradictions. Negative affects were associated above all with the most 'visibly different' refugees from more than a dozen northern and western African countries who had settled in the area over the previous decade. Within the schools, these newcomers – along with refugees from Burma and the Middle East – had presented unprecedented challenges due to the enormous heterogeneity of their backgrounds and often-minimal pre-arrival schooling. As much space as possible has been given to the voices of these students in order to acknowledge, and trouble (White) assumptions about, their experiences, identities, needs and desires.

The third area is spatial and relates to the ways in which multiculturalism in country towns and schools may be understood, valued and lived differently than in metropolitan centres. Most rural and regional areas are considerably less culturally diverse than metropolitan ones, but have larger and long-established Indigenous populations; further, they are *imagined* differently as both social and physical entities. Thus the 'injection' (Hugo, 2008) of a hundred or so refugee families from Africa, Southeast Asia and the Middle East has had unique effects on both the receiving community and the settlers in Easthaven – effects that would not have occurred in another place and at another time. While this is always true in a sense, the study has tried to map some of the distinctive dynamics of lived diversity in regional areas, including the historical White/Black (Anglo/Indigenous) social and cultural hierarchy in many country towns; the fact that, because broader diversity is not the norm, cultural 'others' may be more likely to be perceived as either exotic or problematic; the effects of small numbers of non-Anglo residents ('sprinkles of everything') on discursive and material practices in regard to these 'others'; that there may be greater resistance to change by some rural residents because of the value they place on (rural) stability, order and community cohesion; that some people may value their 'rural' identity more than, say, a professional identity or identity as a 'tolerant Australian'; and how discursive and material practices can combine with prevailing affects, including fear, resentment and indifference, to create new localized hierarchies of belonging.

The fourth aspect, structural, relates to some of the characteristics of regional schools that are linked with their location – such as regional centres' distance from, and greater difficulty in accessing, the resources, specialist services and professional development opportunities available in capital cities. Compared with other OECD nations, Australia's non-metropolitan schools are significantly disadvantaged in this respect (Perry, 2017), due in part to the country's size and urbanization. The structural aspect also includes non-spatial factors such as administration and funding systems, particularly in terms of the separation of multicultural and Aboriginal programmes; teacher training and education; and teachers' age, cultural background and experience, as discussed in the previous chapter. With diversity research overwhelmingly focused on cities, much is yet to be learnt about how 'rurality as a dynamic and multifaceted material and discursive space mediates racialized educational practices and policies' (Pini & Bhopal, 2017, p. 192). This study has sought to add to knowledge in this field – one that warrants considerably more attention in Australia and other Western countries in light of current migration trends.

Looking Forward: Stepping Stones to Better Praxis?

All of the issues and findings outlined above are important in contemplating the future of multicultural education in Australia and to the national curriculum's endeavours to promote intercultural understanding as a core capability for all students. As explained, this study is not intended as a critique of individual teachers but rather seeks to highlight institutional structures and practices that contribute to uneven educational outcomes.

Efforts to create more equitable and genuinely inclusive schools must begin by troubling hegemonic discourses about success, achievement and equality, encapsulated in the following comment by Hillview High principal Neil: 'If you're a good person and you work hard and you're not going to do the wrong thing, then I think you get a fair go . . . in our country'. This is the myth of meritocracy and a trope of Australian identity – land of the 'fair go' (DSS, 2017). Yet school test results – let alone post-school outcomes – continue to show stark differences in performance between Indigenous and non-Indigenous students; urban dwellers and those living in rural and regional areas; those attending private schools and those at public schools; and those from low socio-economic backgrounds and those from well-off, well-educated families (Perry, 2017; Thomson et al., 2016).

As stated in Chapter 3, a central question in this book has been *cui bono* (who benefits) – and a central aim, therefore, to reveal how policies, programmes and practices work to systematically advantage some people and not others in particular spaces. While acknowledging the multiplicity and intersectionality of dimensions of difference, this book has sought to bring attention to the continuing salience of raced thinking, discourses and practices in everyday life, including in schools – that is, to the continuing centrality of race as a social practice, even if it is now often coded as 'cultural difference' (Yosso, 2005). Equally, it has sought to expose how dominant discourses and the practices they promote work to uphold White privilege (Vass, 2014) – because 'white domination is never settled once and for all; it is constantly reestablished and reconstructed by whites *from all walks of life* . . . [including] average, tolerant people'

(Leonardo, 2004, p. 143; emphasis in original). In these endeavours I have followed Povinelli's (1998) counsel that if researchers and scholars are to disrupt hegemonic projects and practices, 'our analyses ... must engage ... the discursive and the global, the microdiscursive, the imaginary, and the corporeal currents through which new relations of social dominance are currently being articulated' (p. 580).

Both critical discourse and race-critical theorists, however, emphasize that analysis and critique are not enough, and that scholarship, in addition, must have an activist dimension and strive for social change (Fairclough, 2003; Hylton, 2012; Ladson-Billings, 2003). With this in mind, I offer some avenues for reflection, discussion and action, including further research. The first is a need to reconceptualize multiculturalism so that it is not seen 'merely as a study of the other, but rather as multiple studies of culture and cultural practices in the lives of humans' (Ladson-Billings, 2003, p. 51). Integral to these 'multiple studies' must be a critical examination of Whiteness and White privilege, and imaginings of 'Australians' and Australian identity – a task that is typically given insufficient attention in antiracism strategies (Nelson, 2015). Multicultural education also needs to be recognized as a *process*, one that explicitly aims to disrupt conventional ways of perceiving, talking about and responding to human differences (Ladson-Billings, 2003). Such an understanding would promote a stronger focus on educational and social outcomes and a commitment to comprehensive evaluation and reporting in this area. This would require significant investments in personnel, systems and other resources – often difficult to secure – and enhanced collaboration and information-sharing across jurisdictions, institutions and academic disciplines (Jakubowicz & Ho, 2013a).

In short, a more equity-driven multiculturalism necessarily implies disruption, which in turn implies a degree (or degrees) of discomfort. This points to a second avenue for change: developing educators' capacities to create spaces for and moderate uneasy conversations about race, racialization and racism. Teaching and learning are affective as well as cognitive, and educators might benefit from being more explicitly equipped to recognize and work with the affectivity of pedagogical practice (Watkins, 2006). The complexity of this work is one reason that schools, despite their role of teaching students about the world around them, often remain coy about the realities of racialization, discrimination and inequality. As Warmington (2009) notes, an argument against race-critical perspectives is that they perpetuate the 'outmoded' concept of race. However, countenancing race and its consequences is not an all-or-nothing proposition: it is not a question of whether we need to talk about race and racism more, or less, but how we can talk about them *more skilfully* (Warmington, 2009, p. 283) – especially in schools.

What 'more skilfully' might look like points to the issue of teacher training more generally. Much has been written in this field and many recommendations made, so here I wish to highlight only a few aspects. The first is the potential value of projects such as this one for participants. There were a number of comments during and at the end of interviews that suggested the process had been of some benefit to participants – comments such as 'Some of the questions I found ... quite challenging, [they] made me think about what we were doing' (Sally, principal, Seaview High) and 'That was really interesting. ... It's nice to talk about all this sort of stuff' (Fiona, NSW DoE consultant), in addition to the hugs and comments mentioned in Chapter 3. On my final visit to Easthaven, I asked the school principals what they had thought of the project and why they had agreed to participate. Both said they hoped their staff would benefit from taking an hour out of their usual routine to reflect on their practice and discuss issues they might not have thought about. Hillview High's Neil also expressed a hope that the research might be useful, in the longer term, to schools beyond his own.

The second aspect is a widely commented upon need for more extensive and intellectually rigorous teacher education programmes (Santoro, 2014; Watkins & Noble, 2021). A crucial objective of these enhanced programmes would be to bring to light educators' (including teacher educators') assumptions about ethnicities, cultures and other human differences – to make visible the ways in which we all 'do' race and ethnicity every day (Moya & Markus, 2010), and yet are all individuals with 'a history and a background and a personality' (Hillview High parent Caryn). As Santoro (2009) has argued, this might productively begin with teacher educators and their charges recognizing and reflecting on the 'ethnic self'. A further objective would be to develop habits of interrogating how racialized discourses, assumptions and expectations impact every day on social and educational practices. Following Edgeworth (2011), I also suggest a need to encourage deeper consideration of the interconnections between space, place and society – including, for example, how the organization of school spaces can affect social relations within a school.

A more robust multiculturalism, then, requires multiscalar change – from an integrated and sustained approach within schools to policy enactments to reform of teacher training and education programmes, classification systems, funding models, evaluation and reporting practices. In many cases, it is not deficits in knowledge but system rigidities, unrealistic time frames, inadequate resourcing and other practical limitations, along with inter- and intratextual tensions, that produce or exacerbate inequities (Chodkiewicz & Burridge, 2013; Vass, 2014). In many contexts there may be a need also to put more structures in place to ensure that social interactions are 'meaningful and relevant to students' lives' (Walton et al., 2013, p. 185), rather than assuming that positive relationships 'naturally' develop in spaces of cross-cultural contact such as African drumming groups or Multicultural Days. Education policies, programmes and practices can help to reduce patterned disadvantage, or they can maintain or intensify it. When the latter is true, the uneven outcomes 'may not be coldly calculated but they are far from accidental' (Gillborn, 2007, p. 499). It is this point that critical discourse and race-critical scholars seek to draw attention to as a necessary first step towards change (Bacchi, 2000; Hartmann, 2015).

A final argument returns to policies' positive framing of diversity. *Contra* current policy exhortations, I recommend Balint's proposal that we – policymakers, researchers and educators – (re)consider 'whether respect and appreciation of difference really is necessary *at all* for the maintenance of a tolerant society' (Balint, 2010, p. 137). As he observes: 'It may be nice to have a tolerant society with no negative attitudes towards differences, but it is far from feasible – the "fact of diversity" (that we don't all want or believe the same thing) necessarily precludes it' (p. 132). Even if social cohesion rather than social justice is the priority in multiculturalism, we need to acknowledge that cultural differences can be unsettling so that those differences and affects do not become sources of conflict and division (Bell & Hartmann, 2007). Being able to negotiate and collaborate across differences may ultimately be more useful in living together than 'expressing empathy, demonstrating respect and taking responsibility' – dispositions the national curriculum identifies as pivotal to the development of intercultural understanding (ACARA, n.d.). Rather than an 'either/or' approach to diversity – that it is a strength or, conversely, a weakness – we need, as a minimum, a 'both/and' orientation, one that holds cultural differences as 'both basic problematics to be worked [out] and opportunities for enrichment' (Grand, 1999, p. 484). The key question for policymakers, researchers and practitioners thus becomes: What kinds of skills do we *all* need now and into the future given the diversity of our ways of perceiving, learning, relating, communicating and so on? Such challenges, as Grand (1999, p. 479) notes, are 'quite beyond good will and tolerance'.

Final Thoughts

Schools can never, on their own, erase social inequalities, but they do have the potential to make a difference in students' lives both during and beyond their school years. Schools are places where young people learn habits of seeing, interpreting, thinking, talking, feeling, acting and interacting. They are places that embed categories, understandings and routines. They cultivate and normalize certain knowledges, beliefs, values and identities, and exclude or sanction others. They are conduits for, but also potential sites of challenge to, hegemonic discourses and practices, such as discourses of meritocracy and categorization processes. They are spaces of differentiation and hierarchy, but also potentially of transformation. There is no singular way forward but rather places to look, as Ball suggests: 'commitment, understanding, capability, resources, practical limitations, cooperation and (importantly) intertextual compatibility'.

The hope is that this book will help signpost some of the particular opportunities and challenges for regional schools and communities as their populations diversify. As noted in the Introduction, the trend towards a more plural rural (Chakraborti & Garland, 2004) is evident across Australia and in other immigrant nations, including the US, Canada and the UK. Given the dominance of 'Anglo-ness' in many rural communities, both in reality and in localized and national imaginaries, bringing Whiteness into visibility takes on a heightened importance. At the same time, it must be recognized that there are many rurals, and more research is needed into the intersections between rurality, racialization and education in different sites (Pini & Bhopal, 2017; Butler, 2020). Detailed ethnographic studies such as this one seem well suited to the complexity of the task (Cohen, 2001).

As the 'Black v Black' discourse and dynamics in Easthaven attest, it is in regional areas that multiculturalism comes most intimately face to face with the legacies of colonialism in Australia – legacies that remain especially burdensome for many Indigenous Australians. As Koleth (2010, p. 2) notes, a crucial influence on race relations in settler societies is the treatment of Indigenous peoples in the past, and their place and welfare within those societies at present. Certainly multiculturalism, overall, has been much more successful in improving outcomes for immigrants than for Aboriginal and Torres Strait Islander Australians. This book has also revealed some of the consequences of the frequent separation of the 'multicultural' and the 'Indigenous' in policy, institutional and academic spheres – a separation that warrants more attention at a theoretical level (adding to the work of scholars such as Anderson, 2000; Povinelli, 1998) as well as a political and practical level.

Here I return to Hillview High, and a NAIDOC Week assembly I observed, for some final concluding thoughts: that 'small actions by small groups of people can lead to enormous change'; that we must 'remember the past, learn from it, and also be inspired by it'; and that 'only a little has been achieved' in terms of improving overall Indigenous outcomes and Indigenous/non-Indigenous relations.[1] Recognizing how far there is to go does not mean losing sight of the gains that have been made (Gillborn, 2007). Continued progress will depend on our ability, individually and collectively, to discern 'shared problems, entangled futures, new principles and structures of feeling' (Amin, 2010, p. 18) – perhaps the sorts of processes Seaview High ESL teacher Richard imagined when he said: 'Integration is accepting [there are] other paradigms of thinking, not just your own, and incorporating that into how you're all communicating with each other. It's a sharing process. That's learning.' That seems a reasonable 'new principle' on which to build a multiculturalism for all.

Notes

Introduction

1. The names of the schools, the town in which they are located and all participants have been changed.
2. National Aborigines and Islanders Day Observance Committee, which was set up to promote recognition of the histories, beliefs, practices and achievements of Indigenous Australians.
3. The terms 'White' and 'Black' are used frequently in this book and their varied meanings are discussed at length in the pages that follow. For now, I note that they are contested, and problematic even if they were not contested – hence the initial inverted commas. Some authors capitalize them, while others do not.
4. In more remote communities, the proportions may be the other way around.
5. Bell raised this question in relation to the United States, not Australia.
6. The federal Racial Discrimination Act was passed in 1975 as part of the turn to multiculturalism.
7. Like Canada and New Zealand, Australia is typically referred to, in both academic and popular discourses, as a 'settler society'. However, the term is contested – for example, with arguments that 'invasion' rather than 'settlement' is the accurate term for what occurred when Europeans arrived on lands (now known as Australia) long occupied by Indigenous peoples (Kerin, 2016; Koerner, 2011). I do not dispute the validity of the 'invasion' perspective, but, as this study is not primarily concerned with Indigenous sovereignty, I use a mix of terms throughout.
8. Known as Kath Walker before she changed her name in 1988 to reflect her ancestry.
9. An initiative introduced and sponsored by the federal government.
10. Under national data standards, students are classified as LBOTE if a language other than English (LOTE) is the main language spoken at home by the student and/or by either of his or her parents/carers (ACARA, 2012).

Chapter 1

1. Organization for Economic Co-operation and Development.
2. Conducted every five years.
3. 'Country' in the Indigenous usage of the word (without a preceding article) – see Chapter 3.
4. While this view is now widespread in the humanities and social sciences, it is not uncontested – see Heng (2011); Smedley (2007).
5. See ABC (2013).

Chapter 2

1. The NSW DoE has updated this policy (August 2022). Its overall focus, however, remains unchanged.
2. The heading is based on one in *The Multicultural Riddle* (Baumann, 1999).
3. A multilingual and multicultural public broadcaster.
4. Like most European countries, Germany has never had an official policy of multiculturalism (Kymlicka, 2012; Lentin, 2014) – underlining again the multiple meanings and usages of the word.
5. 'The genius of Australian multiculturalism' was the original title of the 16 February 2011 speech, and the excerpts quoted are taken from a hard copy. Under a change of government in 2013, the speech was relocated on the internet under a new title, 'Multiculturalism in the Australian context'. It is no longer available online.
6. 'White Australia policy' is the name commonly used to refer to a series of parliamentary acts and government policies – beginning with the Immigration Restriction Act 1901 – that served to protect Australia's European heritage.
7. Grassby, cited in Hage (2000, p. 83).
8. Since 2010, all students in NSW schools are required to complete at least Year 10 and to remain in formal education until they are seventeen (NSW DoE, 2009).

Chapter 3

1. In the 2021 census, respondents could report up to two ancestries; the sum of all ancestry responses may not equal the total number of people in the area.
2. Technical and Further Education – educational institutions focused on vocational education and training.

Chapter 4

1. From the broader interview, it appears that in this sentence Hope was talking about Easthaven rather than Australia, and meaning that 85 per cent of the town's population were of Anglo-Celtic descent. The 'English-American' is difficult to explain, although she did feel that Australian popular culture was heavily influenced by American television.
2. This heading is taken from Brah (1991).
3. 'The Stolen Generation', or generations, refers to the children of Aboriginal and Torres Strait Islander descent who were forcibly removed from their families by government agencies from federation in 1901 through to the 1970s. A range of methods of removal were used, on a range of rationales, with children typically placed in state-run institutions, adopted out to White families and/or used as cheap or unpaid labour (AHRC, 1997).
4. The old name for the topographical feature/tourist attraction that is now more commonly known by its Indigenous name of Uluru. The fact that Reg uses 'Ayers Rock' rather than 'Uluru' suggests an assertion of White linguistic dominance over the landmark, even if other forms of White ownership have been diluted.

Chapter 5

1. Borrowed from Bell and Hartmann (2007).
2. Borrowed from hooks (2006) – see later in this chapter.
3. See also Ahmed (2007a) on the importance of 'following words . . . around' (p. 254) to see what they 'do'.
4. Elaha's comments come from a school document, not a focus group.
5. 'Dago' is a derogatory term that in Australia was mostly reserved for immigrants of Italian descent. It was more ethnically specific than 'wog', and it has not been reappropriated in the same way.

Chapter 6

1. Native plants that were part of the everyday diet of an area's Indigenous inhabitants.
2. Literacy and numeracy tests conducted annually in schools across Australia for students in Years 3, 5, 7 and 9 (National Assessment Program, 2016).
3. This situation has changed since 2004. From 2018, all teachers in NSW schools have had to undertake regular professional development to maintain their accreditation (BOSTES, 2016).
4. Services for the Treatment and Rehabilitation of Torture and Trauma Survivors.
5. Teaching English to Speakers of Other Languages – a certificate requiring four weeks' full-time study.
6. Borrowed from Colic-Peisker and Tilbury (2008).

Conclusion

1. School executive comments.

References

Abbott, T. (2013, August 25). Tony Abbott's campaign launch speech: Full transcript. *The Sydney Morning Herald*. Retrieved from http://www.smh.com.au/federal-politics/federal-election-2013/tony- abbotts-campaign-launch-speech-full-transcript-20130825-2sjhc.html

ABC FactCheck. (2013). *Rupert Murdoch's vision for Australian diversity checks out*. Retrieved from http://www.abc.net.au/news/2013-11-08/rupert-murdoch-diversity-australia/5076168

Abdelkerim, A. A., & Grace, M. (2012). Challenges to employment in newly emerging African communities in Australia: A review of the literature. *Australian Social Work*, 65(1), 104–119.

ABS. (2010). 1301.0 – Year book Australia, 2008 – Aboriginal and Torres Strait Islander population. Retrieved from http://www.abs.gov.au/ausstats/ abs@.nsf/0/68AE74ED632E17A6CA2573D200110075?opendocument

ABS. (2012a). 2011.0.55.001 – Information paper: Census of population and housing – Products and services, 2011 – Changes between the 2006 and 2011 censuses. Retrieved from http://www.abs.gov.au/ausstats/abs@.nsf/lookup/2011.0.55.001Main%20Features22011

ABS. (2012b). 2071.0 – Reflecting a nation: Stories from the 2011 Census, 2012–13 – Cultural diversity in Australia. Retrieved from http://www.abs.gov.au/ausstats/abs@.nsf/Lookup/2071.0main+features902012–2013

ABS. (2016). 2011 Census QuickStats – Greater Sydney. Retrieved from http://www.censusdata.abs.gov.au/census_services/getproduct/census/2011/quickstat/1GSYD?opendocument&navpos=220

ABS. (2018). Estimates of Aboriginal and Torres Strait Islander Australians. Retrieved from https://www.abs.gov.au/statistics/people/aboriginal-and-torres-strait-islander-peoples/estimates-aboriginal-and-torres-strait-islander-australians/latest-release

ABS. (2021a). National, state and territory population. Retrieved from https://www.abs.gov.au/statistics/people/population/national-state-and-territory-population/latest-release

ABS. (2021b). Migration, Australia. Retrieved from https://www.abs.gov.au/statistics/people/population/migration-australia/latest-release

ABS. (2021c). *Section of State*. ABS. Retrieved from https://www.abs.gov.au/statistics/standards/australian-statistical-geography-standard-asgs-edition-3/jul2021-jun2026/significant-urban-areas-urban-centres-and-localities-section-state/section-state

ABS. (2022). Cultural diversity: Census. ABS, Canberra. Retrieved from https://www.abs.gov.au/statistics/people/people-and-communities/cultural-diversity-census/latest-release

ACARA. (2012). *Data standards manual: Student background characteristics* (6th ed.). Retrieved from http://www.acara.edu.au/verve/_resources/DSM_1.pdf

ACARA. (2013). *National report on schooling in Australia 2009*. Retrieved from https://acaraweb.blob.core.windows.net/resources/National_Report_on_Schooling_in_Australia_2009_live.pdf

ACARA. (2014). *State and territory implementation of the foundation to year 10 Australian curriculum*. Retrieved from https://acaraweb.blob.core.windows.net/resources/State_and_Territory_F-10_Australian_Curriculum_Implementation_Timelines_July_2014_v2.pdf

ACARA. (2015). *What does the ICSEA value mean?* Retrieved from http://www.acara.edu.au/_resources/About_icsea_2014.pdf

ACARA. (2016a). Cross-curriculum priorities. Retrieved from http://www.acara.edu.au/curriculum/cross-curriculum-priorities

ACARA. (2016b). General capabilities. Retrieved from http://www.acara.edu.au/curriculum/general-capabilities

ACARA. (n.d.). *Intercultural understanding*. Retrieved from http://v7-5.australiancurriculum.edu.au/GeneralCapabilities/Pdf/Intercultural-understanding

Adams, P. (2015, August 22–23). We're in denial. *The Weekend Australian Magazine*, p. 50.

Adoniou, M., Louden, B., & Savage, G. (2015, September 23). What will changes to the national curriculum mean for schools? Experts respond. *The Conversation*. Retrieved from http://theconversation.com/what-will-changes-to-the-national-curriculum-mean-for-schools-experts-respond-46933

Ahmed, S. (2000). *Strange encounters: Embodied others in post-coloniality*. Abingdon, Oxon: Routledge.

Ahmed, S. (2007a). The language of diversity. *Ethnic and Racial Studies*, 30(2), 235–256.

Ahmed, S. (2008). The politics of good feeling. *ACRAWSA e-Journal*, 4(1), 1–18. Retrieved from http://acrawsa.org.au/files/ejournalfiles/57acrawsa5-1.pdf

Ahmed, S. (2012). *On being included: Racism and diversity in institutional life*. London: Duke University Press.

AHRC. (1997). *Bringing them home: Report of the national inquiry into the separation of Aboriginal and Torres Strait Islander children from their families*. Retrieved from https://www.humanrights.gov.au/sites/default/files/content/pdf/social_justice/bringing_them_home_report.pdf

AHRC. (2016). *Leading for change: A blueprint for cultural diversity and inclusive leadership*. Retrieved from https://www.humanrights.gov.au/sites/default/files/document/publication/2016_AHRC%20Leading%20f or%20change.pdf

AHRC. (2018). Leading for change: A blueprint for cultural diversity and inclusive leadership revisited. Retrieved from https://humanrights.gov.au/sites/default/files/document/publication/Leading%20for%20Change_Blueprint2018_FINAL_Web.pdf

AHRC. (n.d.-a). About constitutional recognition. Retrieved from https://www.humanrights.gov.au/publications/about-constitutional-recognition

AHRC. (n.d.-b). Australia and the universal declaration on human rights. Retrieved from https://www.humanrights.gov.au/human_rights/UDHR/Australia_UDHR.html

AHRC. (n.d.-c). Racism: It stops with me. Retrieved from https://itstopswithme.humanrights.gov.au

Allard, A., & Santoro, N. (2004). Making sense of difference? Teaching identities in postmodern contexts. Paper presented at the *AARE (Australian Association for Research in Education)* annual conference, Melbourne. Retrieved from http://www.aare.edu.au/data/publications/2004/all04561.pdf

Allard, A., & Santoro, N. (2008). Experienced teachers' perspectives on cultural and social class diversity: Which differences matter? *Equity and Excellence in Education*, 41(2), 200–214.

Amin, A. (2002). Ethnicity and the multicultural city: Living with diversity. *Environment and Planning A*, *34*(6), 959–980.
Amin, A. (2010). The remainders of race. *Theory, Culture & Society*, *27*(1), 1–23.
Andersen, M. (1999). The fiction of "diversity without oppression": Race, ethnicity, identity, and power. In R. H. Tai & M. L. Kenyatta (Eds.), *Critical ethnicity: Countering the waves of identity politics* (pp. 5–20). Totawa, NJ: Rowman and Littlefield.
Anderson, K. (2000). Thinking "postnationally": Dialogue across multicultural, indigenous, and settler spaces. *Annals of the Association of American Geographers*, *90*(2), 381–391.
Ang, I. (1994). On not speaking Chinese: Postmodern ethnicity and the politics of diaspora. *New Formations*, *24*, 1–18.
Ang, I. (2001). *On not speaking Chinese: Living between Asia and the West*. London: Routledge.
Ang, I. (2003). Together-in-difference: Beyond diaspora, into hybridity. *Asian Studies Review*, *27*(2), 141–154.
Ang, I. (2014). Beyond Chinese groupism: Chinese Australians between assimilation, multiculturalism and diaspora. *Ethnic and Racial Studies*, *37*(7), 1184–1196.
Ang, I., Brand, J. E., Noble, G., & Sternberg, J. (2006). *Connecting diversity: Paradoxes of multicultural Australia*. Retrieved from http://epublications.bond.edu.au/cgi/viewcontent.cgi?article=1020&co ntext=hss_pubs
Ang, I., Brand, J. E., Noble, G., & Wilding, D. (2002). *Living diversity: Australia's multicultural future*. Retrieved from http://epublications.bond.edu.au/ cgi/viewcontent.cgi?article=1019&context=hss_pubs
Appadurai, A. (1986). Theory in anthropology: Center and periphery. *Comparative Studies in Society and History*, *28*(2), 356–374.
Appadurai, A. (1988). Putting hierarchy in its place. *Cultural Anthropology*, *3*(1), 36–49.
Askins, K. (2009). Crossing divides: Ethnicity and rurality. *Journal of Rural Studies*, *25*(4), 365–375.
Atkin, C. (2003). Rural communities: Human and symbolic capital development, fields apart. *Compare: A Journal of Comparative and International Education*, *33*(4), 507–518.
ATSIC. (2012). 1301.0 – Year book Australia, 1994: Statistics on the indigenous peoples of Australia. Retrieved from http://www.abs.gov.au/ausstats/ abs@.nsf/94713ad445ff1425ca25682000192af2/8dc45512042c8c00ca 2569de002139be!OpenDocument
Audit Office of NSW. (2012). *NSW auditor-general's report: Settling humanitarian entrants in NSW*. Sydney: Community Relations Commission. Retrieved from http://www.audit.nsw.gov.au/Article Documents/245/02_Humanitarian_Entrants_2012_Executive_S ummary. pdf.aspx?Embed=Y
Australian Government. (n.d.). Apology to Australia's Indigenous peoples. Retrieved from http://www.australia.gov.au/about-australia/our-country/our-people/apology-to-australias-indigenous-peoples
Australian Policy Online. (2009). NSW priority schools programs guidelines 2009–2012. Retrieved from http://apo.org.au/resource/nsw-priority-schools-programs-guidelines-2009-2012
Aveling, N. (2007). Anti-racism in schools: A question of leadership? *Discourse: Studies in the Cultural Politics of Education*, *28*(1), 69–85.
Bacchi, C. (2000). Policy as discourse: What does it mean? Where does it get us? *Discourse*, *21*(1), 45–57.
Back, L. (2012). New hierarchies of belonging. *European Journal of Cultural Studies*, *15*(2), 139–154.

Balint, P. (2010). Avoiding an intolerant society: Why respect of difference may not be the best approach. *Educational Philosophy and Theory, 42*(1), 129–141.

Ball, S. (1993). What is policy? Texts, trajectories and toolboxes. *The Australian Journal of Education Studies, 13*(2), 10–17.

Banks, J. (2011). Multicultural education: Dimensions and paradigms. In J. Banks (Ed.), *The Routledge international companion to multicultural education* (pp. 9–32). New York: Routledge.

Barnes, T., & Hannah, M. (2001). The place of numbers: Histories, geographies, and theories of quantification. *Environment and Planning D: Society and Space, 19*, 379–383.

Baum, F. (1999, March 14–17). Social capital and health: Implications for health in rural Australia. Paper presented at the *5th National Rural Health* conference, Adelaide, South Australia. Retrieved from http://www.ruralhealth.org.au/PAPERS/5_schlth.pdf

Baumann, G. (1999). *The multicultural riddle: Rethinking national, ethnic and religious identities*. New York: Routledge.

BBC. (2010). Merkel says German multicultural society has failed. *BBC News*. Retrieved from http://www.bbc.com/news/world-europe-11559451

BBC. (2011). State multiculturalism has failed, says David Cameron. *BBC News*. Retrieved from http://www.bbc.com/news/uk-politics-12371994

Bell, D. (1979). Brown v. Board of education and the interest-convergence dilemma. *Harvard Law Review, 93*, 518–533.

Bell, J., & Hartmann, D. (2007). Diversity in everyday discourse: The cultural ambiguities and consequences of "happy talk". *American Sociological Review, 72*(6), 895–914.

Bennett, S. (2012). 1301.0 – Year book Australia, 2004: The 1967 aborigines referendum. Retrieved from http://www.abs.gov.au/AUSSTATS/abs@.nsf/Previousproducts/1301.0Feature%20Article12004

Betts, K. (2001). Boatpeople and public opinion in Australia. *People and Place, 9*(4), 34–48.

Bloemraad, I., & Wright, M. (2014). "Utter failure" or unity out of diversity? Debating and evaluating policies of multiculturalism. *International Migration Review, 48*(s1), S292–S334.

Boese, M. (2010). Challenging current policy rationales of regionalising immigration. Paper presented at the *Australasian Political Studies Association* conference (date/place not cited). Retrieved from https://www.researchgate.net/publication/267193763_challenging_current_policy_rationales_of_regionalising_immigration

Boler, M., & Zembylas, M. (2003). Discomforting truths: The emotional terrain of understanding differences. In P. Trifonas (Ed.), *Pedagogies of difference: Rethinking education for social justice* (pp. 110–136). New York: RoutledgeFalmer.

Bonilla-Silva, E. (2006). *Racism without racists: Color-blind racism and the persistence of racial inequality in the United States* (2nd ed.). Lanham, MD: Rowman & Littlefield.

BOSTES. (2010). Aboriginal education contexts – Timeline 1967–2007. Retrieved from https://ab-ed.bostes.nsw.edu.au/go/aboriginal-studies/timeline/timeline-1967-2007

BOSTES. (2016). Teacher accreditation: Answering your questions. Retrieved from http://www.nswteachers.nsw.edu.au/current-teachers/accreditation-of-all-teachers/pre-2004-school-teachers/

Bourdieu, P., & Wacquant, L. (1999). On the cunning of imperialist reason. *Theory, Culture & Society, 16*(1), 41–58.

Bowen, C. (2013). *Hearts and minds: A blueprint for modern Labor*. Carlton: Melbourne University Press.

Bowker, G., & Star, S. (2000). *Sorting things out: Classification and its consequences*. Cambridge, MA: MIT Press.

Brah, A. (1991). Difference, diversity, differentiation. *International Review of Sociology*, *2*(2), 53–71.

Brett, J., & Moran, A. (2011). Cosmopolitan nationalism: Ordinary people making sense of diversity. *Nations and Nationalism*, *17*(1), 188–206.

Brown, J., Miller, J., & Mitchell, J. (2006). Interrupted schooling and the acquisition of literacy: Experiences of Sudanese refugees in Victorian secondary schools. *Australian Journal of Language and Literacy*, *29*(2), 150.

Brubaker, R. (2004). Ethnicity without groups. *European Journal of Sociology*, *43*(2), 163–189.

Brubaker, R., & Cooper, F. (2000). Beyond "identity". *Theory and Society*, *29*(1), 1–47.

Brubaker, R., Loveman, M., & Stamatov, P. (2004). Ethnicity as cognition. *Theory and Society*, *33*(1), 31–64.

Bryant, L., & Pini, B. (2009). Gender, class and rurality: Australian case studies. *Journal of Rural Studies*, *25*(1), 48–57.

Buckmaster, L. (2012, September 28). Australian government assistance to refugees: Fact v fiction. Retrieved from http://www.aph.gov.au/ About_Parliament/Parliamentary _Departments/Parliamentary_Library/ pubs/BN/2012-2013/AustGovAssistRefugees

Bulbeck, C. (2004). The "white worrier" in South Australia: Attitudes to multiculturalism, immigration and reconciliation. *Journal of Sociology*, *40*(4), 341–361.

Butler, J. (1997). *Excitable speech: A politics of the performative*. New York: Routledge.

Butler, R. (2020). Young people's rural multicultures: Researching social relationships among youth in rural contexts. *Journal of Youth Studies*, *23*(9), 1178–1194.

Butler, R. (2021). Youth, mobilities and multicultures in the rural Anglosphere: Positioning a research agenda. *Ethnic and Racial Studies*, *4416*, 63–82.

Cadzow, A. (n.d.). A NSW aboriginal education timeline 1788–2007. Retrieved from http://ab-ed.boardofstudies.nsw.edu.au/files/timeline1788-2007.pdf

Cahill, D. (1996). *Immigration and schooling in the 1990s*. Canberra: Department of Immigration and Multicultural Affairs.

Castagno, A. (2014). *Educated in Whiteness: Good intentions and diversity in schools*. Minneapolis, MN: University of Minnesota Press.

Census of India 2011. (2011). Population enumeration data (final population). Retrieved from http://www.censusindia.gov.in/2011census/ population_enumeration.html

Chakraborti, N., & Garland, J. (2004). Introduction. In N. Chakraborti & J. Garland (Eds.), *Rural racism* (pp. 1–13). Cullompton, Devon: Willan Publishing.

Chan, G. (2016). Australia broadly tolerant but pockets of intense prejudice remain, report shows. *The Guardian*. Retrieved from https://www.theguardian.com/australia-news /2016/aug/24/australia- broadly-tolerant-but-pockets-of-intense-prejudice-remain-rep ort- shows?CMP=share_btn_tw

Chodkiewicz, A., & Burridge, N. (2013). Addressing diversity in schools: Policies, programs and local realities. In A. Jakubowicz & C. Ho (Eds.), *For those who've come across the seas: Australian multicultural theory, policy and practice* (pp. 210–222). North Melbourne: Australian Scholarly Publishing.

Clarke, A. (2016). Here's a bunch of things Pauline Hanson has said about Indigenous Australians. *BuzzFeed News*. Retrieved from https://www.buzzfeed.com/allanclarke/ pauline-hanson-and- indigenous-australia?utm_term=.lxmm9GQDO#.euVgvmOAb

Cloke, P. (2004). Rurality and racialised others: Out of place in the countryside? In N. Chakraborti & J. Garland (Eds.), *Rural racism* (pp. 17–35). Cullompton, Devon: Willan Publishing.

Cloke, P., & Milbourne, P. (1992). Deprivation and lifestyles in rural Wales. II. Rurality and the cultural dimension. *Journal of Rural Studies, 8*(4), 359–371.

Cohen, E. (2001). *Re-thinking the "migrant community": A study of Latin American migrants and refugees in Adelaide* (PhD), Adelaide University.

Colic-Peisker, V., & Robertson, S. (2015). Social change and community cohesion: An ethnographic study of two Melbourne suburbs. *Ethnic and Racial Studies, 38*(1), 75–91.

Colic-Peisker, V., & Tilbury, F. (2007). *Refugees and employment: The effect of visible difference on discrimination – Final report*. Retrieved from http://library.bsl.org.au/jspui/bitstream/1/811/1/Refugees%20and%2 0employment.pdf

Colic-Peisker, V., & Tilbury, F. (2008). Being black in Australia: A case study of intergroup relations. *Race and Class, 49*(4), 38–56.

Collins, J. (1993). *Cohesion with diversity? Immigration and multiculturalism in Canada and Australia* (Working paper no. 28). Retrieved from http://www.finance.uts.edu.au/research/wpapers/wp28.pdf

Collins, J. (2013). Multiculturalism and immigrant integration in Australia. *Canadian Ethnic Studies, 45*(3), 133–149.

Collins, J., Reid, C., Fabiansson, C., & Healey, L. (2007). *Tapping the pulse of youth in cosmopolitan south-western and western Sydney – Final report*. Canberra: Department of Immigration and Citizenship.

Colvin, N. (2013). Resettlement as rebirth: How effective are the midwives? *M/C Journal, 16*(5). Retrieved from http://journal.media-culture.org.au/ index.php/mcjournal/article/viewArticle/706

Colvin, N. (2017). "Really really different different": Rurality, regional schools and refugees. *Race Ethnicity and Education, 20*(2), 225–239.

Commonwealth of Australia. (2017). *Executive summary – Coasts*. Retrieved from https://soe.environment.gov.au/theme/coasts

Commonwealth of Australia. (2020). *Migration between cities and regions: A quick guide to COVID-19 impacts*. Retrieved from https://population.gov.au/sites/population.gov.au/files/2021-09/the-impacts-of-covid-on-migration-between-cities-and-regions.pdf

Commonwealth of Australia. (2021). *Australia's permanent migration program: A quick guide*. Retrieved from https://www.aph.gov.au/About_Parliament/Parliamentary_Departments/Parliamentary_Library/pubs/rp/rp2122/Quick_Guides/AustraliasMigrationProgram

Condor, S. (2000). Pride and prejudice: Identity management in English people's talk about "this country". *Discourse & Society, 11*(2), 175–205.

Connell, R. (2009). Good teachers on dangerous ground: Towards a new view of teacher quality and professionalism. *Critical Studies in Education, 50*(3), 213–229.

Connell, R. (2011). *Confronting equality: Gender, knowledge and global change*. Crows Nest, Sydney: Allen & Unwin.

Cowlishaw, G. (2004a). *Blackfellas, whitefellas, and the hidden injuries of race*. Oxford: Wiley-Blackwell.

Cowlishaw, G. (2004b). Racial positioning, privilege and public debate. In A. Moreton-Robinson (Ed.), *Whitening race: Essays in social and cultural criticism* (pp. 59–74). Canberra: Aboriginal Studies Press.

Cowlishaw, G. (2006). Cultures of complaint: An ethnography of rural racial rivalry. *Journal of Sociology, 42*(4), 429–445.

Cox, L. (2014). "You don't migrate to this country unless you want to join our team": Tony Abbott renews push on national security laws. *The Sydney Morning Herald*. Retrieved from http://www.smh.com.au/ federal-politics/political-news/you-dont-migrate-to-this-country- unless-you-want-to-join-our-team-tony-abbott-renews-push-on- national-security-laws-20140818-3dvbx.html

Creagh, S. (2016a). A critical analysis of the language background other than English (LBOTE) category in the Australian national testing system: A Foucauldian perspective. *Journal of Education Policy*, *31*(3), 275–289.

Creagh, S. (2016b). "Language background other than English": A problem NAPLaN test category for Australian students of refugee background. *Race Ethnicity and Education*, *19*(2), 252–273.

Crenshaw, K. (1988). Race, reform, and retrenchment: Transformation and legitimation in antidiscrimination law. *Harvard Law Review*, *101*(7), 1331–1387.

Crowley, M., & Lichter, D.(2009). Social disorganization in new Latino destinations? *Rural Sociology*, *74*(4), 573–604.

Crowley, V. (1999). Towards a postcolonial curriculum for the new millennium. In B. Johnson & A. Reid (Eds.), *Contesting the curriculum* (pp. 100–111). Katoomba: Social Science Press.

Curthoys, A. (2000). An uneasy conversation: The multicultural and the indigenous. In J. Docker & G. Fischer (Eds.), *Race, colour and identity in Australia and New Zealand* (pp. 21–36). Sydney: UNSW Press.

Daley, P. (2016). Why Australia Day and Anzac Day helped create a national "cult of forgetfulness". *The Guardian*. Retrieved from https://www.theguardian.com/australia-news/postcolonial- blog/2016/oct/16/why-australia-day-and-anzac-day-helped-create-a- national-cult-of-forgetfulness?CMP=share_btn_tw

Danaher, G., Schirato, T., & Webb, J. (2000). *Understanding Foucault*. Crows Nest, Sydney: Allen & Unwin.

Davey, M. (2017, January 26). Malcolm Turnbull's Australia Day message recognises Aboriginal people and cultural diversity. *The Guardian*. Retrieved from https://www.theguardian.com/australia- news/2017/jan/26/malcolm-turnbulls-australia-day-message- recognises-aboriginal-people-and-cultural-diversity?CMP=soc_568

Davie, A. (2015). *Engaging young people in regional, rural and remote Australia*. Australian Clearinghouse for Youth Studies. Retrieved from https://docs.education.gov.au/system/files/doc/other/young_people_in_regional_rural_and_remote_australia.pdf

De Finney, S. (2010). "We just don't know each other": Racialised girls negotiate mediated multiculturalism in a less diverse Canadian city. *Journal of Intercultural Studies*, *31*(5), 471–487.

De Lepervanche, M. (1980). From race to ethnicity. *Journal of Sociology*, *16*(1), 24–37.

DFAT. (2015). *Australia's trade in goods and services 2014–15*. Retrieved from http://dfat.gov.au/about-us/publications/trade- investment/australias-trade-in-goods-and-services/Pages/australias-trade-in-goods-and-services-2014-15.aspx

DFAT. (n.d.-a). *About Australia – Indigenous Australia*. Retrieved from http://dfat.gov.au/about-australia/land-its-people/Pages/indigenous-%20australia.aspx

DHA. (2021a). *Permanent migration*. Retrieved from https://www.homeaffairs.gov.au/research-and-statistics/statistics/country-profiles/permanent-migration

DHA. (2021b). *Country profiles*. Retrieved from https://www.homeaffairs.gov.au/research-and-statistics/statistics/country-profiles/overview

DHA. (2022). *Temporary visa holders in Australia*. Retrieved from https://data.gov.au/data/dataset/temporary-entrants-visa-holders

DiMaggio, P. (1997). Culture and cognition. *Annual Review of Sociology, 23*(1), 263–287.
DIMIA. (1998). *Living in harmony – An overview.* Retrieved from http://www.multicultur alaustralia.edu.au/doc/immdept_4.pdf
Dixson, A., & Rousseau, C. (2005). And we are still not saved: Critical race theory in education ten years later. *Race Ethnicity and Education, 8*(1), 7–27.
Dobinson, T., & Buchori, S. (2016). Catering for EAL/D students' language needs in mainstream classes: Early childhood teachers' perspectives and practices in one Australian setting. *Australian journal of Teacher Education, 41*(2), 32–52.
Drury, V., Chiang, P., Esterhuizen, P., Freshwater, D., & Taylor, B. (2014). Researchers' experiences of focus group dynamics in Singapore, Australia and the Netherlands: Troubling multicultural assumptions. *Journal of Research in Nursing, 19*(6), 460–474.
DSS. (2011). The people of Australia: Australia's multicultural policy. Retrieved from http://www.dss.gov.au/sites/default/files/documents/12_2013/people-of-australia -multicultural-policy-booklet_print.pdf
DSS. (2014). Australia today. Retrieved from https://www.dss.gov.au/our-responsibilities /settlement-and-multicultural-affairs/programs-policy/a-multicultural-australia/ national-agenda-for-a-multicultural-australia/why-do-we-need-a-national-agenda/ australia-today
DSS. (2017). *Multicultural Australia: United, strong, successful.* Retrieved from https://www .dss.gov.au/settlement-and-multicultural-affairs/australian-governments-multicultural -statement/australian-governments-multicultural-statement
DSS. (n.d.). Harmony day. Retrieved from http://www.harmony.gov.au
Duff, E. (2015). Ice blamed for terrifying, violent attacks on elderly. *The Sun-Herald.* Retrieved from http://www.smh.com.au/nsw/nervous- of-the-night-the-elderly-community-being-terrorised-by-ice-addicts-20151030-gkn5ys
Dufty, R. (2009). "At least I don't live in vegemite valley": Racism and rural public housing spaces. *Australian Geographer, 40*(4), 429–449.
Dufty-Jones, R. (2014). Rural economies in the "age of migration": Perspectives from OECD countries. *Geography Compass, 8*(6), 368–380.
Dunn, K., Forrest, J., Babacan, H., Paradies, Y., & Pedersen, A. (2008). *Challenging racism: The anti-racism research project – National level findings.* Retrieved from http://www.uws.edu.au/ data/assets/pdf_file/0007/173635/NationalLevelFindingsV1 .pdf
Dunn, K., Kamp, A., Shaw, W. S., Forrest, J., & Paradies, Y. (2010). Indigenous Australians' attitudes towards multiculturalism, cultural diversity, "race" and racism. *Journal of Australian Indigenous issues, 13*(4), 19–31.
Dunn, K., & McDonald, A. (2001). The geography of racisms in NSW: A theoretical exploration and some preliminary findings from the mid-1990s. *Australian Geographer, 32*(1), 29–44.
Dunn, K., Thompson, S., Hanna, B., Murphy, P., & Burnley, I. (2001). Multicultural policy within local government in Australia. *Urban Studies, 38*(13), 2477–2494.
Dwyer, O., & Jones, J. (2000). White socio-spatial epistemology. *Social and Cultural Geography, 1*(2), 209–222.
Dyer, R. (2005). The matter of whiteness. In P. Rothenberg (Ed.), *White privilege: Essential readings on the other side of racism* (2nd ed., pp. 9–14). New York: Worth Publishers.
Edgeworth, K. (2011). *Discourses of inclusion and exclusion: Ethnic minority, Muslim and refugee students in rural schools* (PhD), Charles Sturt University, Australia.
Edgeworth, K. (2014). Black bodies, White rural spaces: Disturbing practices of unbelonging for "refugee" students. *Critical Studies in Education, 56*(3), 351–365.

Edgeworth, K., & Santoro, N. (2015). A pedagogy of belonging: Troubling encounters with ethnic and religious difference. *Cambridge Journal of Education, 45*(4), 415–426.

Education Council (Australia). (2019). *Alice Springs (Mparntwe) Education Declaration*. Carlton South: Education Council Secretariat.

Ekman, P. (1992). An argument for basic emotions. *Cognition and Emotion, 6*(3–4), 169–200.

Essential Research. (2018). *The essential report*. Carlton: Essential Media. Retrieved from https://www.essentialvision.com.au/wp-content/uploads/2018/04/Essential-Report_240418.pdf

Eureka Research. (1998a). *The anti-racism campaign: Quantitative market research to guide campaign development – Project 2115*. Retrieved from https://andrewjakubowicz.files.wordpress.com/2011/11/dimiaantiraci smreportquant1998.pdf

Eureka Research. (1998b). *The anti-racism campaign: Qualitative market research to guide campaign development – Project 2028*. Retrieved from https://andrewjakubowicz.files.wordpress.com/2011/11/dimiaantiraci smreportqual1998.pdf

Fairclough, N. (1989). *Language and power*. Harlow, Essex: Addison Wesley Longman.

Fairclough, N. (1993). Critical discourse analysis and the marketization of public discourse: The universities. *Discourse & Society, 4*(2), 133–168.

Fairclough, N. (1995). *Critical discourse analysis: The critical study of languages*. London: Longman.

Fairclough, N. (2001). The discourse of new labour: Critical discourse analysis. In M. Wetherell, S. Taylor, & S. J. Yates (Eds.), *Discourse as data: A guide for analysis* (pp. 229–266). London: Sage Publications.

Fairclough, N. (2003). *Analysing discourse: Textual analysis for social research*. London: Routledge.

Fanon, F. (1964). *Toward the African revolution: Political essays* (H. Chevalier, Trans.). New York: Grove Press.

Fanshawe, S., & Sriskandarajah, D. (2010, January). *"You can't put me in a box": Super-diversity and the end of identity politics in Britain*. Retrieved from http://www.tedcantle.co.uk/publications/59.pdf

Farrugia, D., Smyth, J., & Harrison, T. (2016). Affective topologies of rural youth embodiment. *Sociologia Ruralis, 56*(1), 116–132.

Fisher, M. (2013). A revealing map of the world's most and least ethnically diverse countries. *The Washington Post*. Retrieved from https://www.washingtonpost.com/news/worldviews/wp/2013/05/16/a-revealing-map-of-the-worlds-most-and-least-ethnically-diverse- countries/?utm_term=.fcfe6354b939

Fiske, S., & Linville, P. (1980). What does the schema concept buy us? *Personality and Social Psychology Bulletin, 6*(4), 543–557.

Ford, M. (2013). Achievement gaps in Australia: What NAPLAN reveals about education inequality in Australia. *Race Ethnicity and Education, 16*(1), 80–102.

Fordham, S., & Ogbu, J. (1986). Black students' school success: Coping with the "burden of 'acting white'". *The Urban Review, 18*(3), 176–206.

Forman, M. (2001). "Straight outta Mogadishu": Prescribed identities and performative practices among Somali youth in North American high schools. *TOPIA: Canadian Journal of Cultural Studies, 5*, 33–60.

Forrest, J., & Dunn, K. (2007). Constructing racism in Sydney, Australia's largest EthniCity. *Urban Studies, 44*(4), 699–721.

Forrest, J., & Dunn, K. (2010). Attitudes to multicultural values in diverse spaces in Australia's immigrant cities, Sydney and Melbourne. *Space and Polity, 14*(1), 81–102.

Forrest, J., & Dunn, K. (2013). Cultural diversity, racialisation and the experience of racism in rural Australia: The South Australian case. *Journal of Rural Studies, 30*, 1–9.

Foucault, M. (1972 [1969]). *The archaeology of knowledge and the discourse on language* (A. M. Sheridan Smith, Trans.). London: Tavistock.

Garbutt, R. (2009). Social inclusion and local practices of belonging. *Cosmopolitan Civil Societies: An Interdisciplinary Journal, 1*(3), 84–108.

Garbutt, R. (2011). *The locals: Identity, place and belonging in Australia*. Bern: Peter Lang.

Garland, J., & Chakraborti, N. (2006). "Race", space and place. *Ethnicities, 6*(2), 159–177.

Gillborn, D. (2007). Education policy as an act of white supremacy: Whiteness, critical race theory and education reform. *Journal of Education Policy, 20*(4), 485–505.

Gillborn, D. (2008). *Racism and education: Coincidence or conspiracy?* Abingdon: Routledge.

Gillborn, D. (2010). The white working class, racism and respectability: Victims, degenerates and interest-convergence. *British Journal of Educational Studies, 58*(1), 3–25.

Goldberg, D. (2006). Racial Europeanization. *Ethnic and Racial Studies, 29*(2), 331–364.

Goodwin, N. (1996). Governmentality in the Queensland department of education: Policies and the management of schools. *Discourse: Studies in the Cultural Politics of Education, 17*(1), 65–74.

Goot, M., & Watson, I. (2005). Immigration, multiculturalism and national identity. In S. Wilson, R. Gibson, D. Denemark, & M. Western (Eds.), *Australian social attitudes: The first report* (pp. 182–203). Sydney: UNSW Press.

Grand, I. (1999). Cultural identities and practices of community. *Futures, 31*(5), 475–485.

Gulson, K. N., & Symes, C. (2007). Knowing one's place: Space, theory, education. *Critical Studies in Education, 48*(1), 97–110.

Hage, G. (2000). *White nation: Fantasies of white supremacy in a multicultural society*. New York: Routledge.

Hage, G. (2008). Analysing multiculturalism today. In T. Bennett & J. Frow (Eds.), *The Sage handbook of cultural analysis* (pp. 488–509). London: Sage Publications.

Hall, S. (1990a). Cultural identity and diaspora. *Identity: Community, Culture, Difference, 2*, 222–237.

Hall, S. (1990b). The emergence of cultural studies and the crisis of the humanities. *October, 53*, 11–23.

Hall, S. (1991). Ethnicity: Identity and difference. *Radical America, 23*(4), 9–20.

Hall, S. (1997). The work of representation. In S. Hall (Ed.), *Representation: Cultural representations and signifying practices* (pp. 13–74). London: Sage Publications in association with The Open University.

Harkins, J. (1990). Shame and shyness in the aboriginal classroom: A case for "practical semantics". *Australian Journal of Linguistics, 10*(2), 293–306.

Harmony Day. (n.d.). Harmony Day. Retrieved from http://www.harmony.gov.au

Hartmann, D. (2015). Reflections on race, diversity, and the crossroads of multiculturalism. *The Sociological Quarterly, 56*(4), 623–639.

Heng, G. (2011). The invention of race in the European middle ages I: Race studies, modernity, and the middle ages. *Literature Compass, 8*(5), 258–274.

Hesse, B. (2007). Racialized modernity: An analytics of white mythologies. *Ethnic and Racial Studies, 30*(4), 643–663.

Hickling-Hudson, A. (2003). Multicultural education and the postcolonial turn. *Policy Futures in Education, 1*(2), 381–401.

Ho, C. (2011). "My school" and others: Segregation and white flight. *Australian Review of Public Affairs*. Retrieved from http://www.australianreview.net/digest/2011/05/ho.html

Ho, C. (2013). From social justice to social cohesion: A history of Australian multicultural policy. In A. Jakubowicz & C. Ho (Eds.), *For those who've come across the seas: Australian multicultural theory, policy and practice* (pp. 31–41). North Melbourne: Australian Scholarly Publishing.

Ho, C. (2020). *Aspiration and anxiety: Asian migrants and Australian schooling*. Melbourne: Melbourne University Press.

Hokari, M. (2012). *Gurindji journey: A Japanese historian in the outback*. Sydney: UNSW Press.

Holloway, S. (2007). Burning issues: Whiteness, rurality and the politics of difference. *Geoforum*, *38*(1), 7–20.

hooks, b. (2006). Eating the other: Desire and resistance. In M. G. Durham & D. M. Kellner (Eds.), *Media and cultural studies: Keyworks* (2nd ed., pp. 366–380). Madden, MA: Blackwell Publishing.

Howitt, R., & McLean, J. (2015). Towards closure? Coexistence, remoteness and righteousness in Indigenous policy in Australia. *Australian Geographer*, *46*(2), 137–145.

Hugo, G. (2000). What is happening in rural and regional populations? Paper presented at the *1st National Conference on the Future of Australia's Country Towns*, Bendigo. Retrieved from http://www.regional.org.au/au/countrytowns/keynote/hugo.htm

Hugo, G. (2008). Immigrant settlement outside of Australia's capital cities. *Population, Space and Place*, *14*(6), 553–571.

Hugo, G., Feist, H., & Tan, G. (2013). Population change in regional Australia, 2006–11. *Australian Population and Migration Research Centre policy brief*, *1*(3). Retrieved from http://www.adelaide.edu.au/apmrc/pubs/policy-briefs/APMRC_Policy_Brief_Vol_1_3_2013.pdf

Hugo, G., & Morén-Alegret, R. (2008). International migration to non-metropolitan areas of high income countries: Editorial introduction. *Population, Space and Place*, *14*(6), 473–477.

Hunt, T. (2012). The virtuous citizen: Patriotism in a multicultural society by Tim Soutphommasane – Review. *The Observer*. Retrieved from http://www.theguardian.com/books/2012/sep/30/virtuous-citizen-review-tim-soutphommasane

Hylton, K. (2012). Talk the talk, walk the walk: Defining critical race theory in research. *Race Ethnicity and Education*, *15*(1), 23–41.

Inglis, C. (2009). Multicultural education in Australia: Two generations of evolution. In J. A. Banks (Ed.), *The Routledge international companion to multicultural education* (pp. 109–120). New York: Routledge.

Jakubowicz, A. (2003). Auditing multiculturalism: The Australian empire a generation after Galbally. Paper presented at the *Annual FECCA* conference, Melbourne. Retrieved from http://www.multiculturalaustralia.edu.au/doc/ma_2.pdf

Jakubowicz, A. (2014). Who gets to write the script for our multicultural future? *The Conversation*. Retrieved from http://theconversation.com/who-gets-to-write-the-script-for-our-multicultural-future-24566

Jakubowicz, A., & Ho, C. (2013a). An agenda for the next decade. In A. Jakubowicz & C. Ho (Eds.), *For those who've come across the seas: Australian multicultural theory, policy and practice* (pp. 277–289). North Melbourne: Australian Scholarly Publishing.

Jakubowicz, A., & Ho, C. (2013b). Preface. In A. Jakubowicz & C. Ho (Eds.), *For those who've come across the seas: Australian multicultural theory, policy and practice* (pp. xi–xvi). North Melbourne: Australian Scholarly Publishing.

James, W. (n.d. [1890]). *The principles of psychology – Volume 1*. Retrieved from http://psychclassics.yorku.ca/James/Principles/prin13.htm

James, W. (2004 [1907]). *Pragmatism: A new name for some old ways of thinking*. Retrieved from http://www.gutenberg.org/files/5116/5116-h/5116- h.htm

Jenkins, R. (1994). Rethinking ethnicity: Identity, categorization and power. *Ethnic and Racial Studies, 17*(2), 197–223.

Jordan, K., Krivokapic-Skoko, B., & Collins, J. (2009). The ethnic landscape of rural Australia: Non-Anglo-Celtic immigrant communities and the built environment. *Journal of Rural Studies, 25*(4), 376–385.

Jørgensen, M. W., & Phillips, L. J. (2002). *Discourse analysis as theory and method*. London: Sage Publications.

Jupp, J. (1995). 1301.0 – Year book Australia, 1995: Ethnic and cultural diversity in Australia. Retrieved from http://www.abs.gov.au/ausstats/ABS@.nsf/ Previousproducts/1301.0Feature%20Article41995?opendocument&tab name=Summary&prodno=1301.0&issue=1995&num=&view=

Jupp, J., & Clyne, M. (2010). Introduction. In M. Clyne & J. Jupp (Eds.), *Multiculturalism and integration: A harmonious relationship* (pp. xiii–xxiii). Canberra: ANU E Press.

Kalantzis, M. (1988). The cultural deconstruction of racism: Education and multiculturalism. *Sydney Studies in Society and Culture, 4*, 90–99.

Kalantzis, M. (1989). The experience of multicultural education in Australia: Six case studies. *Centre for Multicultural Studies, University of Wollongong, Occasional Paper, 20*, 1–47. Retrieved from http://ro.uow.edu.au/ cmsocpapers/16

Kalantzis, M., & Cope, B. (1981). *Just spaghetti and polka?: An introduction to Australian multicultural education*. Sydney: Catholic Education Office.

Kerin, L. (2016). UNSW defends Indigenous guidelines amidst claims of "whitewashing" and "rewriting" history. *The World Today (ABC)*. Retrieved from http://www.abc.net.au/news/2016-03-30/unsw- defends-indigenous-guidelines/7285020

Kirk, A. (2006). Abbott suggests "new paternalism" solution to Indigenous disadvantage. *AM (ABC)*. Retrieved from http://www.abc.net.au/am/content/2006/s1667987.htm

Koerner, C. (2011). *Beyond a white Australia? Race, multiculturalism, Indigenous sovereignty and Australian identities* (PhD), Flinders University, South Australia.

Kohli, R., & Solorzano, D. G. (2012). Teachers, please learn our names!: Racial microaggressions and the K-12 classroom. *Race Ethnicity and Education, 15*(4), 441–462.

Koleth, E. (2010). *Multiculturalism: A review of Australian policy statements and recent debates in Australia and overseas*. Retrieved from http://parlinfo.aph.gov.au/parlInfo/download/library/prspub/272429/ upload_binary/272429.pdf;fileType=application%2Fpdf#search=%22lib rary/prspub/272429%22

Kowal, E. (2015). Welcome to country: Acknowledgement, belonging and white anti-racism. *Cultural Studies Review, 21*(2), 173–204.

Krivokapic-Skoko, B., & Collins, J. (2014). Looking for rural idyll "down under": International immigrants in rural Australia. *International Migration, 54*(1), 167–179.

Kymlicka, W. (2012). *Multiculturalism: Success, failure, and the future*. Washington, D.C.: Migration Policy Institute. Retrieved from http:/www.miguelcarbonell.com/artman/uploads/1/kymlicka.pdf

Ladson-Billings, G. (1998). Just what is critical race theory and what's it doing in a nice field like education? *International Journal of Qualitative Studies in Education, 11*(1), 7-24.

Ladson-Billings, G. (2003). New directions in multicultural education: Complexities, boundaries and critical race theory. In J. Banks & C. McGee Banks (Eds.), *Handbook of research on multicultural education* (2nd ed., pp. 50-65). San Francisco, CA: Jossey-Bass.

Ladson-Billings, G. (2005). The evolving role of critical race theory in educational scholarship. *Race Ethnicity and Education, 8*(1), 115-119.

Ladson-Billings, G., & Tate, W. (1995). Toward a critical race theory of education. *The Teachers College Record, 97*(1), 47-68.

Lakoff, G. (1987). *Women, fire, and dangerous things: What categories reveal about the mind*. Chicago, IL: University of Chicago Press.

Lamb, S., Glover, S., & Walstab, A. (2014, August 3-5). Educational disadvantage and regional and rural schools. Paper presented at the *Quality and Equity: What Does Research Tell Us?* conference, Adelaide. Retrieved from http://research.acer.edu.au/cgi/viewcontent.cgi?article=1228&context= research_conference

Laundy, C. (2016). Our diversity is also one of our strengths. *The Bendigo Advertiser*. Retrieved from http://www.bendigoadvertiser.com.au/story/3798952/our-diversity-is-also-one-of-our-strengths/

Ledesma, M., & Calderón, D. (2015). Critical race theory in education: A review of past literature and a look to the future. *Qualitative Inquiry, 21*(3), 206-222.

Lentin, A. (2006). Replacing "race", historicizing "culture" in multiculturalism. *Patterns of Prejudice, 39*(4), 379-396.

Lentin, A. (2008). Europe and the silence about race. *European Journal of Social Theory, 11*(4), 487-503.

Lentin, A. (2014). Post-race, post politics: The paradoxical rise of culture after multiculturalism. *Ethnic and Racial Studies, 37*(8), 1268-1285.

Leonardo, Z. (2002). The souls of white folk: Critical pedagogy, whiteness studies, and globalization discourse. *Race Ethnicity and Education, 5*(1), 29-50.

Leonardo, Z. (2004). The color of supremacy: Beyond the discourse of "white privilege". *Educational Philosophy and Theory, 36*(2), 137-152.

Letki, N. (2007). Does diversity erode social cohesion? Social capital and race in British neighbourhoods. *Political Studies, 56*(1), 99-126.

Lewis, J. (2003). Design issues. In J. Ritchie & J. Lewis (Eds.), *Qualitative research practice: A guide for social science students and researchers* (pp. 47-76). London: Sage Publications.

Leys, R. (2011). The turn to affect: A critique. *Critical Inquiry, 37*(Spring), 434-472.

Lingard, B., Creagh, S., & Vass, G. (2012). Education policy as numbers: Data categories and two Australian cases of misrecognition. *Journal of Education Policy, 27*(3), 315-333.

Lowenthal, D. (1991). British national identity and the English landscape. *Rural History, 2*(02), 205-230.

Mackellar, D. (2011 [1908]). My country. *dorotheamackellar.com.au*. Retrieved from http://www.dorotheamackellar.com.au/archive/mycountry.htm

Mackenzie, N., & Knipe, S. (2006). Research dilemmas: Paradigms, methods and methodology. *Issues in Educational Research, 16*. Retrieved from http://www.iier.org.au/iier16/mackenzie.html

Maguire, M., & Ball, S. (1994). Discourses of educational reform in the United Kingdom and the USA and the work of teachers. *British Journal of In- Service Education, 20*(1), 5-16.

Malcolm, D. (2004). Outsiders within: The reality of rural racism. In N. Chakraborti & J. Garland (Eds.), *Rural racism* (pp. 63–84). Cullompton, Devon: Willan Publishing.

Mansouri, F., & Jenkins, L. (2010). Schools as sites of race relations and intercultural tension. *Australian Journal of Teacher Education, 35*(7), 93–108.

Mansouri, F., Jenkins, L., Morgan, S., & Taouk, M. (2009). *The impact of racism upon the health and wellbeing of young Australians*. Melbourne: The Foundation for Young Australians. Retrieved from https://www.fya.org.au/app/theme/default/design/assets/publications/Impact_of_Racism_FYA_report.pdf

Mansouri, F., & Percival Wood, S. (2007). The policy of values and the value of policy: Managing cultural diversity in Australian schools. *Education and Society, 25*(2), 51–72.

Markus, A. (2003). Of continuities and discontinuities: Reflections on a century of Australian immigration control. In D. Walker, L. Jayasuriya, & J. Gothard (Eds.), *Legacies of White Australia: Race, culture and nation* (pp. 175–189). Crawley, WA: University of Western Australia Press.

Markus, A. (2010). Attitudes to multiculturalism and cultural diversity. In M. Clyne & J. Jupp (Eds.), *Multiculturalism and integration: A harmonious relationship* (pp. 89–100). Canberra: ANU E Press.

Markus, A. (2013). *Mapping social cohesion 2013: The Scanlon Foundation surveys – National report*. Caulfield East: Monash University. Retrieved from http://scanlonfoundation.org.au/wp- content/uploads/2014/07/mapping-social-cohesion-national-report- 2013.pdf

Markus, A. (2014a). *Mapping social cohesion 2013: The findings*. Paper presented at the Mapping Social Cohesion forum, State Library, Sydney.

Markus, A. (2014b). *Mapping social cohesion 2013: The Scanlon Foundation surveys – Local areas report*. Caulfield East: Monash University. Retrieved from http://scanlonfoundation.org.au/wp-content/ uploads/2014/07/mapping-social-cohesion-local-areas-report-2013.pdf

Markus, A. (2015). *Mapping social cohesion: The Scanlon Foundation surveys 2015*. Caulfield East: Monash University. Retrieved from http://scanlonfoundation.org.au/wp-content/uploads/2015/10/2015- Mapping-Social-Cohesion-Report.pdf

Markus, A. (2016). *Australians today: The Australia@2015 Scanlon Foundation survey*. Caulfield East: Monash University. Retrieved from http://scanlonfoundation.org.au/australians-today/

Markus, A. (2018). *Mapping social cohesion: The Scanlon Foundation Surveys 2018*. Caulfield East: Monash University. Retrieved from https://scanlonfoundation.org.au/wp-content/uploads/2018/12/Social-Cohesion-2018-report-26-Nov.pdf

Markus, A. (2021). *Mapping social cohesion 2021*. Caulfield East: Monash University. Retrieved from https://scanloninstitute.org.au/sites/default/files/2021-11/Mapping_Social_Cohesion_2021_Report_0.pdf

Massey, D. (1992). Politics and space/time. *New Left Review, 196*, 65–84.

Massey, D. (2005). *For space*. London: Sage Publications.

Massey, D. (2008). *New faces in new places: The changing geography of American immigration*. New York: Russell Sage Foundation.

Massumi, B. (1995). The autonomy of affect. *Cultural Critique, 31*, 83–109.

Matias, C., & Zembylas, M. (2014). "When saying you care is not really caring": Emotions of disgust, whiteness ideology, and teacher education. *Critical Studies in Education, 55*(3), 319–337.

Matthews, J. (2008). Schooling and settlement: Refugee education in Australia. *International Studies in Sociology of Education, 18*(1), 31–45.

McCarthy, C. (2003). Contradictions of power and identity: Whiteness studies and the call of teacher education. *International Journal of Qualitative Studies in Education*, *16*(1), 127–133.

McCarthy, J. (2008). Rural geography: Globalizing the countryside. *Progress in Human Geography*, *32*(1), 129–137.

McIntosh, P. (1989). White privilege: Unpacking the invisible knapsack. *Peace and Freedom*, *49*(4), 10–12.

McIntosh, P. (2010). "White privilege: Unpacking the invisible knapsack" and some notes for facilitators. Retrieved from https://nationalseedproject.org/white-privilege-unpacking-the-invisible-knapsack

McKenzie, K., & Scheurich, J. (2008). Teacher resistance to improvement of schools with diverse students. *International Journal of Leadership in Education*, *11*(2), 117–133.

McLeod, J., & Yates, L. (2003). Who is "us"? Students negotiating discourses of racism and national identification in Australia. *Race Ethnicity and Education*, *6*(1), 29–49.

Mence, V., Gangell, S., & Tebb, R. (2015). *A history of the department of immigration: Managing migration to Australia*. Canberra: Commonwealth of Australia. Retrieved from https://www.border.gov.au/ CorporateInformation/Documents/immigration-history.pdf

Mertens, D. (2009). Donna Mertens on research methods. Interview recorded at *Mixed Methods* conference, Harrogate. Retrieved from https://www.youtube.com/watch?v=8_AMAbK7wcU

Michell, M. (2014). NSW – The failing multicultural state. Retrieved from https://www.nswtf.org.au/files/nsw_the_failing_multicultural_state.pdf

Miles, R., & Brown, M. (2003). *Racism* (2nd ed.). London: Routledge.

Miller, J., Mitchell, J., & Brown, J. (2005). African refugees with interrupted schooling in the high school mainstream: Dilemmas for teachers. *Prospect*, *20*(2), 19–33.

Mills, C. (2008). "I don't have much of an ethnic background": Exploring changes in dispositions towards diversity in preservice teachers. *International Journal of Pedagogies and Learning*, *4*(3), 49–58.

Mitchell, L. (2011). *Domestic violence in Australia – An overview of the issues*. Retrieved from http://parlinfo.aph.gov.au/parlInfo/download/library/prspub/1246402/upload_binary/1246402.pdf;fileType=applicat ion/pdf#search=%22background%20note%20(p arliamentary%20librar y,%20australia)%22

Modood, T. (2013). The strange non-death of multiculturalism. Paper presented at the *Max Weber Programme* lecture series, Fiesole. Retrieved from http://cadmus.eui.eu/bitstream/handle/1814/ 26814/MWP_LS_2013_03_Modood.pdf

Modood, T. (2014). Understanding "death of multiculturalism" discourse means understanding multiculturalism. *Journal of Multicultural Discourses*, *9*(3), 201–211.

Morin, R. (2013). The most (and least) culturally diverse countries in the world. Retrieved from http://www.pewresearch.org/fact-tank/2013/07/18/the-most-and-least-culturally-diverse-countries-in-the-world/

Morrison, N. (2014). How schools are breaking down the language barrier for EAL students. *The Guardian*. Retrieved from https://www.theguardian.com/teacher-network/teacher- blog/2014/mar/05/teaching-eal-foreign-languages-students-integration-schools

Moya, P., & Markus, H. (2010). Doing race: An introduction. In H. Markus & P. Moya (Eds.), *Doing race: 21 essays for the 21st century* (pp. 1–102). New York: W.W. Norton.

Multicultural NSW. (n.d.-a). Grants. Retrieved from http://multicultural.nsw.gov.au/grants/

Multicultural NSW. (n.d.-b). Welcome to the multicultural NSW community profile. Retrieved from http://multiculturalnsw.id.com.au

Museum of Australian Democracy. (n.d.). Documenting a democracy – Commonwealth of Australia Constitution Act – Amendment to Section 127, page 24. Retrieved from http://foundingdocs.gov.au/amendment-amid-21.html

Nakata, M. (2000). History, cultural diversity and English language teaching. In B. Cope & M. Kalantzis (Eds.), *Multiliteracies: Literacy learning and the design of social futures* (pp. 106–120). Abingdon and Oxford: Routledge.

Nakata, M. (2007). The cultural interface. *The Australian Journal of Indigenous Education*, 36(S1), 7–14.

Nakata, M. (2010). The cultural interface of Islander and scientific knowledge. *Australian Journal of Indigenous Education*, 39(S1), 53–57.

National Assessment Program. (2016). About. Retrieved from https://www.nap.edu.au/about

Neal, S. (2002). Rural landscapes, representations and racism: Examining multicultural citizenship and policy-making in the English countryside. *Ethnic and Racial Studies*, 25(3), 442–461.

Nelson, J. (2015). "Speaking" racism and anti-racism: Perspectives of local anti-racism actors. *Ethnic and Racial Studies*, 38(2), 342–358.

Nieto, S. (1995). From brown holidays and heroes to assimilationist agendas: Reconsidering the critiques of multicultural education. In C. E. Sleeter & P. L. McLaren (Eds.), *Multicultural education, critical pedagogy and the politics of difference* (pp. 191–214). Albany: State University of New York Press.

NMAC. (1999). *Australian multiculturalism for a new century: Towards inclusiveness.* Retrieved from http://www.multiculturalaustralia.edu.au/doc/mcc_1.pdf

Noble, G., & Poynting, S. (2010). White lines: The intercultural politics of everyday movement in social spaces. *Journal of Intercultural Studies*, 31(5), 489–505.

Norrie, J. (2006). You're not welcome, town tells refugees. *The Sydney Morning Herald*. Retrieved from http://www.smh.com.au/news/ national/youre-not-welcome-town-tells-refugees/2006/12/14/ 1165685828180.html

NSW DoE. (2009). *New school leaving age: Information for parents and secondary school students.* Retrieved from http://www.childrenscourt.justice.nsw.gov.au/Documents/stuinfosheet.pdf

NSW DoE. (2014). *English as an additional language or dialect: Advice for schools.* Retrieved from https://www.det.nsw.edu.au/policies/ student_serv/equity/comm_rela/eald_advice.pdf

NSW DoE. (2016a). Aboriginal education and training policy. Retrieved from https://education.nsw.gov.au/policy-library/ policies/aboriginal-education-and-training-policy

NSW DoE. (2016b). Anti-racism policy. Retrieved from https://education.nsw.gov.au/policy-library/policies/anti-racism-policy

NSW DoE. (2016c). Multicultural education policy. Retrieved from https://education.nsw.gov.au/policy-library/policies/multicultural- education-policy

NSW DoE. (2021a). 2021 schools – Language diversity in NSW. Retrieved from https://data.cese.nsw.gov.au/data/dataset/schools-language-diversity-in-nsw/resource/ec1eeca2-1d39-406c-bbf0-56270aaf657a

NSW DoE. (2021b). Schools and students: 2020 statistical bulletin. Retrieved from https://education.nsw.gov.au/content/dam/main-education/about-us/educational-data/cese/2020-schools-and-students-statistical-bulletin.pdf

NSW DoE. (n.d.). Welcome to country and acknowledgment of country: Guidelines and protocols for NSW public schools and TAFE NSW institutes. Retrieved from https://www.det.nsw.edu.au/media/ downloads/dethome/yr2005/welcomecountry.pdf

NSW Government. (2015). *Multicultural NSW Act 2000 No 77*. Retrieved from http://www.legislation.nsw.gov.au/inforcepdf/2000-77.pdf?id=1149872b-2d24-4592-a299-ddf65dd8c048

OECD. (2023). *Foreign-born population*. Paris: OECD. https://data.oecd.org/migration/foreign-born-population.htm.

Ogbu, J. (1992). Understanding cultural diversity and learning. *Educational Researcher*, *21*(8), 5–14+24.

Overington, C. (2007). Duo succeeds in changing town's tune on Sudanese. *The Australian*. Retrieved from http://www.theaustralian.com.au/news/nation/duo-succeeds-in- changing-towns-tune-on-sudanese/story-e6frg6nf-1111112843265

Overington, C. (2012,). Not so black and white. *The Australian*. Retrieved from http://www.theaustralian.com.au/life/weekend- australian-magazine/no-so-black-and-white/story-e6frg8h6- 1226305047298

Oxford Dictionaries. (2016). Cultural diversity. Retrieved from http://www.oxforddictionaries.com/definition/english/cultural- diversity?q=cultural+diversity

Panelli, R., Hubbard, P., Coombes, B., & Suchet-Pearson, S. (2009). De-centring white ruralities: Ethnic diversity, racialisation and Indigenous countrysides. *Journal of Rural Studies*, *25*(4), 355–364.

Paradies, Y. (2006). Beyond black and white essentialism, hybridity and indigeneity. *Journal of Sociology*, *42*(4), 355–367.

Park, B., & Judd, C. (2005). Rethinking the link between categorization and prejudice within the social cognition perspective. *Personality and Social Psychology Review*, *9*(2), 108–130.

Pedersen, A., Clarke, S., Dudgeon, P., & Griffiths, B. (2005). Attitudes towards Indigenous Australians and asylum seekers: The role of false beliefs and other social-psychological variables. *Australian Psychologist*, *40*(3), 170–178.

Perkins, M. (2016). Turnbull Islamic council visit marks shift for Muslims under pressure. *The Age*. Retrieved from http://www.theage.com.au/victoria/turnbull-islamic-council-visit- marks-shift-for-muslims-under-pressure-20160307-gnclas.html

Perry, L. (2017). Educational disadvantage is a huge problem in Australia – we can't just carry on the same. *The Conversation*. Retrieved from http://theconversation.com/educational-disadvantage-is-a-huge- problem-in-australia-we-cant-just-carry-on-the-same- 74530?utm_source=twitter&utm_medium=twitterbutton

Phillips, T. (2004). Multiculturalism's legacy is "have a nice day" racism. *The Guardian*. Retrieved from http://www.theguardian.com/society/ 2004/may/28/equality.raceintheuk

Piller, I. (2016). *Linguistic diversity and social justice: An introduction to applied sociolinguistics*. New York: Oxford University Press.

Pini, B., & Bhopal, K. (2017). Racialising rural education. *Race Ethnicity and Education*, *20*(2), 192–196.

Pini, B., Price, R., & McDonald, P. (2010). Teachers and the emotional dimensions of class in resource-affected rural Australia. *British Journal of Sociology of Education*, *31*(1), 17–30.

Popke, J. (2011). Latino migration and neoliberalism in the US South: Notes toward a rural cosmopolitanism. *Southeastern Geographer*, *51*(2), 242–259.

Povinelli, E. (1998). The state of shame: Australian multiculturalism and the crisis of indigenous citizenship. *Critical Inquiry, 24*(2), 575–610.

Premier, J., & Miller, J. (2010). Preparing pre-service teachers for multicultural classrooms. *Australian Journal of Teacher Education, 35*(2), 35–48.

Priest, N., Walton, J., White, F., Kowal, E., Fox, B., & Paradies, Y. (2016). "You are not born being racist, are you?" Discussing racism with primary aged-children. *Race Ethnicity and Education, 19*(4), 808–834.

Probyn, E. (2005). *Blush: Faces of shame*. Minneapolis, MN: University of Minnesota Press.

Prout, S., & Howitt, R. (2009). Frontier imaginings and subversive Indigenous spatialities. *Journal of Rural Studies, 25*, 396–403.

Putnam, R. D. (2007). E pluribus unum: Diversity and community in the 21st century: The 2006 Johan Skytte Prize Lecture. *Scandinavian Political Studies, 30*(2), 137–174.

Puwar, N. (2004a). *Space invaders: Race, gender and bodies out of place*. Oxford: Berg Publishers.

Puwar, N. (2004b). Thinking about making a difference. *The British Journal of Politics & International Relations, 6*(1), 65–80.

Racism No Way. (2015). About racism – Australia's cultural diversity – Diversity of language – Australian Indigenous languages. Retrieved from http://www.racismnoway.com.au/about-racism/population/index- Diversit-2.html

Ramzan, B., Pini, B., & Bryant, L. (2009). Experiencing and writing Indigeneity, rurality and gender: Australian reflections. *Journal of Rural Studies, 25*(4), 435–443.

Reiner, A. (2010). *Literature review – Background paper for African Australians: A review of human rights and social inclusion issue*. Retrieved from https://www.humanrights.gov.au/sites/default/files/content/ africanaus/papers/africanaus_literature_review.pdf

Salter, P., & Maxwell, J. (2016). Navigating the "inter" in intercultural education. *Discourse: Studies in the Cultural Politics of Education*. https://doi.org/10.1080/01596306.2016.1179171

Santoro, N. (2009). Teaching in culturally diverse contexts: What knowledge about "self" and "others" do teachers need? *Journal of Education for Teaching, 35*(1), 33–45.

Santoro, N. (2014). "If I'm going to teach about the world, I need to know the world": Developing Australian pre-service teachers' intercultural competence through international trips. *Race Ethnicity and Education, 17*(3), 429–444.

Santoro, N., & Smyth, G. (2010). Researching ethnic "others": Conducting critical ethnographic research in Australia and Scotland. *Intercultural Education, 21*(6), 493–503.

SBS. (2014). Media release: SBS commissioned study shows Australia is changing and brands need to change too. Retrieved from http://media.sbs.com.au/home/upload_media/site_20_rand_166646255 4_media_release_sbs_commissioned_study_shows_australia_is_changing_ and_brands_need_to_change_too.pdf

Screen Australia. (2016). *Seeing ourselves: Reflections on diversity in Australian TV drama*. Retrieved from https://www.screenaustralia.gov.au/ getmedia/157b05b4-255a-47b4-bd8b-9f715555fb44/TV-Drama- Diversity.pdf

Seidman, S. (2013). Defilement and disgust: Theorizing the other. *American Journal of Cultural Sociology, 1*(1), 3–25.

Shah, S. (2004). The researcher/interviewer in intercultural context: A social intruder! *British Educational Research Journal, 30*(4), 549–575.

Shaw, W., Herman, R., & Dobbs, G. (2006). Encountering Indigeneity: Re-imagining and decolonizing geography. *Geografiska Annaler: Series B, Human Geography, 88*(3), 267–276.
Shepherd, T. (2012). Inquiry swamped with racist submissions. *news.com.au*. Retrieved from http://www.news.com.au/national/ inquiry-swamped-with-racist-submissions/ story-fndo4eg9- 1226476936303
Shnukal, A. (2001). Torres Strait Islanders. In M. Brandle (Ed.), *Multicultural Queensland 2001: 100 years, 100 communities, a century of contributions*. Brisbane: Department of Premier and Cabinet. Retrieved from http://www.multiculturalaustralia.edu.au/doc/ shnukal_torres_strait.pdf
Shouse, E. (2005). Feeling, emotion, affect. *M/C Journal, 8*(6). Retrieved from http:// journal.media-culture.org.au/0512/03-shouse.php
Sibley, D. (2006). Inclusions/exclusions in rural space. In P. Cloke, T. Marsden, & P. Mooney (Eds.), *Handbook of rural studies* (pp. 401–410). London: Sage Publications.
Smedley, A. (2007). The history of the idea of race – and why it matters. Paper presented at the *Race, Human Variation and Disease: Consensus and Frontiers* conference, Warrenton, VA. Retrieved from http://www.understandingrace.org/resources/pdf/ disease/smedley.pdf
Smith, L. (1999). *Decolonizing methodologies: Research and indigenous peoples*. London: Zed Books.
Smith, Z. (2016). On optimism and despair. *The New York Review of Books*. Retrieved from http://www.nybooks.com/articles/2016/12/ 22/on-optimism-and-despair/
Sparrow, J. (2015, August 7). If black lives really mattered in Australia, it's time we owned up to our history. *The Guardian Australia*. Retrieved from http://www.theguardian .com/commentisfree/2015/aug/07/if-black-lives-really-matter-in-australia-its-time-we -owned-up-to-our-history
Starr, P. (1992). Social categories and claims in the liberal state. *Social Research, 59*(2), 263–295.
Stratton, J., & Ang, I. (1994). Multicultural imagined communities: Cultural difference and national identity in Australia and the USA. *Continuum, 8*(2), 124–158.
Swanton, D. (2005). *Iranians in Vancouver: "Legible people"/irredeemable others/migrant stories*. Working paper series No. 05-21. Retrieved from http://mbc.metropolis.net/ assets/uploads/ files/wp/2005/WP05-21.pdf
Swanton, D. (2010). Sorting bodies: Race, affect, and everyday multiculture in a mill town in northern England. *Environment and Planning A, 42*(10), 2332–2350.
Taksa, L. (2013). Opening address. Paper presented at the *Cultural Diversity@Work: Engaging with Inter-cultural Relations and Communication* symposium, Sydney.
Taylor, S. (2004). Researching educational policy and change in "new times": Using critical discourse analysis. *Journal of Education Policy, 19*(4), 433–451.
The Guardian. (2005). Britain "sleepwalking to segregation". *The Guardian*. Retrieved from http://www.theguardian.com/world/2005/ sep/19/race.socialexclusion
The Nationals. (n.d.). What we stand for. Retrieved from http://nationals.org.au/about/ what-we-stand-for/
Thomas, L. (1995 [1979]). *The medusa and the snail: More notes of a biology watcher*. London: Penguin.
Thomsen, S. (2017). Here is prime minister Malcolm Turnbull's Australia Day address. *Business Insider Australia*. Retrieved from http://www.businessinsider.com.au/here-is -prime-minister-malcolm-turnbulls-australia-day-address-2017-1

Thomson, S., De Bortoli, L., & Underwood, C. (2016). *PISA 2015: A first look at Australia's results*. Retrieved from https://www.acer.edu.au/files/PISA- First-Look.pdf

Thrift, N. (2004). Intensities of feeling: Towards a spatial politics of affect. *Geografiska Annaler: Series B, Human Geography, 86*(1), 57–78.

Tilbury, F., & Colic-Peisker, V. (2006). Deflecting responsibility in employer talk about race discrimination. *Discourse & Society, 17*(5), 651–676.

Timperley, H., & Robinson, V. (2000). Workload and the professional culture of teachers. *Educational Management Administration & Leadership, 28*(1), 47–62.

Tomkins, S. (1962). *Affect, imagery, consciousness. Volume I: The positive affects*. New York: Springer.

Tomkins, S. (1963). *Affect, imagery, consciousness. Volume II: The negative affects*. New York: Springer.

Troyna, B., & Williams, J. (2012). *Racism, education and the state*. Abingdon, Oxon: Routledge.

Tsolidis, G. (2016). Researching school choice in regional Australia: What can this tell us about the ethnographic imaginary? *International Journal of Qualitative Studies in Education, 29*(1), 29–43.

Uptin, J., Wright, J., & Harwood, V. (2013). "It felt like i was a black dot on white paper": Examining young former refugees' experience of entering Australian high schools. *The Australian Educational Researcher, 40*(1), 125–137.

US Census Bureau. (2012). *Hispanic origin – Main*. Retrieved from http://www.census.gov/population/hispanic/

US Census Bureau. (2020). *United States Census 2020*. Retrieved from https://www2.census.gov/programs-surveys/decennial/2020/technical-documentation/questionnaires-and-instructions/questionnaires/2020-informational-questionnaire-english_DI-Q1.pdf

Valentine, G. (2008). Living with difference: Reflections on geographies of encounter. *Progress in Human Geography, 32*(3), 323–337.

Valentine, G. (2010). Prejudice: Rethinking geographies of oppression. *Social & Cultural Geography, 11*(6), 519–537.

Valentine, G., & Sadgrove, J. (2014). Biographical narratives of encounter: The significance of mobility and emplacement in shaping attitudes towards difference. *Urban Studies, 51*(9), 1979–1994.

van Dijk, T. (1992). Discourse and the denial of racism. *Discourse & Society, 3*(1), 87–118.

van Dijk, T. (1993). Principles of critical discourse analysis. *Discourse & Society, 4*(2), 249–283.

Vass, G. (2014). The racialised educational landscape in Australia: Listening to the whispering elephant. *Race Ethnicity and Education, 17*(2), 176–201.

Vaught, S. E., & Castagno, A. E. (2008). "I don't think I'm a racist": Critical race theory, teacher attitudes, and structural racism. *Race Ethnicity and Education, 11*(2), 95–113.

Vertovec, S. (2007). Super-diversity and its implications. *Ethnic and Racial Studies, 30*(6), 1024–1054.

Vertovec, S. (2023). *Superdiversity: Migration and Social Complexity*. London and New York: Routledge.

VicHealth. (2013). *How cultural diversity can be good for business – Information sheet*. Carlton South: Victorian Health Promotion Foundation.

Walsh, M. (1993). Languages and their status in aboriginal Australia. In M. Walsh & C. Yallop (Eds.), *Language and culture in Aboriginal Australia* (pp. 1–13). Canberra: Aboriginal Studies Press.

Walton, J., Paradies, Y., Priest, N., Wertheim, E. H., & Freeman, E. (2015). Fostering intercultural understanding through secondary school experiences of cultural immersion. *International Journal of Qualitative Studies in Education, 28*(2), 216–237.

Walton, J., Priest, N., Kowal, E., White, F., Fox, B., & Paradies, Y. (2016). Whiteness and national identity: Teacher discourses in Australian primary schools. *Race Ethnicity and Education*. https://doi.org/10.1080/13613324.2016.1195357

Walton, J., Priest, N., & Paradies, Y. (2013). Identifying and developing effective approaches to foster intercultural understanding in schools. *Intercultural Education, 24*(3), 181–194.

Warmington, P. (2009). Taking race out of scare quotes: Race-conscious social analysis in an ostensibly post-racial world. *Race Ethnicity and Education, 12*(3), 281–296.

Warren, S., & Vincent, C. (2001). "This won't take long…": Interviewing, ethics and diversity. *International Journal of Qualitative Studies in Education, 14*(1), 39–53.

Watkins, M. (2006). Pedagogic affect/effect: Embodying a desire to learn. *Pedagogies, 1*(4), 269–282.

Watkins, M. (2011). Complexity reduction, regularities and rules: Grappling with cultural diversity in schooling. *Continuum, 25*(6), 841–856.

Watkins, M., Ho, C., & Butler, R. (2017). Asian migration and education cultures in the Anglo-sphere. *Journal of Ethnic and Migration Studies. 43*(14), 2283–2299.

Watkins, M., Lean, G., Noble, G., & Dunn, K. (2013). *Rethinking multiculturalism/reassessing multicultural education: Project report number 1: Surveying New South Wales public school teachers*. Penrith South: Western Sydney University. Retrieved from http://www.multiculturaleducation.edu.au/wp-content/uploads/ 2012/02/RMRME -Report-1-web.pdf

Watkins, M., & Noble, G. (2016). Thinking beyond recognition: Multiculturalism, cultural intelligence, and the professional capacities of teachers. *Review of Education, Pedagogy, and Cultural Studies, 38*(1), 42–57.

Watkins, M., & Noble, G. (2019). Lazy multiculturalism: Cultural essentialism and the persistence of the multicultural day in Australian schools. *Ethnography and Education. 14*(3), 295–310.

Watkins, M., & Noble, G. (2021). *Doing diversity differently in a culturally complex world: critical perspectives on multicultural education*. London: Bloomsbury.

Watkins, M., Noble, G., & Wong A. (2019) *It's complex! Working with students of refugee backgrounds and their families in New South Wales public schools*. Surry Hills: NSW Teachers Federation.

Wesley, M. (2009). *Building an Asia-literate Australia: An Australian strategy for Asian language proficiency*. Retrieved from https://www.griffith.edu.au/ australian-strategy-asian-language-proficiency/report/skills-shortfall

Wike, R., Stokes, B., & Simmons, K. (2016,). Europeans not convinced growing diversity is a good thing, divided on what determines national identity. *Pew Research Center*. Retrieved from http://www.pewglobal.org/2016/07/11/europeans-not-convinced -growing-diversity-is-a-good-thing-divided-on-what-determines-national-identity/

Wilkinson, J., & Langat, K. (2012). Exploring educators' practices for African students from refugee backgrounds in an Australian regional high school. *The Australasian Review of African Studies, 33*(2), 158–177.

Williams, C. (2007). Revisiting the rural/race debates: A view from the Welsh countryside. *Ethnic and Racial Studies, 30*(5), 741–765.

Williams, R. (2002 [1958]). Culture is ordinary. In B. Highmore (Ed.), *The everyday life reader* (pp. 91–100). London: Routledge.

Wilson, C. (2016). *Cultural learning for aboriginal and Torres Strait Islander children and young people: Indigenous knowledges and perspectives in New South Wales schools* (PhD), Southern Cross University.

Wilson, H. (2013). Learning to think differently: Diversity training and the "good encounter". *Geoforum, 45,* 73–82.

Winant, H. (2000). Race and race theory. *Annual Review of Sociology, 26,* 169–185.

Winders, J. (2008). Nashville's new "sonido": Latino migration and the changing politics of race. In D. S. Massey (Ed.), *New faces in new places: The changing geography of American immigration* (pp. 249–273). New York: Russell Sage Foundation.

Wise, A. (2011). Moving food: Gustatory commensality and disjuncture in everyday multiculturalism. *New Formations, 74,* 82–107.

Woods, E. (2013). Wise words from Australian indigenous mentoring experience finalists. *The Sydney Morning Herald*. Retrieved from http://www.smh.com.au/national/wise-words-from-australian-indigenous-mentoring-experience-finalists-20131204-2yqzt.html

Yosso, T. (2005). Whose culture has capital? A critical race theory discussion of community cultural wealth. *Race Ethnicity and Education, 8*(1), 69–91.

Zembylas, M. (2010). Racialization/ethnicization of school emotional spaces: The politics of resentment. *Race Ethnicity and Education, 13*(2), 253–270.

Zerubavel, E. (1993). *The fine line: Making distinctions in everyday life.* Chicago, IL: University of Chicago Press.

Zerubavel, E. (1996). Lumping and splitting: Notes on social classification. *Sociological Forum, 11*(3), 421–433.

Zizek, S. (2010). Liberal multiculturalism masks an old barbarism with a human face. *The Guardian*. Retrieved from https://www.theguardian.com/commentisfree/2010/oct/03/immigrati on-policy-roma-rightwing-europe

Index

Abbott, T. 48
Aboriginal-African tensions 173–7
Aboriginal education 149–50
   external review 159–60
   Hillview High's school leaders
      on 150–4
   inclusion and engagement 159
   objectives 160, 161
   Seaview High's school leaders
      on 154–5
   teachers' perspectives and
      practice 159–62
Aboriginal Education and Training Policy
      (NSW DoE) 44, 45
Aborigine/Aboriginal people 4–5, 8, 16;
      see also Indigenous Australians
   education policy 44–5
   policies and programmes 50
   as real problem 133–4
   schema 24
Adams, Phillip 51
affect/emotion 12, 31–4; *see also* spaces
   diversity discourses (*see* diversity
      discourses)
   Ekman on 33
   as embodied phenomena 33
   Massumi on 33
   negative 60
   number and universality 33–4
   performance of 33
   Tomkins on 33
   Watkins on 32
African American 100–2
African immigrants/refugees 1–2, 6, 12,
      38, 74, 80, 82, 94, 96, 102, 104–9,
      114, 117, 125, 130–2; *see also* Black/
      Blackness; diversity discourses;
      Sudanese
   being darker black 118, 119
   discrimination 140–2
   growth of 69
   topographies of 142–3

Ahmed, S. 31, 34, 60, 124
Amin, A. 180
ancestry 19–20
Ang, I. 12, 42, 47, 48, 53, 57, 58, 119,
      145
Anglo-Australian 3, 4, 10, 19, 28, 47, 48,
      70, 77, 78, 82, 102, 109–15; *see also*
      diversity discourses; Whiteness
   characteristics 111
   on culturally diverse 91–4
   fantasies 106–7
   multiculturalism and 51, 53, 54
   as norm 28
   refugee-background students
      and 113–14
   resentments 39
   schemas 111
   taken-for-granted dominance
      106
   threats to 106
   White Australia policy 51
   White flight 29
anti-discrimination laws 3
ANZAC (Australian and New Zealand
      Army Corps) 72
appearance 25, 95–7
Asia literacy 21
Asian migrants to Australia 17, 21
assimilation/integration 126–8
attitudes 52–63
   actions 59–61
   negative 59–60
   teachers 61–3
Australian Bureau of Statistics (ABS) 4,
      21, 30, 67
Australian Census 19–20
Australian Constitution 30
Australian Curriculum, Assessment
      and Reporting Authority
      (ACARA) 27–8, 155
Australian Standard Classification of
      Cultural and Ethnic Groups 20

Australian Statistical Geography Standard   67
Australians Today survey/study   59, 61, 140

Back, L.   50
Balint, P.   184
Ball, S.   9, 45, 179–80, 185
Barnes, T.   65–6
Baum, F.   38
Baumann, G.   30, 32, 98, 113
Bell, D.   3, 10, 50–1
Bell, J.   9, 18, 97, 123
belonging   34
   racialized hierarchies   109
   topographies   142–3
Black/Blackness   31, 99–108
   discriminatory discourse   140–2
   mulattoes   20
Blackfella Films   31
'Black v Black'   173–7
   aggressive behaviour   174
   competition for resources   177
   cultural performances   175
   old and new (temporal dimension)   176–7
   Whiteness and   177
Boler, M.   12, 62–3, 118, 119, 139, 144
Bonilla-Silva, E.   144
Bourdieu, P.   10–11
Brett, J.   60
Britain   35
Brown, M.   25
Brown v Board of Education   10, 50–1
Brubaker, R.   12, 16, 17, 20, 23–4, 30, 32
Bryant, L.   35
Burmese   131
Butler, R.   7

Cameron, D.   46
Castagno, A.   123–4, 170
categories   17–18, 30–4
   census   19–20
   classical view   22
   concept   17
   consequences   20
   deployment   23
   as interventions   25
   micropolitics   30
   naturalness   18, 23
   overview   12, 16
   as powerful technologies   17
   race, culture, and ethnicity   25–7
   schemas and   23–4
   spatial management   34
   stereotypes   32
categorization   12, 23–4
   education or school system   27–9
   as group-making processes   30
   lumping   24
   sophisticated systems   27
   splitting   24
celebrations   171–3
celebration/tolerance model   63
Centre for Population   68
Chakraborti, N.   35, 37, 127
Challenging Racism   54
Chinese immigrants/migrants   17, 21
classification, as macro-level categorization process   12
classroom practices   163–70
Cloke, P.   35
colonial-era narratives   138
colonization   11
colour-blind racism   144
Cope, B.   6
Covid-19   67–8
Cowlishaw, G.   26–7, 38–9, 100, 135, 153–4
Crenshaw, K.   163
critical discourse   9–11
Critical Discourse Analysis (CDA)   42–3
Critical Legal Studies (CLS)   10
Critical Race Theory (CRT)   10–11
   Whiteness as property   11
Crowley, V.   108
cultural differences   3, 184–5
cultural diversity   2–8, 90–4; *see also* diversity discourses
   commonsense meaning   4
   defined   4
   dimensions   4
   educational benefits   121–5
   measuring   19–20
   official positivity   10
   as a potential threat   18
   promoting and celebrating   3
   as visual phenomenon   19

cultural identity   97–9
culturally diverse   90–4
cultural maintenance   49, 53–4, 128
cultural performances   171–3
culture(s)
    defined   4
    domains   15–16
    operationalizing   19
    as social construct   26
    as values   23
curriculum   61, 149
    as intellectual property   170

data analysis   84–7
data collection   75–84
decolonization   3, 8
De Lepervanche, M.   3, 48, 89
denial/sameness model   63
developed nations   26
DiMaggio, P.   23
discourse
    Fairclough on   42–3
    Foucault on   42
    hegemony and   44
    as language in action   42
    policies and   43–4
diversity discourses   119–44
    ambivalent   125–6
    educational benefits (diversity as a strength)   121–5
    fear of the 'other'   139–44
    food/culinary   119–20
    generational differences   128–30
    media   132
    model minority   122–3
    patterns and themes   118–19
    real and leading problem   133–5
    refugee-background students   132–3
    White victimology   136–9, 144
Dixson, A.   143
Dufty, R.   7
Dunn, K.   57–60
Dyer, R.   110–11
Dyirbal   23

Edgeworth, K.   108
Ekman, P.   33

emotion; *see* affect/emotion
Englishness   35
equality and equity   162–3
    distinction   163
    misconceptions   162–3
    neoliberal discourses   163
ESL tuition   156–9
ethnic fractionalization   17
ethnicity   19, 26, 117; *see also* culture(s); race
ethnographic observation   75
Eureka Research   54–6, 60

Fairclough, N.   12, 27, 42–3, 45, 62, 85, 119, 124, 170
Fanshawe, S.   30
fear of the 'other'   139–44
Feist, H.   67
Fiske, S.   36
Forrest, J.   57–60
Foucault, M.   42, 43, 45
Fraser, M.   49

Garbutt, R.   107
Garland, J.   35, 37, 127
genocide   26
Gillborn, D.   123, 143
Goldberg, D.   22, 97
Grand, I.   185
Grassby, A.   49

Hage, G.   12, 22, 34, 45–6, 49–52, 104–5, 137
Hannah, M.   65–6
Hanson, P.   154
Harkins, J.   175
Harmony Day   5, 15, 19, 55, 76, 79, 137, 156, 171, 172
Hartmann, D.   9, 18, 46, 97, 123
hegemony   44
Hickling-Hudson, A.   31
Hillview High   3, 75, 77, 80–4; *see also* multicultural education; schools; teachers
Ho, C.   29
Holloway, S.   154
Howard, John   47
Howitt, R.   68–9, 71–2
Hugo, G.   2–3, 37, 67

identification 12, 97–8
identities 97–9
immigrants/immigration 7, 11, 12, 16, 17, 21–2; *see also* African immigrants/refugees; refugee-background students
  attitudes (public opinion) towards 53–7
  economic growth and 22, 47
  identities 19
  nation-building and 47
  non-European backgrounds 22
  programmes and services 19
  residing in cities 21
  settlement and integration 7–8
  'too many' 34, 126
  underrepresentation 22
Index of Community Socio-Educational Advantage (ICSEA) 28–9
Index of Relative Socio-Economic Disadvantage 68
Indian Census 20
Indian immigrants/migrants 17, 21
Indian language 21
Indigeneity 4
Indigenous Australians 68–9; *see also* Aboriginal education; Aborigine/Aboriginal people; Torres Strait Islander
  Census and 30
  colonial-era narratives 138
  Constitution and 30
  political power 30–1
  social justice agenda and 48
  as a special group 31
Indigenous culture 4
Indigenous languages 20
Intensive English Centres (IEC) 156, 157
intercultural understanding 6, 149–50
intersectionality 10
Islamic terrorism 132

James, W. 65
James Ruse Agricultural High School 28
Jenkins, L. 61, 62, 74
Jenkins, R. 25, 30
Jones, Alan 17
Jørgensen, M. W. 8, 18, 85

Kalantzis, M. 6
Koerner, C. 9
Koleth, E. 185

Ladson-Billings, G. 6, 10, 26, 170
Lakoff, G. 12, 16, 22–3
Langat, K. 176
language backgrounds other than English (LBOTE) students 6
  categorized or classified as 27–9
  government schools enrollment 21
  Hillview High's students 80
  Seaview High's students 78, 80
languages 16–18, 20
lateral violence 177
Lentin, A. 26
Leonardo, Z. 92, 141, 178
Lingard, B. 28
Linville, P. 36
Living in Harmony 55, 61
Loveman, M. 12, 16, 17, 20, 23–4, 30, 32
Lowenthal, D. 36

McCarthy, C. 41
McIntosh, P. 137
McKenzie, K. 167
McLeod, J. 85, 152
Mansouri, F. 61, 62, 74
Mapping Social Cohesion (MSC) surveys 53–4, 56, 60
marginalization-through-indifference 113
Markus, A. 15, 53, 54, 56–9, 140
Massey, D. 12, 34
Massumi, B. 33
Matias, C. 33
Matthews, J. 108
Merkel, Angela 46
Mertens, D. 66
migration programmes 7
Miles, R. 25
model minority 122–3
Moran, A. 60
MSC, *see Mapping Social Cohesion (MSC)* surveys
mulattoes 20
Multicultural Australia: United, Strong, Successful 18

Multicultural Day   1–2, 4, 6, 11, 19, 152, 154, 171, 179, 184
multicultural education   149–50, 183; *see also* aboriginal education
   Hillview High's school leaders on   150–4
   Seaview High's school leaders on   154–5
   teachers' perspective and practice (*see* teachers)
   whole-school approach   171–3
Multicultural Education Policy (NSW DoE)   44, 45, 153, 154
multiculturalism   45–59
   challenges   179–80
   description *vs.* prescription   46
   governments' commitment to   18
   Hage on   45–6, 49
   international context   46
   multiscalar change   184
   national context   46–7
   as national identity   5, 9
   public opinion   52–9
   small print   47–9
   virtues and strategies   49–52
Multiculturalism Act   44
Multicultural NSW Act 2000   5, 44
multicultural policies   3, 9, 18, 43–5; *see also* multicultural education
   Labor government and   18, 47
   settler-society history and   8
Murri   39, 153–4
Muslims   130, 132, 143
myths about non-metropolitan Australia   2–3

NAIDOC Week   2, 76, 79, 81, 136, 157, 171, 186
National Multicultural Advisory Council (NMAC)   54
natural response/biological model   63
negative other-presentation   162
Nelson, J.   51, 52
New South Wales (NSW)   21
   overseas-born population   21
Noble, G.   52, 123, 141–2
non-metropolitan areas
   colonial narratives   4
   myths   2–3
   settler histories   4

Noonuccal, O.   5
nostalgia   138–9

OECD countries   16, 148
one-drop rule   20
overseas-born population   16
   English-speaking countries   17
   living in capital cities   21

Panelli, R.   35–6
The People of Australia   5, 15, 18–20, 41, 43–7, 55
Pew Research Centre   52–3
Phillips, L. J.   8, 18, 85
Phillips, T.   46, 52
physical appearance; *see* appearance
Pini, B.   35
places; *see* spaces
policies; *see also* multicultural policies
   as discourse   43
   as texts   43
Popke, J.   38
population; *see also specific population group*
   portrayal   19
   statistics   16–17
positive self-presentation   162
Povinelli, E.   183
Poynting, S.   141–2
principle of interest convergence   10
Prout, S.   68–9, 71–2
public opinion   52–9
   immigrants' background   55–7
   respondents' background   57–9
Puwar, N.   119

race; *see also* culture(s); ethnicity
   biological notions   25
   changing category label   26–7
   concept   25–6
   genealogy   25
   as modern construct   25
   as pigment of imagination   26
   UNESCO on   26
race-critical approach   9–11
Racial Discrimination Act   49
racial identities   11
racialization   3, 26
   rural communities   7

racialized hierarchies   109
racism/racial discrimination   3, 143–4
    colour-blind racism   144
    experiences   59–60
    rural communities   7
    segregation   10
    urban bias in   7
Ramzan, B.   35, 71
refugee-background students   132–3
    antisocial behaviour   134–5
    assistance offered to   175–6
    diversity celebrations   171–2
    ESL tuition   156–9, 176
    extracurricular engagement   175–6
    focusing on professional careers   176
refugee resettlement policy   37
refugees   17
Refugee Week   2, 76, 81, 171
religion   20
resegregation   10
reverse racism   162
Rousseau, C.   143
Rudd, Kevin   47
rural space   35–8

Santoro, N.   62, 73, 86, 87, 168, 184
Saulwick, Irving   55
Scanlon Foundation surveys   54
schemas   23–4
    as hierarchically organized   24
    as knowledge structures   23
    rural space   35–8
Scheurich, J.   167
school leaders   150–5
    Hillview High   150–4
    Seaview High   154–5
Seaview High, NSW, Australia   1–3, 75, 77–80; see also multicultural education; schools; teachers
Second World War   3, 16, 26, 48, 128
Seidman, S.   131
sentiments   33
September 2001 terrorist attacks   46, 143
settler societies   8
    decolonization in   3
    modern discourses   3–4
    Whiteness as property   11
shame   175

skin colour   25, 92, 96, 99, 100, 108, 140, 173
Smyth, G.   73, 86, 87
social cognition   24
social interactions   10
spaces   34–9
    defining and naming   34
    ideas and images   35
    rural   35–8
Special Broadcasting Service (SBS)   45
Sriskandarajah, D.   30
Stamatov, P.   12, 16, 17, 20, 23–4, 30, 32
Stanner   170
Starr, P.   20, 29–30
stereotypes   32, 144
Sudanese   70, 95, 104, 105, 108, 112, 114–15, 128, 129, 131, 140, 158, 172, 174; see also African immigrants/refugees
Syrian refugees   17

Tan, G.   67
Tate, W.   6, 10, 26, 170
Taylor, Charles   30
teachers   6, 61–3
    Aboriginal education   159–62
    autonomy   166
    classroom practices   163–70
    critical reflection   168–70
    education and training   61, 62, 167–8, 183–4
    equality and equity   162–3
    ESL students   156–9
    ethos towards diversity   62
    hegemony and notions of deficit   166–7
    interpersonal behaviour   61
    quality of training   167–8
technological competency   6
temporary visas   17
Thomas, L.   65
tolerance   51
Tomkins, S.   33
topographies of belonging   142–4
Torres Strait Islander   4–5, 16, 19, 20, 24, 27, 29–31, 56, 68, 71, 149, 161, 186; see also Indigenous Australians
Tsolidis, G.   83
Turnbull, M.   5, 18, 47, 55

United Nations Educational, Scientific and Cultural Organization (UNESCO) 26
United Nations High Commissioner for Refugees (UNHCR) 17
United States
   Brown v Board of Education 10, 50–1
   mulattoes 20
   racial segregation 10
   September 2001 terrorist attacks 46
Universal Declaration of Human Rights 48
US Census 20

Valentine, G. 38, 60
van Dijk, T. 12, 24, 42, 44, 45, 51, 52, 85, 118
Vaught, S. E. 170
victims of racial vilification 141–2

Wacquant, L. 10–11
Watkins, M. 32, 52, 61–2, 74, 123, 153
White Australia policy 48–51, 188 n.6
White benevolence 138
Whiteness 11, 109–15
   'Black v Black' and 177
   extraordinary ordinariness 108
White privilege 137, 162
White superiority 25
White victimology discourse 136–9, 144
White worrier 137–8
whole-school approach 171–3
Wilkinson, J. 176
Williams, C. 35
Williams, R. 19, 40
Winant, H. 25
Winders, J. 35

Yates, L. 85, 152

Zembylas, M. 12, 33, 62–3, 118, 119, 139, 144
Zerubavel, E. 12, 16, 17, 24, 102
Zizek, S. 126

www.ingramcontent.com/pod-product-compliance
Lightning Source LLC
Chambersburg PA
CBHW071835300426
44116CB00009B/1545